SCANDINAVIA
PROFILED

Essential facts on society, business and politics
in Scandinavia

Edited by Barry Turner

MACMILLAN

This edition published in the United Kingdom by

MACMILLAN REFERENCE LIMITED, 2000
25 Eccleston Place, London, SW1W 9NF, UK
and Basingstoke
Associated companies throughout the world

http://www.macmillan-reference.co.uk

British Library Cataloguing in Publication Data
Scandinavia profiled
    1. Scandinavia - Politics and government.
    2. Scandinavia - Civilization
    Turner, Barry, 1937 -
    948

    ISBN: 0–333–80060–5

Typeset in the United Kingdom by Florence Production Ltd, Stoodleigh, Devon.
Printed and bound in the United Kingdom by Polestar Wheatons Limited, Exeter.

Contents

The Faroe Islands

Colour maps fall between pages 156 and 157

HISTORICAL INTRODUCTION

Omitting Iceland, the lonely outpost in the North Atlantic, the other four Scandinavian or, more properly, Nordic countries form a territorial entity which extends 1,900 km (1,200 miles) from the Danish-German frontier to the northernmost part of Norway. Their land area is about 1,165,000 sq. km (450,000 sq. miles), greater than Britain, France and Spain put together. But the balance changes dramatically when people, not acres, are counted. Vast expanses of northern Finland, Norway and Sweden are given over to mountains and forest, while most of volcanic Iceland is uninhabitable. Those who can properly call themselves Nordic number just under 22m. and are to be found living mostly along the coasts or in the rich agricultural areas of the south where nearly all the big towns are located.

The Faeroes, an outcrop of rocky islands in the Atlantic north of the Shetlands, and Greenland come under Danish jurisdiction but enjoy a large measure of home rule. Greenland is distinguished by being the world's largest island but since in defiance of its name most of it is covered in ice, it also has one of the smallest proportions of habitable land. The Arctic Svalbard island group is administered by Norway and certain Antarctic territories are also Norwegian possessions.

When the glaciers retreated some 15,000 years ago they left behind a landscape that was, at best, patchy in quality. The soil was at its most fertile in Denmark and in southern Sweden but over the rest of Sweden and in Finland and Norway it was too stony to be of value to farmers. Norway has only three per cent of its land under cultivation. More wealth has been extracted from the sea than from land. This is as true today as at any other time, though in the modern scheme of things the emphasis has extended from fish to oil. The rich harvests from the Lofoten fishing grounds off northern Norway have sustained the costal communities for centuries while the great fishing banks near Iceland are still the mainstay of that country's economy.

Until this century the entire region was virtually devoid of energy resources. It was only when advantage was taken of the numerous rivers and waterfalls to create hydro-electric power and a secure foundation for commercial expansions that the potential for developing a prosperous and advanced society was finally realized. By the Second World War, Norway was the world's second largest user per capita of hydro-electric power, with Sweden and Finland not far behind. Since then, the tapping of North Sea oil has once again transformed that Norwegian economy. The most remarkable source of energy in Scandinavia is also the oldest; Iceland's hot springs. Over 70 per cent of Icelanders have geothermal heating in their homes.

The sub-Arctic region of Norway, Sweden and Finland is the home of the Samia or Lappish people. There are less than 45,000 Lapps: 22,000 in Norway, 17,000 in Sweden, 3,500 in Finland and less than 2,000 in northern Russia, just over the Finnish border. But though few in number and widely dispersed, they have a distinctive culture which can be traced back to the Romans. Originally a coastal people, the Lapps turned inland when they found they could get food, clothing and shelter by staying close to the wild reindeer herds. Reindeer hides were draped around poles to make simple tents; skins were turned into shoes, furs and bags; reindeer horn made buckles and knife handles and the animals were killed for their meat. It was a way of life which kept the Lapps on the move, following the herds from their winter grazing in the forests to the summer pasture on the mountains. As practised Arctic travellers they pioneered the use of skis, a word which derives from Skridfinrna, the old Scandinavian word for Lapland; *skrid* or *skrida* meaning to slide.

Although Greenland is not strictly speaking part of Europe, it has strong links with Scandinavia. The first inhabitants were Eskimos from north America, but Nordic settlement started in the tenth century when a group of Icelanders found their way to the fertile fjords of south-west Greenland, the only part of the island that really justified its name. While owing allegiance to the Dano-Norwegian kingdom, distance and the absence of exploitable resources permitted the colony almost complete independence. It survived for about five hundred years and was then unaccountably wiped out, possibly by an epidemic or by clashes with the Eskimos. Nordic communications with Greenland were not resumed until the beginning of the eighteenth century. Intermarriage with migrants from the American continent created a mixed race identified by its Mongolian features. But the prevailing religious and social influences were from Scandinavia which meant that Greenland again became part of the Dano-Norwegian state and remained with Denmark along with Iceland and The Faeroes after 1814 when Norway was ceded to Sweden.

Danes, Norwegians, Icelanders and Swedes all speak north Teutonic languages related to the German and Anglo-Saxon tongues and derived from a common language which was still spoken about a thousand years ago. This was the time of the Vikings, a collective term for those intrepid Scandinavians who left their homes to seek their fortunes in distant lands. From Sweden, the Vikings ventured eastwards following the rivers into Russia to establish a short-lived colony in the region of Novgorod. The Norwegian Vikings sailed to the Atlantic islands, Scotland and Ireland, and also colonized Iceland which had become an independent state by the middle of the tenth century. The Danes conquered England, and for a short time under Canute the Anglo-Danish kingdom was one of the leading European powers.

Not all Scandinavians were Vikings. To equate the two is as simplistic as referring to all seventeenth-century Englishmen as buccaneers. Moreover, not all Vikings were plunderers. Contemporary sources give a lurid portrait of savage marauders, their minds set on rape and pillage. But where trade or settlement could be achieved, the Vikings were not slow to take up the peaceful option.

What has never been in dispute was their brave determination to beat formidable odds in their overseas excursions. One of the many whose exploits were faithfully recorded by the saga writers was Eric the Red who discovered Greenland and, with a promoter's eye to attracting settlers from Iceland, gave the island its name. His son, Leif Erikson, combined piety with great courage, the first part of his reputation being acquired by his missionary zeal on behalf of Christianity (Greenland remained the last outpost of Nordic paganism), the second by his voyage of discovery across the Davis Strait, to America. The expedition was entirely peaceful, motivated by the desire to set up trading posts for timber and fur and to find new land for cattle farming.

Achievement of a different sort distinguished Iceland when the first democratic national assembly, the Althing, was founded in about 930. Soon after their arrival, the Norwegian colonists set up local *things* or assemblies of freemen to resolve disputes. Then, in about 927, one of their number returned to Norway to study law and to prepare a code for all of Iceland. The adjudicating body was the Althing, the only national *thing* to be created by the northern peoples. It served also as a legislature and as a fair, a marriage mart, and a national celebration in which a large proportion of the Icelandic population participated for two weeks each June. The first notable event in its history occurred in 1000 when, by majority decision, Christianity was adopted as Iceland's official religion.

The first steps towards centralized rule were taken by Harold Fairhair who extended his rule along the coastal region of Norway. Battles with rival chieftains culminated in about 900 when Harold was proclaimed king of the Norwegians. His successors were less assertive and by the mid-tenth century the country was effectively under the suzerainty of Harold Bluetooth, king of Denmark and

Skåne. It was Bluetooth's grandson, Canute the Great, who fought successfully to incorporate England into his North Sea Empire before setting his sights on Sweden, then the most backward of the Scandinavian countries. But the limitations of royal authority were shown on the death of Canute when the English, unchallenged, simply chose their own king while the Danish and Norwegian nobles decided that whichever of their own monarchs lived longest should take power in both countries, an agreement which for a time resulted in a Norwegian ruler for Denmark.

However unsettled the style of government, the Nordic kings, supported by the Church, created a form of patchwork nationalism. By 1200 Norway, Denmark and Sweden had developed into clearly defined if loosely organized kingdoms with largely the same borders as they have today except that Skåne, Halland and Blekinge in the south of Sweden formed part of Denmark; Jämtland, Härjedalen and Bohuslän in the west of Sweden belonged to Norway, and the southern border of Denmark was at the Eider in what is now northern Germany. Though there remained a large measure of linguistic overlap, Danish, Swedish and Norwegian henceforth developed their own forms of dialect and spelling while the Icelanders, culturally marooned in the Atlantic, kept to the ancient speech which today is incomprehensible to other Scandinavians.

In the thirteenth century, the expansion of fishing to satisfy the demand from Catholic Europe in turn stimulated agriculture and other basic industries. This new-found prosperity brought with it a passion for building – particularly churches and cathedrals – and a desire by the wealthy to copy the fashions of the German and French aristocracy. Economic growth strengthened German influence. Under the protection of a monopolistic association known as the Hanseatic League, German entrepreneurs secured important trade concessions for herring, salt and grain from Denmark and played a leading role in that country's turbulent political affairs. Norway, too, was infiltrated by German traders. To maintain the supply of corn the port of Bergen became a Hanseatic base for controlling the north-Atlantic trade routes. Stockholm contained a large German population, and further down on the south-east coast of Sweden, Kalmar and the offshore island of Gotland were virtually run by German immigrants. Gotland was the last link in the chain of Hanseatic trading posts to the east. This included Finland, which by a gradual process of colonization, was brought into the Swedish kingdom. That she remained there for almost five hundred years fully justifies her inclusion in the Nordic sphere of influence even though the origins of the Finns are anything but Scandinavian. Finnish is not related to any of the great European languages but together with Estonian and Hungarian forms part of the Finno-Ugrian group. Early Swedish influence, however, established a second line of cultural development, so that even today Swedish retains the status of a second official language and six per cent of the population use it as their first language.

With the growing power of centralized government it was only a matter of time before a Scandinavian monarch challenged the privileges of the Hanseatic League. When the moment came the Germans were doubly discomfited because it was one of their own who struck the blow. Valdemar Atterdag, who claimed to be the 'true heir to the throne of Denmark', had been raised in the Imperial German court. But Atterdag was soon to prove he was his own man, prepared to devote his energy to uniting Denmark under his leadership.

Success inevitably brought him into conflict with Sweden over the disputed southern provinces of Skåne, Halland and Blekinge. His strategy was to attack Gotland, hoping thereby to secure a base for further assaults on the Swedish mainland, and at the same time to show the Hanseatic League who was master in Scandinavia. In 1361 Gotland was taken in one of the bloodiest battles in Nordic history.

Safe within their walled city of Visby, the Hanseatic merchants
watched the massacre of the Goths before making haste to buy
protection with a large donation to the Danish exchequer. Retaliation
came in the form of an unsuccessful rebellion against Atterdag and a
Hanseatic assault on Danish positions along the Sound which
consolidated German control over the approaches to the Baltic.

Valdemar Atterdag had no obvious male successor but he did
have a very able and ambitious daughter, Margaret, who was
married to Håkon of Norway. When the Danish king died in 1375 she
claimed the throne on behalf of her five-year-old son, Olav. It was the
first step towards establishing her personal rule over all three
Scandinavian kingdoms. The prospect was not unrealistic. National
identities were not yet so strong as to preclude a single royal
authority and fear of further encroachment by the Germans, the real
outsiders, offered a cause for unity. A contributing factor was the
Black Death which took off between a third and a half of the
population, leaving Scandinavia vulnerable to attack.

Acting for her son, Margaret became regent of Denmark and, on
the death of Håkon, regent of Norway. By then she had gained a
reputation for standing up to the Hanseatic League which endeared
her to that section of the Swedish nobility who had opposed the
election of a German claimant, Albrecht of Mecklenburg, to the
Swedish throne. Confirmed as regent of Denmark and Norway,
Margaret defeated Albrecht, thus clearing the way to a Nordic union.
With the death of her son and unable to take the triple crown for
herself, she nominated her five-year-old nephew, Erik of Pomerania,
as king of all three countries. His election was formalized at Kalmar in
1397.

Margaret worked hard to cement the union. While there was never
any doubt that Denmark ranked first in the territorial hierarchy, she
was careful not to over-exploit her Danish connections. Nonetheless,
it needed more than a generation of enlightened rule to create a

single Scandinavian state. Soon after Margaret's death in 1412, Erik found himself in trouble with the Swedish nobles who resented being taxed to finance Danish wars in north Germany. By now, Sweden was strong enough to resist Danish efforts to drain her of revenue. Erik finally abdicated and was succeeded by another union king but after 1450 Denmark was rarely able to impose her will.

As the first in a long line of Swedish nationalists, Sten Sture, who was made regent in 1470, defeated the Danes at Brunkeberg just outside Stockholm. Following this success he worked on Swedish nationalist sentiment with grand and defiant gestures like the public display of a huge wood carving of St George slaying the dragon (now on view in Stockholm cathedral) or, of more lasting influence, the setting up of the first Swedish university, at Uppsala. Norway on the other hand had no choice but to remain part of Denmark, even after the disintegration of the Kalmar union. Her economy was weak, and though adventurers were prepared to try their chances against the Danes, the country lacked a ruling class.

After the Reformation, when all five countries were converted to Lutheranism, shared values introduced a high degree of uniformity into the development of state administrations and legal systems. By the sixteenth century Europe was accustomed to thinking of Scandinavia as two states, Denmark-Norway (including Iceland and Greenland) and Sweden-Finland. The ruling languages were Danish in the west and Swedish in the east. Finland was so permeated by Swedish culture at this period that it became an integral part of Scandinavia.

Relations between the two sides were seldom amicable. Sweden-Finland felt herself to be hedged in between Denmark and Norway and the two nations were rivals for control of Baltic trade. Intermittent fighting in the second half of the century resulted in few territorial changes but Sweden was weak and vulnerable when Gustavus Adolphus 'the Dragon King', inherited the crown in 1611. A leader who combined military prowess with outstanding intellectual abilities, Gustavus set about raising the country to the status of a great power first by consolidating his hold on strategic points on the Russian side of the Baltic and later by taking his armies into northern Europe to play a critical role in holding back the Catholic advance in the Thirty Years War. This enterprise cost him his life but gained for Sweden large possessions in the north of Germany.

The fortunes of Denmark, meanwhile, had shifted into reverse with the loss of Gotland and the Norwegian territories of Jämtland and Härjedalen to her old enemy. In 1660 Sweden finally conquered Skåne, Halland and Blekinge which nowadays are thought to be intrinsically Swedish but then were just as naturally part of Denmark. Further Swedish gains in Norway included the province of Bohuslän in the southeast just below Oslo, an acquisition which tidied up the border to give Sweden the overwhelming strategic advantage if she resolved on further dismemberment of Denmark or Norway. In fact, this was probably what Charles X, the warrior king, had in mind, but even if his ambitions had not been cut short by fatal illness, Britain and Holland's interest in Baltic trade would have counted decisively against Swedish dominance of the Scandinavian peninsula.

By now the internal boundaries of Scandinavian were set firm, though the political division was still between Denmark-Norway and Sweden-Finland. Sweden went on to further military glories but her days as a great power were numbered by the emergence of Russia as a formidable rival. In the early part of the eighteenth century Sweden was forced to give up her Baltic territories including a part of Finland and all her north-German possessions except west Pomerania.

The restoration of the balance of power in Scandinavian brought a lull in dynastic rivalry and even encouraged thoughts of cooperation in the interests of security. As a foretaste of things to come, the two monarchies joined in a policy of armed neutrality to defend their merchant shipping from the contenders in the Seven Years War. But it was not the time for any serious move towards unity on the Kalmar model. Though Sweden was reasonably secure in her possession of Finland, at least in so far as the Finns showed no enthusiasm for transferring their allegiance to a Russian master, there were tensions within Denmark-Norway created by the buildup of German nationalism on the southern border and by the growing confidence of a Norwegian middle class who resented the privileges of the Copenhagen business elite. There was even talk in Oslo of union with Sweden. The opportunity to test this alternative came sooner than anyone expected with the dramatic rejuggling of Scandinavian allegiances caused by the Napoleonic wars.

Undeterred by the Franco-Russian alliance of 1807, Sweden held to a policy of cooperation with Britain while that same year, Denmark, smarting under the British bombardment of Copenhagen, allied herself to Napoleon. Accordingly, Sweden was trapped in a Baltic pincer movement. After an inglorious campaign which led to a coup in Stockholm and the overthrow of the Gustavian monarchy, Finland was ceded to Russia. The terms, for the Finns, were generous, a pledge being made by Tsar Alexander to govern as Grand Duke and to protect their established laws and liberties.

Sweden now looked towards Norway for compensation for her losses in the east, and the choice of a new ruler, a cousin of the Danish king, was partly determined by his influence with those Norwegians who favoured a transfer of allegiance. But within a year Christian August had died of a stroke and the succession was open once again. This time it was complicated by the need to take into account the wishes of Napoleon with whom Sweden had lately made peace. After some curious machinations involving the duplication of couriers dispatched to sound out views in Paris, the choice fell on one of Napoleon's marshals, Bernadotte, who became king under the name of Karl Johan in 1810.

So entered one of the most remarkable Nordic leaders, who, though never learning Swedish or Norwegian, identified immediately with the interests of his adopted country. When Napoleon punished Sweden for engaging in an extensive but illicit trade with the British by annexing Swedish Pomerania, Karl Johan used the excuse to line up with the enemies of France. He was in powerful company because now the Russians were also in league against Napoleon. Karl Johan's first objective was to win Russian agreement for the return of Finland but when this proved unacceptable he settled for a promise that if their joint enterprise was successful, the Tsar would support a union of Sweden and Norway. This was the price Denmark was forced to pay for clinging to her alliance with France. By the treaty of Kiel, 1814, King Frederik signed away his rights in Norway, although he was allowed to retain Iceland, Greenland and The Faeroes and even made some small gains in Germany by way of compensation.

But no one had thought to take account of the wishes of the Norwegians. The frustration of being treated as a backward province found expression in a bid for independence and the proclamation of a liberal constitution. Karl Johan sent his army across the border to hasten a submission. In November 1814, the king of Sweden was 'unanimously elected and recognized' by the Storting as the king of Norway. But the constitution remained to ensure that government from Stockholm was less intrusive than government from Copenhagen.

Before long, Denmark had to face the prospect of further territorial losses, this time in the south, where German nationalism was pressing hard against Schleswig-Holstein. The duchies had been attached to Denmark for four hundred years but the official language was German, and Holstein was actually a member of the German confederation. A revolution in 1848 was contained by the great powers acting in concert against the Germans. In 1863 Denmark conceded the impracticability of holding on to Holstein by giving the duchy its own constitution and cutting it out of Danish affairs. At the same time Schleswig was bound more closely to Denmark. The German confederation objected, Prussian and Austrian troops went on the offensive, the greater powers stood aside and Schleswig and Holstein were both lost.

The consequences of the war for Denmark can be measured in the loss of two-fifths of her territory, most of it rich agricultural land, and nearly a million inhabitants. For a time there was some doubt as to whether Denmark had any future at all as an independent state. And yet within a few years the country managed to pull itself back from one of the lowest points in its history. The economy benefited from a huge land-reclamation programme in the sandy region of Jutland which increased the acreage under cultivation until it fully compensated for that ceded to the Germans in Schleswig.

This remarkable assertion of national will was in large measure inspired by the teachings of Bishop Grundtvig, founder of the folk high-schools. In the winter months the children of farmers and small-holders extended their learning beyond basic literacy by engaging in what Grundtvig called 'the living word'. Stories and songs from Denmark's great past inspired a sense of pride in the country's achievements and idealism for the future. But unlike most other nationalist propaganda it was not pure chauvinism that Grundtvig was imparting. His greatest accomplishment was to reconcile patri-otism with a reduced status for Denmark in European affairs. If he did not go so far as to claim that small is beautiful, he at least got across the message that it is not necessary to be big to be virtuous. Denmark still had much to contribute to the world but her people needed faith in their own genius. The lesson was not lost on the rest of Scandinavia.

In Norway successive steps towards self-government within the union culminated in a referendum in which the overwhelming majority of Norwegians voted for separation. In October 1905 Oscar II renounced his title to the western provinces and a month later a Danish prince was confirmed as Haakon VII of free Norway. The Icelanders too built up a formidable campaign for independence. But though near complete home rule was conceded at the beginning of the century, the country remained part of the kingdom of Denmark until the Second World War. Both settlements were achieved peace-fully.

All five countries were late industrial developers. A shortage of minerals, especially coal, meant that for most of the nineteenth century their overseas trade was founded on the supply of primary products to the more commercially advanced nations. Timber was the leading revenue-earner. Demand was such that in Norway it led to the virtual denudation of the most accessible forests along the southern coastline.

Conditions changed radically towards the end of the century when there was a great burst of economic activity. Of a number of contrib-utory factors, the early utilization of hydro-electric power was the most important. The improvement in communications achieved by the railways and steam-driven ships brought boom markets within easy reach of industries like pulp, paper, agriculture and fishing. A rapid increase in population created the pool of labour that was essential to the growth economy.

Sweden was in the best position to exploit the opportunities. She already had a small industrial base centred on a modest output of iron-ore. Shipbuilding and textiles were well established and, with other infant enterprises, supported a thriving banking system. The introduction of the steam-driven sawmill coincided with an increase in British demand for timber products from tar and resin to telegraph poles and pit props which Norway and Canada, the traditional suppliers, were unable to satisfy. A boost to exports was achieved at the cost of decimating the northern landscape. But by the end of the century, when timber accounted for almost half of the country's total exports, the development of a chemical process for converting wood into good quality paper ensured a less wasteful exploitation of Sweden's forests. The first chemical pulp factory was set up in Bergvik in 1872. By the First World War, Sweden sold more pulp than any other country.

Mining also benefited from new industrial techniques. The Bessemer process, partly developed in Sweden, stimulated production of good-quality steel, while the Gilchrist method, which brought into productive use iron-ore of high phosphoric content, opened up the prospect of mining in the far north, around Kiruna and beyond the Arctic Circle. Engineering came to lead the growth industries, its reputation for quality products nourished by an enthusiasm for innovation and a gift for invention. To the Swedes goes credit for making the first ball-bearing, the first adjustable spanner, the first cream separator and the first primus stove, not to mention the first safety match and, somehow linked to it in the imagination if not in strict historical fact, the first stick of dynamite.

The Danes sought prosperity in the expansion of agriculture. It was not easy. With the opening up of the North American prairies and the Russian wheatlands, European prices collapsed and Danish farmers faced ruin. The only way to recovery was to adapt to animal husbandry and the export of perishable dairy products. The success of this turnabout (within 20 years, Denmark was a net importer of grain) owed much to the cooperative movement. By joint investment in dairies, bacon factories and other support services, economies of scale were achieved without risk to the social cohesion of the small family farms. A healthy trade balance allowed for plentiful imports of coal and iron which in turn stimulated the growth of shipbuilding and high-grade engineering on the Swedish pattern.

With no agriculture surplus to speak of and limited timber resources the Norwegians put much of their effort into making a living from the sea. The fishing industry had several natural advantages: a long, ragged coastline afforded good harbours, the waters were ice-free and the continental shelf accommodated rich spawning grounds. When times were hard there were more volunteers for Arctic sealing and whaling expeditions, a hazardous occupation in which Norway established a world lead. The first floating factory whaler was launched from a Norwegian dock in 1905.

Young Norwegians found it difficult to avoid the sea. If they were not fishermen, likely as not they were merchant sailors. At more than one and a half million tons, the merchant fleet was bigger than all the other Nordic fleets put together. Conversion to steam was complete by 1900 when, notwithstanding the growth of shipbuilding and the pulp and paper industries, Norway still had more seamen than factory workers.

While Denmark, Sweden and Norway were in the throes of economic change, Finland was still locked into a pre-industrial social structure which was as primitive as it was poor. In terms of the Finnish national income, textiles was an industry of note but there were only three mills and these were almost exclusively at the service of the Russian market. Timber accounted for about two-thirds of the export trade. Most Finns lived on what they could get from the land, which was precious little. As late as 1867–69, bad harvests led to famine which killed off eight per cent of the population.

The Icelanders were scarcely more prosperous. At the beginning of the century there was not a factory in the country, scarcely a passable road, no bridges, no man-made harbour and very few stone-built houses. Hopes were pinned on adapting the fishing fleet from open rowing boats to decked vessels capable of venturing to more distant waters.

With late industrialization some of the worst features of mass production were simply not encountered. Scandinavian industry remained essentially a small-town affair. At the time the trade unions were beginning to gather strength, living standards were improving, and though feelings against employers and right-wing governments could run high, the biggest fear of the ordinary worker was that by pushing his masters too far he would drive himself into unemployment and poverty. The other powerful antidote to the threat of social disruption was the easy availability of a boat-ticket to the new world. From 1865–70 one in ten of United States immigrants was Scandinavian, and though the proportion was never to be so high again, the numbers of those departing increased sharply when times were really bad. The disastrous harvests of 1867–69 caused 80,000 to leave from Sweden alone.

The much admired Scandinavian model for labour relations began to emerge in the last year of the century. It was then that Danish employers and unions put their signatures to the September Compromise, a deal which was enforced throughout the country. Employers were confirmed in their right to run their companies in the way they thought fit, and that included the freedom to hire and fire. But there was a joint commitment to strive for 'peaceful, stable and good working conditions', a responsibility employers took more seriously as they came to realize they had more to gain from a contented work force. Gradually the terms of the agreement were changed to allow the unions a stronger voice and to open the way for government intervention in industrial bargaining. After 1910 a government mediator could step in when unions and employers failed to agree.

The September Compromise turned out to be a formula for peaceful economic growth. It was copied in all the other Nordic countries. In Sweden the Saltsjöbaden Agreement between unions and employers became the basis for the most comprehensive framework for centralized collective bargaining to be found anywhere in the Western world. After the unions' humiliating defeat in the 1909 general strike there was a long period in which employers and labour were hardly on speaking terms. But attitudes were modified as the social-democratic party gained sufficient support to claim a share in government. The interests of the national economy demanded that the unions and employers should talk sensibly to each other, a precept which the 1932 social-democrat government was prepared, if necessary, to back up with legislation. Neither side was prepared for this, with the result that they settled down to working out a mutually acceptable procedure for dealing with disputes.

Social democracy had its start as the political offshoot of the trade unions, in particular the craftsmen, the establishment of the working class, supported by the radical intellectuals. Their leading spokesman was a distinguished Swedish scientist, Hjalmar Branting, who was destined to be the first Scandinavian socialist prime minister. Inspiration in shaping a political programme came from Germany where conditions corresponded with those in Scandinavia. The struggle in Russia against a corrupt autocratic regime had scarcely any bearing on the Nordic experience.

The exception was Finland, which lived in the shadow of Russian autocracy. Though it was almost entirely a rural economy socialism took a strong hold in the first years of the century. Under Alexander II Finland had contrived to build on her status as a grand duchy, so that by the 1880s she even had control over her own army. It was all too much for the Russian military, who feared that moves towards Finnish separatism would make more difficult their task of defending the long western border. With the appointment of General Bobrikov as governor general in 1898 a start was made on bringing Finland back into the imperial fold. The army was put under Russian command, the Russian language was made compulsory for the civil service and for schools and decision-making reverted to the Tsar's appointees.

Resistance first took the form of non-cooperation (less than half the Finns of military age responded to a general conscription) but as the Russian revolutionary movement gathered pace, their allies in Finland became bolder. In June 1904 Bobrikov was assassinated and in 1916 the Marxists won an absolute majority in a parliamentary election. It was a short-lived victory but the far left held its popular appeal.

Elsewhere in Scandinavia, social-democratic parties found themselves allied to governments of more or less liberal persuasion in support of moderate constitutional and social reforms. By these tactics the Danes secured state loans for smallholders wanting to buy their land, the Swedes brought in restrictions on child and female labour, and the Norwegians insured their merchant sailors and fishermen against accident. All three countries introduced old-age pensions and free elementary education.

The guns of August 1914 were quickly followed by declaration of neutrality from Sweden, Norway, Denmark and Iceland. Finland's foreign policy was decided by her Russian masters. The collapse of the Russian autocracy in March 1917 brought about the immediate restoration of Finland's ancient constitutional rights but left open the question as to who should exercise them. The socialists, who held a majority in the Eduskunta, demanded full independence and for a short time it looked as if the Russians might accede. But the advance of the Germany armies in mid-1917 and the presence of Finnish volunteers among the invading forces soured negotiations. When the Russians refused to deliver, the socialists were at a loss to know what to do next except to follow the extremists along the path of direct action.

They were pushed further in this direction by events in Russia where, in November, the Bolsheviks seized power. Ironically, it was Lenin who came to the aid of the moderates by granting Finnish independence, which he saw as a step towards a closer relationship rooted in a shared Marxist destiny. But at this point, the non-socialist Eduskunta decided to restore order with the appointment of General

Mannerheim, a Finnish but Russian-speaking aristocrat who was a long-serving officer in the imperial Russian army, as military commander. In early 1918 he launched his campaign against the socialists or Reds with an enthusiasm and energy that convinced his opponents of the imminence of a bourgeois coup. In a quick counter-action, the socialist party council gave the signal for taking over the government. Finland was thrown into civil war.

In three months it was all over. The Reds, though supplied with arms and equipment by the Russians and controlling all the big industrial towns of the south, were no match for the professional White forces led by officers trained in the Swedish or Russian armies. As the enemies of Bolshevism the Whites gained sympathy and support abroad, while at home they succeeded in associating their cause with pride in Finland as an independent state. The war, though short, was fought with terrible ferocity. To the seven thousand who were killed in open battle must be added at least as many who fell before the execution squads, and a similar number again who died of starvation or disease in detention camps. Yet in the immediate aftermath, creative political forces were quickly reasserted. In March 1919, with Mannerheim installed as regent, elections were held for a parliament whose first task was to draft a new constitution. The socialists won 80 seats, more than any other single party but had to work together with the centre whose representatives held the balance. The compromise was a constitution which combined the democratically elected assembly characteristic of the European parliamentary tradition with a strong president to perform the executive role, as in the United States.

The president was to be elected for six years as against three (later four) years for the legislature. There was no way in which he could be dismissed and no limitation on the number of terms he could serve. Legislation was the business of the Eduskunta but the president was allowed what amounted to a free hand in implementing the laws, and there was a wide area of government where he could act on his own prerogative. In placing foreign policy in this category, the architects of modern Finland, though recognizing the importance of the relationship with the Soviet Union, could not have guessed at the priority it would take in later years and the role the president was to assume in making it work. Meanwhile, Finland found herself with the most highly centralized and, in many ways, the most authoritarian government in Scandinavia.

The early post-war period was a frustrating decade for the Swedish social democrats who formed three governments up to 1926 but found themselves implementing liberal policies. Whenever they attempted socialist measures, by a direct attack on unemployment, for instance, they came up against the rural vote. The lesson learned from the twenties was to try more seriously to attract the support of the centre, which really meant the farmers, for policies which could be clearly shown to benefit the entire nation. As it happened, it was a tactic which was ideally suited to the economic conditions of the following decade when social democracy really came into its own.

Danish social democrats went through a similar transformation. Having supported a radical government on extending the vote to all over 25, they cooperated to bring about the eight-hour day and make it easier for would-be smallholders to acquire land. Their first chance to lead came in 1924, when recession gave them a powerful boost. Thorvald Stauning, who became prime minister of a minority government, naturally looked to the radicals to give the same support as he had given them in the early post-war years. He was to be disappointed. At a time when unemployment was rising to 25 per cent, proposals for direct aid to industry and a tax on high earners were rebuffed. The failure led to a temporary break-up in a long-standing political alliance, but out of power the social democrats and radicals agreed a policy on which they could work together without offending free-market economics. When Stauning returned as prime minister in 1929 it was to lead a coalition capable of uniting rural and urban interests in one of the most ambitious programmes of social reform ever mounted.

Norway was something else. There the leftist movement took a far stronger hold. First, it had an outstanding leader in Martin Transmael who emigrated to America at the beginning of the century and saw the face of capitalism in its toughest and most uncompromising phase. He returned to Norway convinced that his mission was to destroy the system that dehumanised labour. Conditions favoured Transmael's brand of politics. Of all the Nordic countries, Norway had experienced the most rapid transformation from a rural to an industrialized society. The huge majority of those working in the factories or on the new power-plants had been brought up in tiny villages or on isolated farms. They were easily convinced that all their efforts were going into making a few individuals vastly rich. In 1918, Transmael forced out the labour old guard and was elected secretary of the party. Two years later his followers gained a majority on the congress of the trade union federation. So successful was Transmael in promoting Marxism that he was able to take the Norwegian socialists into the Third International.

It was all too much for the right wing, who broke away to form their own social-democrat organization. After a series of damaging strikes failed to rally working-class support, opinion soon shifted in favour of the Danish and Swedish model for advancing democracy. The labour and social-democrat parties joined forces and in 1928 had their first if fleeting experience of power – they were out after two weeks. But the union held, and though the party stayed well to the left of Scandinavian politics, conditions in the thirties encouraged the evolution of a broad-based programme of reform.

By the early thirties the parallel evolution in the politics of the three central Scandinavian states was unmistakable. The parliamentary status of the social democrats gradually shifted from that of junior to senior partner in administrations aimed at holding the middle ground. Critical to this transformation was the toning down of socialist policy to a point where such basic principles of capitalism as the right to private ownership were accepted without question. Their appeal to the electorate rested in the claim that a government of the left could make capitalism work better for more people.

The twenties and early thirties were for Finland a period when the class antagonism inherited from the civil war remained the dominant political issue. For the victorious Whites, communism was next to treachery and social democracy was next to communism. This made it all but impossible for the centre to work constructively with politicians on the moderate left. Though persecuted throughout the twenties the communist party continued as an effective electoral machine, operating from its strongholds in the poor rural districts of the north and east. In November 1929, the communist youth movement chose to hold a demonstration in Lapua, a deeply conservative small town in the heart of Österbotten, where Mannerheim had first rallied his supporters to fight the Red menace. The subsequent riot was the signal for other more serious acts of violence. In mid-1930 the communist members of the Eduskunta were arrested and a full catalogue of anti-communist laws approved.

The moderate socialist and non-socialist parties finally came together in 1937 to form a government. But it was too late in a decade ending in war for the domestic achievements of the partnership to be anything but modest. Knee-jerk defensive measures against recession such as cuts in wages caused greater suffering in Finland than in any other of the Scandinavian countries.

The Second World War put a huge strain on relations between the Scandinavian countries. Sweden avoided the Nazi occupation suffered by Norway and Denmark by seeming to favour the German cause. Even when, later on, she provided a refuge for thousands of

Danish Jews and gave military training to Norwegian and Danish
exiles, the feeling that somehow Sweden had opted out from her
responsibilities came easily to the surface.

Meanwhile as Europe was waiting for the central drama to begin,
the Finns were taking up arms to resist Moscow's territorial demands.
Outnumbered and outmatched in arms and equipment, their hopes
were pinned on foreign involvement. When this failed to materialize,
there was nothing for it but to give the Russians all they wanted
including the Karelian Isthmus. The 1940 treaty which ended the
Winter War required the resettlement of no less than 12 per cent of
the entire Finnish population. Not surprisingly, within the year Helsinki
had opened up contacts with the Germans, allowing transit for
military traffic much as the Swedes were doing, in return for food and
armaments.

There followed the German invasion of Russia, an adventure
which Mannerheim, in justifying the active participation of his army,
described as a 'holy war' to restore Finnish borders. Having achieved
this objective with remarkable ease, the Finns wanted out, a desire
which became all the more determined as the German advance
ground to a halt at Stalingrad. But there was no basis for a settlement
and the Finns could only wait for the inevitable Russian counter-
attack. When it came, retreating Germans took revenge by
devastating everything in their path.

Sweden

As the Nordic country to emerge strongest from the war, Sweden was
well set to re-open for business. In six years her gross national
product had risen by 20 per cent. Her industries were unscathed, her
labour force well trained and her commercial leaders eager for
expansion. A start was made on dismantling the rationing system,
import controls were lifted and building regulations liberalized. One
or two in office wanted to push the country more to the left – Gunnar

Myrdal as minister of commerce was all for going further, faster in that direction – but they were no match for prime minister Hansson, the gentle innovator and supreme mediator.

After Hansson's unexpected death in 1946, a strong section of social-democrat opinion favoured a younger man for the job – someone who would brighten up the image of a government currently dominated by politicians whose ideas were moulded by pre-war experience. Interest centred on Tage Erlander, minister of education. At 45, he was of the right generation, an intellectual with a feeling for practical politics. It turned out to be a wise choice, confirmed by a record 23 years of unbroken power and a lasting reputation as a leader who governed by consensus.

Erlander kept up the drive for growth despite a high rate of inflation. The jump in prices in the early fifties was 20 per cent in 1951 alone. A scarcity of labour pushed up wages by no less than 25 per cent between 1950 and 1952. The prime minister responded by devaluing the krona by a massive 30 per cent. What would have been judged elsewhere as an economic disaster was justified as part of a broad strategy guaranteeing increased productivity and full employment.

The government looked set for an overwhelming vote of confidence in the 1956 elections. The economy was booming, unemployment at a minimum, poverty almost eradicated. Sweden shared with Switzerland the distinction of being the richest country in Europe. Her welfare system was the envy of less affluent states. Even the rate of inflation was down to manageable proportions. But the success of social democracy carried a penalty. Voters felt sufficiently secure to look more closely at what the right-wing opposition parties had to offer. The social democrats remained the single biggest party but governed with a wafer-thing majority. It brought out the best in Erlander. Every Riksdag vote was a challenge to his ability as a parlia-mentary tactician and he survived them all. The social democrats did well in the 1964 election and even better in 1968, when reaction to the

Russian invasion of Czechoslovakia brought in a welcome bonus vote from disaffected communists. But then Erlander decided to retire. In choosing a successor the party made a break with the past. Olof Palme was a youngish left-wing intellectual. New thinking was expected and a more turbulent period predicted for Swedish politics.

Denmark

In the early post-war years, political leaders depended for their appeal less on programme or ideology than on their war record. But unlike Norway, where there was close accord on priorities between politicians of different colours, Denmark started with a government of diverse personalities who managed, between them, to offer conflicting views on almost every important question.

A start on economic recovery had to wait on America's decision to pump dollar aid into Europe. With its share of the Marshall Plan, Denmark entered on a new industrial revolution. By the mid-fifties manufacturing capacity equalled that of agriculture. But in parallel with Swedish and Norwegian experience the race for affluence brought with it short-run economic problems such as a high rate of inflation.

After a succession of light-weight coalition governments the 1953 election brought the social democrats back into power where they remained, more or less securely, until the mid-sixties. Their problem was to maintain rapid economic growth, which entailed a further switch away from agriculture as the first export industry, while at the same time trying to maintain a stable currency. A policy of muddling through, usually with the help of foreign loans, tended to disguise the real economic gains and to concentrate the public's attention on their daily tribulations – higher taxes and prices. By the mid-sixties the ratio of inflation in Denmark was higher than in any comparable industrial country, and among OECD members was only exceeded in Iceland and Turkey.

The government's strongest card was its leader – Jens Otto Krag. Still only in his forties when he took over as prime minister, he combined political intelligence with a lifestyle that was more appropriate to a film star than a solemn parliamentarian. He generated excitement and attracted the young voters when the youth cult was at its height. Like Erlander, he preferred to govern by consensus. Unions, employers and agricultural interests came together to advise the government on any aspect of policy it thought fit to discuss. Among its earlier recommendations was a centralized wages policy, which was remarkably successful in stabilizing of incomes, prices and profits.

But even Krag was unable to beat the odds against a stable moderate government. His only means of staying in power was to work with the far left. Their coalition held until late 1967 when a jerk in the rate of inflation was accompanied by a run of foreign reserves. To hold down consumption Krag proposed a suspension of the annual cost-of-living adjustment to wages and pensions. It was too much for the far left. At the general election, an anti-labour coalition came out ahead.

The change of government did not signify an early change in strategy. Hopes of lower taxes were soon disappointed, and promises to bring down public expenditure were soon diluted to allow for extensions to social welfare, such as the raising of the school-leaving age and a cost-of-living supplement on pensions. When the next election came in 1971, the social democrats picked up votes from those who were either disillusioned with the government's general handling of the economy or persuaded that Krag would get the best deal in negotiations with the EEC. Having secured a narrow lead, Krag was able to take his country into Europe, an achievement which made Copenhagen the bridge between all the Nordic capitals and Brussels.

Norway

Norway's first post-war prime minister had spent four years in a concentration camp. Einar Gerhardsen had been vice-chairman of Oslo city council until he became leader of the underground anti-Nazi movement in the early days of the occupation. As recently elected social democrat leader he was the natural choice to head the 1945 caretaker government.

He and his mixed-party group of ministerial colleagues agreed on the basics for an economic plan. The action needed to restore Norway's prosperity was apparent to everyone: to make good the heavy losses in the merchant fleet; to increase the output of hydro-electricity; and to develop new industries. The chief worry for the social democrats was the likely impact of communists who had gained credit for leading the resistance. Talks on a possible merger of the parties were as unproductive as parallel negotiations in Denmark, but the electoral results of each party's going its own way were markedly different in the two countries. More confident of their purpose, the Norwegian social democrats took the electorate by storm, increasing their share of the popular vote in the 1945 election by close on ten per cent. Their advance gave them the one prize that eluded their colleagues everywhere else in Scandinavia – an absolute majority and the freedom to govern without always looking over their shoulder.

The government was supported wholeheartedly by the trade unions. In return for price controls and food subsidies, which stabilized the cost of living for almost five years, and the guarantee of full employment, the unions accepted compulsory arbitration for all wage disputes and virtually foreswore the use of the strike weapon. Returned in 1949 with an increased majority, the social democrats were able to point to a rise in productivity and living standards well beyond that achieved by most other Western countries. But the general increase in world prices triggered by the Korean War meant that Norway had to pay much more for her essential imports. The use of subsidies to counteract the adverse balance of trade reached its limit when they became the largest item in the national budget. In 1950, food prices were allowed to get closer to their market level, the cost of living started on an upward curve, leading to a 30 per cent increase over three years, and industrial investment suffered a sharp cutback.

The social democrats held on to power until the mid-sixties when a centre right coalition took over. Per Borten, centre party leader, became prime minister. It was not an adventurous government but it suited the mood of the time. By 1969 the social democrats had recovered much of their lost ground. But it was not enough to stop the return of the coalition government. With a majority of two it struggled on, until the EEC issue shook Norwegian politics to its roots.

Finland

Having fought first against Russia then against Germany, the country emerged from the war defeated, demoralized and in political disarray. The peace treaty with the Soviet Union was still to be agreed, but the terms of the 1944 armistice – the surrender of one-twelfth of Finnish territory and reparations to be paid in goods valued at three hundred million dollars at 1938 prices – suggested that Russia had no inhibitions about leaning heavily on her weaker neighbour.

If the public looked anywhere for a lead it was to the presidency, and to Field-Marshal Mannerheim. Revered as a national hero by the right, Mannerheim extended his reputation by bringing his country through the Winter War and by his initial success in the renewed hostilities with Russia in 1941. Though he was not much loved by the Soviets they acknowledged Mannerheim's unique personal authority.

Carl Enckell, a close and trusted associate of Mannerheim for many years, took charge of foreign affairs. Like the president he had been trained as an officer in the Russian army but resigned at the height of the Tsarist oppression and transferred to the Finnish diplomatic corps. As a realist in international politics Enckell had nothing to teach the new prime minister, Juho Paasikivi, who returned to the job he had held briefly early in the century. His political skills were in demand once again on the eve of the Second World War, when he returned to Moscow to negotiate a joint defence plan against threatened German aggression. Paasikivi was instructed by his government to reject plans for handing over key strategic areas, a rebuff which set Finland on course for the Winter War. Given more freedom it is likely that Paasikivi would have tried to go some way to meet the Russians. In any event, his relations with the Soviet leaders were firm enough for him to be welcomed as envoy to Moscow in the peace period between the Winter War and the Continuation War, his return to the premiership in 1944 was at the insistence of the Russians, who overrode Mannerheim's objections.

The 1945 election confirmed Paasikivi and Enckell in their jobs and a cabinet was formed giving roughly equal representation to the social democrats, communists and the farmers' party. When Mannerheim, who had turned 78 and was ailing fast, was persuaded to stand down in mid-term of his presidency, Paasikivi was the obvious successor. The issue was so clear-cut it was decided to forego the formality of a popular election and instead invite parliament to authorize Paasikivi's elevation. He needed no instruction on the working of the Finnish constitution. Power was centred on the presidency – or rather, on the man who had enough strength of character to use the presidency for all it was worth.

The peace treaty with Russia was signed on February 1947. Though severe, the terms confirmed what had already been provisionally agreed by the 1944 armistice. Finland was to lose 12 per cent of her border territory to the Soviet Union, including the country's second largest city of Viipuri and the port and province of

Petsamo on the Arctic coast. With a large part of the province of Karelia taken over by the Russians the frontier was moved back from a distance of only 19 miles from Leningrad to a new line 112 miles from the former Soviet capital. Four hundred thousand people had to be resettled. The Åland Islands were to remain demilitarised and limitations were imposed on the size of the Finnish armed forces and on the weapons they could use.

The Russians then raised the stakes with an 'invitation' to negotiate a mutual assistance agreement. It seemed as if nothing less than an administration directly answerable to Moscow would satisfy the Russians. Paasikivi opened negotiations by arguing that the interests of the Soviet Union on her north-western border (the only part of Finland that really mattered to the Russian military) could best be served by a sovereign Finland whose sympathetic relations with her eastern neighbour precluded her territory being used as a platform for attack. Skilfully, Paasikivi shifted the emphasis away from Russian ambitions for making Finland an ally towards the far more attractive prospect of the two countries' entering into a joint security arrangement which would allow Finland to stand aside from big power politics.

In the end it was all a matter of interpretation. Finland promised to defend herself against an attack from Germany or an allied state, to confer with Russia in case of war or threat of war and, if necessary, to accept Russian aid. Great play was made of Finland's ambition 'to remain outside the conflicting interests of the great powers'.

The popular view in Europe was that Finland had tied herself to the Soviet Union and was as much under the control of Moscow as any of the communist satellites. Paasikivi did his best to counteract this impression and reacted decisively if there was any hint of a threat to his own authority. When in the spring of 1948 there were rumours that the communists were planning to seize power, he dismissed the powerful minister of internal affairs, Yrjö Leino. But the president was hyper-sensitive to Moscow's needs for reassurances of Finnish good faith. The press was told to tone down criticism of the Soviet Union.

In this uncertain political climate the economy entered its first painful stage of recovery. Fortunately, most of the nation's productive capacity had survived the war intact, and the export demand for wood products was strong. But paying off reparations in goods the Russians wanted meant a big transfer of resources to the engineering industry. All this had to be achieved without a share in Marshall aid, though US loans totalling 150 million dollars were channelled through in other ways. Skilled labour and consumer goods were both in short supply with the inevitable consequence that wages and prices climbed steeply, each one feeding off the other to send inflation soaring. In 1948 prices were eight times their pre-war level.

The communists were well placed to take advantage of the government's troubles. In the summer of 1949 they disrupted industry with a series of strikes which split the trade-union movement and raised fears of an imminent coup. Paasikivi promptly replaced the social democrat government with one formed by the agrarians under the leadership of Urho Kekkonen. It was a wise choice.

Like Paasikivi, Kekkonen worked hard to establish good personal relations with the Russians. But he was not content merely to be an echo of his master's voice. In 1952 he put up a plan for 'a neutral alliance between the Scandinavian countries', which 'would remove even the theoretical threat of an attack ... via Finland's territory'. In reality, a Scandinavian alliance, neutral or otherwise, was impracticable since Denmark and Norway had only recently joined NATO. But the gain to Kekkonen was approval from the Soviet Union. Moscow was delighted by an unsolicited rejection of the Atlantic pact by a north European state and congratulated Finland on pursuing the course of 'strict neutrality'. This was one of the strongest indications so far that Russia was prepared to recognize Finland as neutral, and though Soviet commentators generally referred to that country as 'striving for neutrality' rather than having achieved the objective, Kekkonen's initiative put relations between the two nations on an entirely new footing.

In 1955, two years after the death of Stalin had brought the first signs of an easing in the cold war, Finland negotiated the return of the Porkkala base near Helsinki, which had been leased to the Soviet Union for 50 years. This meant the departure of the last Soviet troops on Finnish territory – the most powerful boost to national morale of the early post-war years. The concept of neutrality was beginning to take on real substance. That same year Finland joined the United Nations – but stayed out of the latest formation of Soviet defence, the Warsaw Pact.

In 1956 Kekkonen succeeded Paasikivi as president. A succession of weak governments consolidated presidential power and confirmed Kekkonen as the only leader capable of handling the Russians. Enjoying his enhanced prestige he was soon back on course with his policy of trying to establish Finland as an independent neutral.

At a time when the cement had barely set on the Berlin wall and the Soviet nuclear tests had climaxed with the detonation of a 50-megaton bomb, Kekkonen chose to go off to America where, as evidence of his country's freedom of action, he suggested that recent membership of EFTA was a prelude to a deal with the European Community. The Soviet Union promptly activated article 2 of the 1948 Treaty by demanding consultation on measures to ensure the defence of their frontiers. It was the most serious challenge yet to Finnish neutrality. It had been said so often that article 2 could be acted upon only when *both* parties agreed that a threat existed, it came as a shock to realize that a unilateral declaration of interest by the stronger partner was sufficient to start the process of military consultation. If the Soviet claim went uncontested Finnish independence would be seen as a sham.

Western observers expected the worst; nothing less than military bases on Finnish soil would satisfy Moscow. But Kekkonen remained placid. When he arrived back in Helsinki he was ready with a compromise strategy calling for a postponement of military talks in favour of discussions aimed at reassuring the Kremlin that Finland would remain true to her foreign policy. The strategy failed to satisfy the Russians. The only chance of persuading them to take the broader view was to appeal directly to Khrushchev. The crisis brought out the best in Kekkonen. He had nothing to give except the sure knowledge that if military consultations went ahead there would be a war scare in Scandinavia, possibly leading to counter-measures by the West. Why take the risk of creating another international trouble spot when all that was needed to guarantee the northern frontiers was a reaffirmation of the Finnish commitment to the 1948 treaty?

The sense of relief in Helsinki when Khrushchev agreed to postpone military talks was so great that nothing could detract from Kekkonen's prestige as the country's saviour. He was elected for a second six-year term by an overwhelming majority on the first round of voting.

Iceland

Iceland decided on 1944 as the year of its unilateral declaration of independence. The news was not well received in occupied Denmark, even though the termination of the union was little more than a formality. Home rule had been conceded in 1918 as part of a constitutional package which allowed either country to cut loose entirely after another 25 years. Even if the Icelanders were anticipating events by four years, the German invasion of Denmark in 1940 had effectively ended that country's responsibility for Iceland's foreign relations.

Independence meant that the Icelanders were on their own when it came to dealing with the Americans. The country was occupied peacefully by Britain in 1940, but US troops took over a year later. They poured money into the economy, improved roads and docks, built an airport and employed a large number of local people at high wages. Now, the first question for the free state to consider was an American request for a long-term lease on three military bases.

The government was sympathetic. With no means of defending herself, another world conflict would put Iceland at the mercy of whichever power could get to her first. But the continuing presence of American forces at the strength envisaged by Washington somehow gave the lie to the independence so recently celebrated. The answer was to recruit Iceland to NATO. Objection to the Americans' operating the Keflavík airbase were gradually withdrawn and in 1951 a separate defence agreement with the United States allowed for an increase in the number of troops brought in 'to defend Iceland and . . . to ensure the security of the seas around the country'.

When Icelandic politicians were not concerned with Americanization, the debate invariably turned to the state of the fishing industry. Fish was central to the economy, accounting for 90 per cent of the export trade. But over-dependence on a single product led to sensitive political nerves. Soon after the war there was concern that other nations were taking too large a share of the Icelandic catch. In 1948 the demarcation of new fishing zones was made subject to Icelandic jurisdiction. Two years later one mile was added to the three-mile offshore zone which Iceland had administered since 1901. This was just acceptable to other fishing nations but when, in 1958, the limit was extended to 12 miles, Britain sent naval vessels to protect trawlers from harassment and arrest. This was the first Cod War, a cat-and-mouse game between the British navy and coastguard patrols which continued up to 1961. At that point Britain and West Germany, the other fishing nation involved in the dispute, accepted the 12-mile zone on condition that if Iceland intended to widen her jurisdiction still further she had to give six months' notice of her intention and, if challenged, refer her claims to the International Court at The Hague.

In 1971, however, a left-wing government fulfilled its promise to do something about over-fishing by unilaterally extending the offshore zone to 50 miles. Despite a clear contravention of treaty commitment, Iceland gained sympathy as the tiny nation fighting the giants. There was something else working in her favour. Other countries including Britain and members of the European Community wanted to extend their jurisdiction over the continental shelf. A limit of 200 miles seemed to gain favour, a claim which put the Icelandic declaration into modest perspective.

In fact, such was the speed at which international opinion changed that in 1975 Iceland felt strong enough to make real what others were still speculating about. Britain protested at the 200-mile limit but when the talks reached stalemate in December 1976, British vessels were nevertheless banned from Icelandic waters.

EFTA and the EEC

After negotiations on Britain's entry to the EEC broke down in 1958, thoughts turned to an alternative trade alliance. The only counter-grouping to make any sense was one which brought together those who favoured a loose association with the EEC – Norway, Sweden, Denmark, Britain, Austria, Switzerland and Portugal, or the Outer Seven, as they were soon to be called. Between Britain and the Scandinavians there was already a strong basis for cooperation. Britain was the region's single most important customer. After preliminary talks between trade ministers a draft convention was approved at a ministerial meeting in Stockholm in July 1959 and signed the following January.

The Stockholm Convention adopted the same timetable for the reduction of tariffs as set by the EEC. The target year for the abolition of duties was 1970. Agriculture and fishing were excluded from the agreement. The status of Finland presented a problem. Finland was attracted to any proposal which allowed her to diversify her trade and made her less dependent on the Soviet Union. This was to continue a trend started in the fifties, soon after the completion of reparation payments when Russia accounted for 20 per cent of Finnish exports. By 1960 the proportion had dropped to fifteen per cent, with the difference being made up by sales to Western Europe. Imports too showed an increasingly western bias as tariff reductions secured by GATT (Finland joined in 1949) began to take effect. But it was in the Soviet interest that Finland, a rich export market with easy access to western technology, should continue to develop her economy.

With the tacit approval of the Soviet Union, it was made clear that Finland was not so much seeking to join EFTA as to secure an entirely new free-trade association, with the Seven as one party to the agreement and Finland as the other. The Russians felt reassured. It was a reminder to all that Finland was different.

In late 1968 Iceland asked to join EFTA but on terms that were favourable to the expansion of her infant industries. Eventually the EFTA partners settled for an immediate 30 per cent cut in Iceland's domestic tariffs with further gradual reductions leading to abolition in ten years. The Seven became Eight plus Finland in March 1970.

The Nordic countries did best out of EFTA. In the first decade trade between the EFTA members increased by 186 per cent; but between Norway, Sweden, Denmark, Finland and Iceland the gain was 284 per cent. The most remarkable advance was the proportion of Finnish trade with EFTA, which rose to over 50 per cent by the end of the sixties.

The preoccupation of the Nordic countries with their own trade diverted attention from important changes in the British attitude to the rest of Europe. It came as a surprise when, in 1961, Britain declared her conversion to the Treaty of Rome and her wish to reopen negotiations with the Community. The response from her Nordic partners in EFTA revealed the wide differences in attitudes towards European integration. Denmark gave unqualified approval to a move which promised to secure freer access to her two best markets, Britain and West Germany. Her own request to be admitted to the EEC was snapped in to arrive in Brussels at the same time as that from Britain. Norway was more reserved. The business sector had gained sufficient confidence to see exciting possibilities in being part of a wider Europe but the farmers and fishermen felt threatened by EEC policies which affected their interests, and the opinion polls showed barely 25 per cent of the electorate in favour of EEC membership. In the Storting, however, a majority wanted to follow Britain. The government promised that the final verdict on EEC membership would be subject to a referendum. In April 1962, nine months after Britain declared her commitment to Europe, Norway too announced that she wanted to be part of the Community.

Expectations that Sweden and even Finland might follow soon faded. Both refused to compromise their neutrality. But before serious talking began there was a crisis in Anglo-French relations which put into doubt the whole future of an enlarged European Community. France complained that Britain was attempting to change the rules of the Common Market. The point at issue was Britain's acceptance of American Polaris warheads to be installed in British-built submarines. President de Gaulle was now able to assert that by acting alone Britain had proved her unreliability as a prospective European partner. It was the breaking-point in the negotiations.

Early in 1967, the British government felt confident enough to resume negotiations on entry to the European Community. Again, France objected. Then, in April 1969 de Gaulle resigned. His successor, Georges Pompidou, made it clear that if Britain cared to resume her efforts to join the Common Market, France would not stand in her way. Referenda on the European issue in Denmark and Norway led to a decisive 63·3 per cent in support for Denmark entering the EEC but a narrow victory for the anti-marketeers in Norway. The remaining EFTA countries, led by Sweden, sought a free-trade agreement without political strings.

On 1 July 1977 the relationship between the EEC and the remaining seven EFTA countries – Austria, Finland, Iceland, Norway, Portugal, Sweden and Switzerland – took on a new significance. It was on that date that the remaining duties on most industrial products traded between the two blocs were finally removed, so creating the largest free-trade area in the world.

All the EFTA agreements with the EEC, except Finland's, covered a willingness to extend cooperation beyond trade. In Sweden's case this clause was open-ended, and her negotiators made it clear that they were prepared to consider any area of collaboration where neutrality was not at issue. A strong representation at Brussels was soon complemented by an elaborate network of bureaucratic contacts, which brought Sweden in on almost every new development programme from telecommunications and computer techniques to environment protection and food technology.

The evolutionary clauses for Norway and Iceland (like those for Austria and Switzerland) were restricted to economic matters. Norway in particular was keen to keep a distance between herself and the Community. But as the seventies advanced there was less concern about the risks of getting involved with the EEC and more about the dangers of being left out. The immense wealth from North Sea oil raised national self-confidence and at the same time revealed weaknesses in the country's economic base which could only be corrected by attracting technological expertise from the big industrial powers. Talks started on simplifying rules of origin, stimulating trade in agricultural products and exchanging information on state purchasing.

Spared any further anguish on the Common Market, the Norwegian government now had to face up to an even greater challenge. The discovery and extraction of oil from the bed of the North Sea coincided with the leading producers in the Middle East working together to control the world market for an essential product. Almost overnight, the value of oil off the Norwegian coast assumed a value undreamt of by the first prospectors.

When talks with the oil companies began in the early sixties generous tax concessions were needed to start exploration of 78 blocks south of the 62nd parallel. There followed four years of disappointment, relieved only marginally by discoveries of gas condensate. Then just before Christmas 1969, the Phillips Group announced a major find in the Ekofisk field. The first oil was brought ashore in June 1971. It was at this point that the government started to take a closer interest in what was obviously a valuable national resource. After 1972, when the publicly owned Statoil company was set up, a system of co-ownership and profit-sharing was developed which gave the state up to 66 per cent of the revenue from gas and oil production.

At the beginning of the decade Norway was ninth in the world league of wealthy nations. By 1975, her national income boosted by the rising price of oil, she was well on the way to enjoying the highest standard of living in the world. But this was not altogether pleasing news. There was a fear that oil riches would damage the social framework by inflating the economy, destroying old-established industries and changing the commercial shape of the coastline to the detriment of fishermen and farmers.

The government dithered. There was no denying the advantages that oil gave to Norway. Yet those who urged prudence were not entirely motivated by old-world nostalgia. The 1977 Bravo blowout which, given less favourable weather, could have turned into a major disaster, underlined the risks of moving ahead faster than technical competence.

As for Denmark, the EEC insider, agricultural policy made her a Common Market beneficiary. By the late seventies Denmark's net annual gain from the Community budget was in the region of seven hundred million pounds, better than any other member. But the oil recession and recurring economic crises linked to the country's heavy borrowing overseas led the Danes to *feel* less well off. With the contrast of a relatively stable Sweden and a booming Norway just next door, the first instinct was to fasten on the EEC as the source of their troubles. Laws made in Brussels were said to encroach on basic freedoms and to pull Denmark more securely into the Franco-German sphere of influence.

The standard assumption of the Nordic political scene, that it was stable and predictable, was shattered in the early seventies by the rise of populism. The widespread disillusionment with established government brought on by the recession caused by the 1974 oil crisis showed itself in the dramatic gains made by the rural party in Finland, the progressive party and the centre democrats in Denmark and the Anders Lange party in Norway. Icelandic voters gave unexpectedly strong support to a new left-wing grouping. Only Sweden failed to produce a party of dissidents, but this was only because the centre party broadened its appeal to attract a strong populist element.

Sweden

When Erlander retired in 1969 after 23 years as social-democrat leader, there was only one serious contender for his job. Olof Palme was an intellectual and a visionary whose forthright pronouncements on the shortcomings of Swedish society put him to the left of most of his colleagues. He had served a ten-year apprenticeship as personal assistant to Erlander and then, after entering parliament in 1963, had quickly advanced to ministerial status, first in communications and latterly in education.

Within months of his taking office Palme was leading his party into one of the bitterest election campaigns in living memory. That Erlander had gone seemed to act as a release on frustrations which had been bubbling away beneath the normally placid surface of Swedish democracy. An unofficial strike in the state-owned LKAB mines at Kiruna, led by relatively well-paid skilled workers who were protesting against the general levelling of incomes, was a warning to the party and to the trades union confederation (LO) that their efforts on behalf of lower-paid workers were by no means universally applauded. But Palme stuck to his ideals for greater equality and for a 'low-income profile' for future wage settlements.

If Palme was under attack from the right, matters were hardly more settled at the other end of the political spectrum. The new prime minister understood and sometimes spoke the language of Marxism and he had taken up the most cherished course of the highly organized and vocal student movement – opposition to US involvement in Vietnam. But many feared that by giving the far left a sympathetic hearing, Palme was putting his future and that of his party in jeopardy.

The election gave the social democrats 163 seats. The parties of the right collected 170 seats between them, with the centre moving ahead strongly to return 71 members. But there were also the communists to take into account. They had been expected to fall victim to the new constitutional rule that to qualify for representation in the Riksdag a party must secure four per cent of the national vote or 12 per cent in any one constituency. But since condemning the Russian invasion of Czechoslovakia the communists had rediscovered some of their old vitality. Carried forward on a wave of anti-capitalist and anti-American sentiment, chiefly among young voters, they won 17 seats, enough to put the social democrats back into office, only this time as a minority government.

Dissatisfaction among skilled and professional workers soon spread beyond the iron-mining region of the north. The trouble really started when the two biggest white-collar unions put in for salary increases of up to 23 per cent and demanded separate bargaining machinery. Here was a major revolt by middle-class unionists against the whole concept of centralized wage negotiations. Palme surprised everybody by reacting quickly and strongly. He flatly refused to compromise, and a limited strike was countered by a lockout which affected the railways, schools, welfare services and even the armed forces, and threw the country into chaos. The crisis in what was normally held up to be a model industrial environment, attracted front-page news round the world.

After nearly two months of fruitless negotiations, the government rushed through emergency legislation which banned all strikes and lockouts for six weeks. Union resolve crumbled and a settlement was patched together which did little to satisfy white-collar aspirations.

If anything, middle-class complaints became more vocal over the following months. This was not so much a reflection on Palme's radical policies – though his promise to bring democracy to the shop floor raised a few managerial hackles – as a reaction to a general downturn in the economy. In the approach to the 1973 election the opposition attacked what they saw as the underlying contradictions of social democracy. Though professing the freedom of the individual, the social-democrat party, it was claimed, had come to behave like an arrogant big brother – fussy and over-protective, telling others how best to run their affairs and then, if frustrated, resorting to bullying tactics.

The politician who gained most from the discomfort of the social democrats was the leader of the centre party, Thorbjörn Fälldin. There were a lot of jokes made about Fälldin. Closely identified with his northern rural background, his small-town image, accentuated by a fondness for home-spun philosophy delivered in a ponderous monotone, put him at the other end of the political line from Palme, the sophisticated internationalist. But that did not make him a nonentity.

The same people who worried about Palme's cleverness found Fälldin's honesty refreshing and endearing. So obviously not part of the Stockholm establishment, he was a persuasive advocate of decentralization and a convincing defender of the rights of the individual against state bureaucracy.

The election turnout of over 90 per cent was the highest ever recorded. The centre party made a great advance, particularly in the metropolitan areas and the social democrats fell back yet again, but the dramatic polarization that many had expected did not take place. Instead there was deadlock with 175 members elected to each side. What evidence there was of electoral preference suggested that Palme, the leader of the largest party, should try to keep his government together, at least until the Riksdag decreed otherwise.

On basic issues the government could usually patch together a majority. An urgent package of economic measures was followed by a series of all-party consultations to discover what other proposals might win broad acceptance. The main question was how the economy could absorb the doubling of oil prices. Sweden ranked first in the world in energy consumption per head of population, and with 70 per cent of her needs met by oil imports the price spiral of 1973–74 added some eight thousand million krona to her trade bill.

One possible solution was to find a substitute for imported energy. Sweden was further ahead than most with plans for a network of nuclear reactors. Up to this point there was no hint of public nervousness. It was a different matter when, in the wake of the oil crisis, the expansion programme was revised upwards to allow for a chain of 15 reactors to be completed by 1985. Suddenly the country realized the extent of its commitment and the hazards involved. Critics like the writer Eva Moberg and the Nobel prize-winner Professor Hans Alfvén, who had been accustomed to speaking into thin air, now found themselves with eager audiences. And to Thorbjörn Fälldin arch-opponent of the centralized decision-making process which allowed the nuclear lobby to flourish, the spokesman for rural Sweden and the champion of the anti-pollution movement, they offered a cause into which he could throw himself body and soul.

He toured the country calling for the end of a government which, by its shortsighted policy, was prepared '… to endanger our children and grandchildren for thousands of years to come'. His almost religious devotion to the anti-nuclear crusade – 'I will not take part in a government that starts one more reactor' – re-established Fälldin as the leading alternative to Palme even though his prospective coalition partners, the liberals and conservatives, were much more sympathetic to nuclear development.

With another election fast approaching, the social democrats were further tarnished when in January 1976 the film director Ingmar Bergman was taken from rehearsals at the Royal Dramatic Theatre in Stockholm to be interviewed by the police about his taxes. After spending some time recovering from what he described as 'nearly unbearable humiliation', Bergman announced he was leaving Sweden to work abroad. Before doing so he launched a blistering attack on the social democrats' 'ideology of grey compromise' which pointed up the virtue of expensive programmes of social reform while ignoring the dangers of a bureaucracy spreading 'like a fast-spreading cancer'. If they did not know it before, Swedish taxpayers were now aware that revenue inspectors could enter their offices and homes (the former without even a court order), require banks to surrender statements of accounts and even see private medical records – all with the law on their side.

For the opposition the tax issue was their strongest electoral card. Industrialists complained that workers were staying away because they were expected to pay well over 50 per cent in marginal tax. The position was even worse for the self-employed, who had to pay their own social security. Their plight became a matter for public debate when Astrid Lindgren, the much-loved children's writer, was assured by the tax board that she was bound to pay them 102 per cent of her year's income. The writer of fairy tales responded by publishing in a popular daily a story about a never-never land where the rules of logic were infinitely adaptable to allow people as many per cents as they wanted. The news value of these events was enhanced by the knowledge that both Bergman and Astrid Lindgren were life-long social democrats.

In the run-up to the election Fälldin made his famous pledge to abandon nuclear power within ten years. It was enough to deprive the social democrats of their majority and to give Fälldin his chance. The shaping of the coalition was surprising painless. Of the policy deals to be made, the most urgent was in the sensitive area of nuclear development, where Fälldin had cried 'Stop!' too often to be allowed to forget his commitment – or so it was thought. Despite accusations of betrayal, he settled for the nuclear programme to remain on the drawing board while a special commission examined future energy supply and alternatives to nuclear power.

The promise to increase individual freedom and choice was quickly translated into lower taxes on small businesses. But the cynics noted that the first non-socialist budget in 44 years allowed for thirty-five thousand more public-sector jobs. And there was no understating the commitment to 'carry on a policy of social reform', which included new measures to help the underprivileged, better working conditions and further moves towards sex equality.

A pledge to keep unemployment below two per cent required a record level of state intervention to help companies ride out the latest crisis. One industry after another – shipyards, steel, textiles, glass, shoes – asked for and received loans and grants which soon reached an annual total of three billion dollars, an outlay about equal to the country's total industrial profits. By the end of its life the coalition had accomplished more nationalization than all previous administrations put together – quite an achievement for a supposedly right-wing government.

The unions accepted the need to hold down consumer spending, allowing a VAT increase and a double devaluation – six per cent in March 1977 and ten per cent in August – without much in return except a price freeze. With wages pegged, the combined effect was to reduce the real living standards. As part of the second devaluation, the coalition took Sweden out of the European snake, the linking arrangement for a group of currencies which had effectively over-valued the krona by tying it to the deutschmark. The unions were rewarded for their forbearance by news of order books refilling and an impressive reduction in the trade deficit.

But it was the energy issue that wrecked the government. The leader who not two years earlier had pledged that nuclear power would be phased out by 1985 had to decide whether to go ahead with fuelling two new reactors. The prospect was anathema to the hardliners in the centre party, who were not prepared to budge at least until the popular view had been tested. But Fälldin's coalition partners were not ready for a referendum. Fälldin was trapped. Just two years after he had achieved one of the most remarkable victories in Swedish election history, he had no choice but to resign.

The fall of the government put the social democrats into a quandary. They were unwilling to push for an election when they were constitutionally bound to repeat the performance in less than ten months' time. The alternative of a coalition with the liberals on the West German and latterly the Danish model was not even considered by a party hierarchy which remained convinced that the 1976 defeat was an electoral aberration soon to be corrected. On the right, it was conceded that the centre party had to remain out of government until the current parliament had run its course.

Palme and the liberal leader, Ola Ullsten, concluded that the only possibility was for the liberals to govern alone. It was an extraordinary turn of fate that the most junior of the party leaders, heading the second smallest parliamentary group (only the communists had fewer seats), should be asked to run the country. On paper, Ullsten headed one of the weakest minority governments in Europe. But looking beyond parliament the prospects were more encouraging. Just a few days before his departure Fälldin detected the first signs of economic recovery. Industrial production had started rising again, the trade balance was once more in surplus and, with devaluation aided by wage restraint, Sweden had regained the edge in international competitiveness. The scene was set for the liberals to stimulate private consumption with a package of tax cuts and improved family allowances – all good vote-winners.

For a few weeks after the fall of the coalition, the minority government drafted an energy bill which allowed for a stop on the expansion of the nuclear industry once 12 reactors were operating. It seemed as if the humiliation of Fälldin was complete. But, before the government had a chance to act, an event on the other side of the world caused the whole of Swedish nuclear policy to be thrown back into the melting pot.

The reactor leak at Three Mile Island near Harrisburg, Pennsylvania, in 1979 made a stronger impact in Sweden than in the United States. That no one suffered any ill-effects from the accident was barely detectable in Sweden. The affair was like a tonic to Fälldin; but before he had the chance to recover fully, Palme reacted to prevent a split in his own ranks and to stop short a centre-party revival. In April the social-democratic leadership conceded that a referendum on nuclear energy was not such a bad idea after all, as long as it was held after the election. This turned out to favour a centre-right coalition (assuming it could be formed) with a one-seat advantage. There followed a month of party wrangling while Fälldin gradually reasserted his authority. Having reached accord the ruling triangle barely had time to agree ministerial appointments and to promise a mildly reformist programme before they were plunged back into electioneering on the narrow but vital question of energy policy.

The nuclear referendum took place in March 1980. Three proposals were offered, two of them advocating a doubling in the number of reactors but nevertheless projecting a long-term phasing out of nuclear power, while the third called specifically for a phasing out within ten years. The social democrats and the liberals backed proposal two, which differed from proposal one (the conservative preference) only in stipulating that all new power plants must be publicly owned. In wanting an early phase-out as in proposal three, the centre found itself an ally of the communists.

Split three ways on an issue that was central to economic strategy, it seemed unlikely that the coalition could long survive the referendum, whatever the result. But when the voters gave the decisive yes to nuclear development – the first two proposals got respectively 18·7 and 39·3 per cent – Fälldin did not resign. In sticking to his job he could comfort himself that after activating the two new reactors which were ready for service, it would be some time before other sensitive decisions were required.

If others in the government had their doubts, they were deterred from expressing them by the conviction that they were alone capable of dealing with Sweden's economic problems, notably the challenge of trying to apply a wages policy at a time when the country's high labour costs were causing her to lose international competitiveness. With inflation moving back over ten per cent, the unions pitched their demands at the same level. The employers argued that the economy could not stand an increase of more than three per cent. An attempt to bridge the gap was made with a government offer to freeze prices for nine months and to reduce taxes if the unions temporized. Their refusal inaugurated the biggest labour conflict in Sweden's history, with strikes and lockouts shutting down most of the country's industry and public services.

Clearly, the industrial relations machinery which had served Sweden so well over the years was proving inadequate for an economy where growth could no longer be assumed. It was not so much tinkering with the system that was needed as a wholly new philosophy of political management.

Each Nordic country had its own particular reason for registering an anti-establishment vote in the early to mid-seventies – the Common Market issue in Norway, taxation in Denmark, the poverty of the regions in Finland, inflation in Iceland and over-government in Sweden. As the leading party the social democrats suffered most, but there were also dramatic changes on the right, with extremist parties making their strongest advances in Norway and Denmark.

So was it just coincidence that all of Scandinavia should be thrown off political balance at about the same time? Ignoring the occupational groups with special grouses, the newly affluent were the most easily deflected from their normal loyalties–typically the youngish couple on the suburban housing estates, those who had done well out of social democracy but who now feared that any further moves towards the egalitarian society could only be achieved at their expense. It had to be accepted on the left that its working-class foundation was fast contracting, and with it the number of voters who were prepared to take the system as they found it.

But there was a deeper problem. In central Scandinavia, where the social democrats had enjoyed a long run of uninterrupted power, there was an uncomfortable feeling that the party had taken on a life of its own, controlling and directing the nation's affairs as best suited its own interests. It was an interpretation of events which the left angrily rejected. In the age of the computer and the centralized data bank it was natural to assume that the state had too much power to manipulate and control. But by international acclaim, Scandinavia boasted the most open system of government in the world. Hardly any official activity was closed to public scrutiny, and consultation with relevant interest groups was assumed to be an essential preliminary to decision-making at all levels.

Yet something was lacking. The middle-class Dane who complained that their taxes were too high did not feel adequately represented in the power structure; nor did the Swedish anti-nuclear campaigners or the Norwegian farmers and fishermen, who resented the assumption that they were bound to do well out of the Common Market. Ideas for extending the freedom of the individual soon figured on every party agenda and brought into much sharper focus the differences between left- and right-wing parties.

Economic Reform

As the mid-seventies recession wore on it became clear to Scandinavian governments that they could not always spend their way out of trouble. Leading areas of the economy were coming under pressure from low-cost competitors in the developing countries like Brazil, Hong Kong, Korea and Taiwan, a feature of international commerce that was likely to get more serious in the years ahead. It came to be recognized that support for ailing industries was an unproductive as well as an expensive exercise.

A prime example was shipbuilding, important to Sweden, Denmark and Finland, where it accounted for up to ten per cent of total exports, but more so to Norway where the figure was more than 20 per cent, without including revenue from her merchant fleet, the fifth largest in the world. After investing in bulk cargo carriers and tankers in the early seventies to cater for the expected growth in trade an increase in oil consumption in the west, all four countries had spare capacity. Then, as the depression cut into the profits of shipping lines, the construction side of the business saw the gaps in the order books widening to frightening proportions. The Norwegian and Swedish governments rushed in with loans and subsidies to assist a hard-pressed industry. By the end of 1977 Sweden had put in over a billion dollars, while Norway contributed four hundred million dollars in that year alone. But this was only the beginning. By 1979, demand was running at under one third of potential output. A Norwegian royal commission estimated that 1985 might be a realistic date to expect a recovery in shipping, and even then it was not likely to be easy. The time had come to think about adapting the industry to take account of real world demand.

An example of what could be achieved without intervention from the state was provided by Finland, where no yards were closed and where, between 1973 and 1978, the labour force fell by less than one ninth. A big factor in the survival of Finnish shipping was the steady flow of orders from the Soviet Union; but early specialization in the building of icebreakers, arctic offshore vessels, container ships and – the most promising bet for the future – oil and gas drilling rigs and ships also played a major part in maintaining a healthy industry.

In 1978 Norway started to let the air out of the subsidy cushion with a reduction of state support from an average of 20 per cent for each contract to 12 or 15 per cent. At the same time it was acknowledged that the merchant fleet would get smaller, tumbling from its fifth place in world ranking. To ease the shock, the shipping companies were helped to buy second-hand vessels, many of which were available on the international market at knock-down prices, with loan guarantees of up to 30 per cent of the purchase price. The Swedish government took a similar line, tempering generosity with hard commercial sense by proposing to hand over two of the largest yards to maintenance and repair work and adapting others to heavy engineering. Employment in shipping and shipbuilding, having dropped 30 per cent from 1975 to 1978, continued its downward slide. It was much the same story with other staple industries, including steel and engineering, textiles and even pulp and paper, where the effects of over-capacity at a time of recession were magnified by the dramatic advance of American competitors.

But few observers of the Scandinavian scene were persuaded that the latest economic revolution had gone anywhere near far enough. The main point at issue was the size of the state sector. As the world economy went into recession, the right-wing parties called for tax cuts and a tougher line on welfare handouts as a way of stimulating entrepreneurial skills. But the social democrats were reluctant to change the principles of a lifetime. This was not simply a case of political myopia. Many of their supporters worked in the state sector which in Sweden, for example, accounted for over half the labour market. They were not likely to vote for policies that reduced their security or living standards. In any case, criticism of the tax burden in Sweden, then the highest in the Western world, was tempered by a regard for a welfare system that others could only envy.

The social democrats temporised. While proclaiming a renewed belief in the freedom of the individual, by proposing a bigger share for workers in the running of their industries, say, or by putting more resources into lifelong learning, the party chose to ignore the mounting national debt, arguing that more investment in export-led manufacturing would promote economic growth which, in turn, would bring in the tax revenue needed to sustain the welfare infrastructure. As a last resort, the economy could be brought back on track by a currency devaluation. This happened in 1987 when the Swedish krona was allowed to fall by a full 16 per cent, leading to a welcome boost to exports. But as the opposition was quick to point out, it would not be long before this option was ruled out by the world-wide move towards free trade and the ending of exchange controls. Worries about a future in which Sweden would be forced to live within its means raised the conservative vote and made that party the natural leader of any future right-wing coalition, a prospect that would have been unthinkable a decade earlier. Meanwhile, the social democrats held on to power by the narrowest of margins.

The same challenge had to be faced in Denmark where foreign debt was an incredible 40 per cent of GDP. But there, the political scene changed dramatically in the eighties, not least because as a member of the European Union since 1972, the country had had to face economic realities. A centre-right coalition headed by the conservative leader, Poul Schlüter, came to power in 1982 with a mandate to cut the public sector and to introduce tax reforms to make the economy more competitive. The government was not strong enough to push through radical measures – income tax remained at around 60 per cent – but a firmer grip was imposed on state expenditure which kept inflation in line. The lesson was not lost on the social democrats, led by Roul Nyrup Rasmussen, when they returned to power in the early nineties. Changes to the welfare system including tougher conditions for unemployment benefits, an end to generous paid leave schemes and tighter criteria for early retirement, helped to bring the national budget back into surplus. Unemployment fell and economic growth caught up with and eventually outpaced the rest of Europe.

The age of innocence in Sweden ended in 1986 with the assassination of Olof Palme. That the prime minister could be gunned down in a public thoroughfare came as a huge shock to a people who thought they lived in a secure and open society. It was made worse for them by the failure of the police to establish a motive or to bring a convincing case against any of the suspects. There were more shocks along the way. Palme's deputy, Ingmar Carlsson, took over as head of government at a time when industrial production was falling, unemployment was on the increase and the budget deficit was mounting at a frightening rate. To add to the government's discomfort the Chernobyl nuclear disaster revived the energy debate at a time when over half the country's electricity was nuclear based.

More pragmatic than the idealistic Palme, and less wedded to socialist dogma, Ingmar Carlsson embarked on a programme of gradual reform. Various measures to encourage small businesses as the best prospect for creating jobs included a dumping of time- and money-wasting regulations and the ending of currency controls. Taxes remained high but there was a shift of emphasis from income to sales. A start was made on transferring state-owned business to the private sector. The problem with 'market socialism' was that it upset hardcore supporters of the government while falling long short of the demands of the radical right.

Popular dissatisfaction surfaced in the 1991 election when Carl Bildt, the young and forceful conservative leader, emerged as the only serious rival to Ingmar Carlsson. After the votes were counted, the social democrats stepped aside in favour of a right-centre coalition with Carl Bildt as prime minister. His accession coincided with a period of international upheaval. With the collapse of Soviet communism, the reunification of Germany and the ending of the Cold War, Sweden had to rethink its place in the world. Strict neutrality no longer made any sense, particularly for business people who saw their best opportunities for expansion within the European market.

Bildt did much to prepare the Swedish economy for a closer involvement with Europe by carrying forward a programme of dereg- ulation and privatisation. Capital gains taxes were reduced and taxes on dividends scrapped. Even the once sacrosanct welfare system had to accept change with cuts in sickness and unemployment benefits.

The swing to the right was also evident in Norway where, after being in power all but seven years between 1935 and 1981, the social democrats surrendered office to a minority conservative government. The shock to the system that the politicians had to contend with was the slide in oil prices. Facing up to the realization that Norway was not quite so rich as it liked to think, led to modest cuts in government expenditure. But radical measures were inhibited by growing unemployment. In 1986 the social democrats, led by Mrs Gro Harlem Brundtland, took up the challenge of coping with a worsening economic crisis. An austerity programme including a tight restraint on wages held down inflation and improved exports. But Norway was still left with the problem of over-dependence on oil revenue.

Finland too suffered from the collapse of oil prices but for contrasting reasons. Oil was the currency with which Russia paid for Finnish imports. When the price dropped, Russia could afford to buy less. The comfort was in knowing that, with Perestroika, there was no longer any constraint on developing markets outside the Soviet sphere of influence. Finnish independence was acknowledged by Gorbachev 'without equivocation'. But transforming the economy to appeal more to buyers in the West was bound to take time. A start-up on a range of technology-based industries was eventually to make Finland the big success story of the EU but before that happened the news had to get worse. Exports to Russia fell again, yet more sharply, as the Soviet empire began to fall apart. GDP slumped 13 per cent in the three years up to 1993. Unemployment increased to over 20 per cent. It was a case of boom to bust on the fast track.

However, by 1994 there were already signs of recovery. It began with Finland's push for EU membership. This, in turn, was helped along by the agreement between the EU and EFTA, to which Finland was associated, to create the European Economic Area of free trade. Norway and Sweden also lodged applications for full membership of the EU. Negotiations proceeded smoothly but in subsequent referenda only Finland and Sweden secured majorities for joining. Norway again decided to remain aloof though along with Iceland she remained part of the EEA. Another step towards Nordic and European integration was taken when Finland embraced the common currency. Sweden and Denmark were more cautious but while there was vocal opposition, particularly from the left which feared pressure to dismantle the welfare state, both countries adopted monetary policies which effectively tied them to the Euro. A final decision is likely to be made before Sweden takes over the EU presidency in 2001.

NORDIC CO-OPERATION

Governmental co-operation between the Nordic countries developed after the Nordic Council was established in 1952. This is an advisory body which deals with questions concerning co-operation in the economic, legislative, social and cultural fields and issues regarding environmental protection and communications.

The Plenary Assembly, which is the central body of the Nordic Council, is composed of 87 parliamentary members elected by their respective parliaments, and government representatives nominated by the Nordic governments. Government representatives do not take part in the voting.

A further step was taken in 1971 with the setting up of the Nordic Council of Ministers. All decisions are made unanimously although a country can abstain from voting. Consultations are held on such matters as trade policy and relations between the Nordic countries and the ITO, OECD and UNCTAD. Consultations are also held on matters concerning co-operation with developing countries. The Nordic countries have joint representation in certain international organizations.

Laws concerning contracts, purchase of goods, instalment purchases, instruments of debt, commercial agents and travellers, are now almost identical. The same can be said about the laws on copyright, patents, trademarks and industrial design, as well as transportation and maritime law.

An agreement establishing a common Nordic labour market was concluded in 1954. Nordic nationals are able to work and to settle in another Nordic country without a work permit or permanent residence permit.

The Nordic countries are treaty-bound to keep each other informed of measures planned to ensure full employment.

Within the framework of this common labour market, about 1m. persons have migrated over the Nordic borders. A Nordic convention on social security covers all forms of social benefits. A Nordic citizen receives the social benefits of the country in which he lives, without regard to his nationality. Persons living in one Nordic country who are visiting another are covered for medical care.

In 1954 the Nordic countries signed an agreement creating a passport union in the area. Nordic citizens can travel across Nordic frontiers without presenting passports. Since then, it has been agreed that non-Nordic citizens need present their passports only on entering the Nordic area but not when crossing borders between the Nordic countries.

In 1996 Denmark, Finland and Sweden signed an agreement of accession to the EU Schengen agreement, which upon its entering into force will imply free movement for persons within Europe from Finnmark (Arctic Norway) in the north to Gibraltar in the south. Iceland and Norway, which are not EU members, negotiated special agreements of co-operation with the Schengen countries. The Nordic passport-free area will be retained.

In 1971 the Nordic countries signed a Cultural Treaty. The aim of this Treaty is to further Nordic cultural interests and to increase the combined effect of the countries' investments in education, research and other cultural activities.

In 1988 an action plan was adopted to further Nordic cultural co-operation. One aim of the plan is to develop a single Nordic educational area, another is to improve mutual understanding of the Nordic languages.

In 1975 the Nordic countries agreed to establish a joint Nordic Investment Bank. The bank has its head office in Helsinki, Finland, and its purpose is to finance investment and export projects of common Nordic interest. A Nordic Development Fund has been set up in order to provide long-term, interest-free loans for development projects of Nordic interest.

A Nordic Fund for Technology and Industrial Development supports projects which concern the development of materials, products, processes or the solution of technical problems with industrial applications.

Intra-Nordic co-operation is well established in the supply of electrical energy. The power grids of Denmark, Finland, Norway and Sweden are inter-connected and power producers co-operate via Nordel.

A joint airline company, the Scandinavian Airlines System (SAS), is operated by public and private capital from Denmark, Norway and Sweden.

A post and telecommunications union operates between the Nordic states.

Recent co-operation has focused on efforts to expand the Nordic communications infrastructure in the construction of new road and railroad networks, air and sea routes, as well as data communication channels. The task of building a bridge/tunnel over the Öresund between Sweden and Denmark has been completed and the bridge/tunnel was to open in July 2000.

THE NORDIC CULTURAL TRADITION

Until modern times, Scandinavia was characterized by small, often isolated communities which remained true to their rustic origins, even where factories, mills or mines provided the main source of income. A sense of belonging extending further than the next valley or forest came from a shared language and religion and from a pride in a common history. This feeling for the past expressed in story and song attracted the interest of political leaders who saw in the exploitation of folk culture the best prospects for arousing nationalist sentiment. In Sweden and Denmark it was chiefly a reaction to a declining influence in international politics.

Rediscovering the past appealed just as strongly to the subordinate members of the Nordic family, but for them cultural self-respect was linked to a specific objective – the achievement of independence. Central to their cause was the promotion of language as a symbol of national identity. The revival of interest in Finnish, which over the years of Swedish sovereignty had been held in contempt by the educated classes, was promoted by the publication in 1835 of the *Kalevala*, a volume of folk poems collected by Elias Lönnrot on his trips into the rarely travelled Finnish hinterlands. It is difficult how to appreciate the impact of the *Kalevala* on the intellectual imagination. But for a country with little in the way of recorded history, except as a subject state, it came as a revelation to read of the adventures of Finns who, in pagan times, had owed allegiance to no one outside their own community. That the *Kalevala* was also judged to be a literary masterpiece proved what had hitherto been seriously in doubt – that the Finnish language had a soul which could inspire the finest artists. Other folklore collectors soon followed in Lönnrot's footsteps, urged on by nationalist politicians like Johann Snellman, who acknowledged the debt owed to the peasants as the custodians of true Finnish culture. 'So long as a nation loves its own history, its own antiquity, so long will it also have hope for its future,' he told his followers.

With patriotic fervour still rising against the evicted overlords, the Swedes, whose cultural influence long survived their physical departure, and against their successors, the Russians, few paused to question the authenticity of the *Kalevala* or of other folk literature. It was left to a later generation of researchers to show that Lönnrot had given as much to the *Kalevala* as had the ancients whose thoughts and beliefs he sought to recapture. Without his literary talent the poetic fragments which formed the basis of his work would have remained just fragments, and while it was widely assumed that he had restored the poems to their original form not even Lönnrot believed this to be true.

The idea of using language as a nationalist weapon found strong favour in Norway, another subject country which had lately exchanged masters. There the source of colonial authority had shifted from Copenhagen to Stockholm. Efforts to establish a national language by the gradual modification of Danish were not discouraged by the Swedes who, like the Russians in Finland, saw an opportunity to wean their recently acquired citizens off their traditional cultural loyalties. But the concept of a separate linguistic identity attracted such enthusiasm that the advocates of *riksmål*, or 'language of the realm', soon found themselves upstaged by those who favoured the creation of a wholly national language based on Old Norse as preserved in the rural dialects of the remote fjord country of western Norway. *Landsmål* ('language of the land') attracted nearly a third of the population, a victory for regionalism which set off a long-running dispute between urban and rural Norway.

Even the *landsmål*-speaking Norwegians did not go the whole way in their search for linguistic origins. If they had done so they might well have ended up making common cause with the

Icelanders. In boasting the oldest and the least adulterated of the Nordic languages, the Icelanders had to concede that it was almost certainly acquired from the Norwegian colonizers who came to the island in the ninth and tenth centuries. In fact, the Icelandic and Norwegian languages did not become markedly different until the fourteenth century, when Norwegian started adapting first to Danish and then later to Swedish influence. Though Iceland was governed by the Danes it was more isolated and so protected from linguistic innovation. Where Danish was spoken it was generally as the language of commerce. Icelanders therefore had no difficulty in preserving their spirit of individuality – only in asserting it politically. The first tremors of nationalism in the early years of the nineteenth century, when war between England and Denmark nearly brought ruin to the country, gained force with economic recovery and the weakening of Danish rule. Poets and scholars from the Icelandic Literary Society, the National Library and the Northern Text Society, all founded within a few years of each other, explored the Norse heritage, to reveal that from the tenth to the thirteenth centuries the literature produced by this tiny country ranked with the best in the world. Moreover, it had stood the test of time not just as poetry but, in the sagas, as a vivid and dramatic early history of an extraordinary nation. The significance for the nationalists was quickly recognized, and it is no coincidence that Jón Sigurdsson, Iceland's popularly acknowledged leader for most of the second half of the century, combined political work with a study of the saga literature, bringing it to a wider public at home and abroad.

The Nordic countries embarked on the twentieth century with a strong sense of cultural identity. Superbly effective as an instrument of nationalism, folk culture was also a great equalizer. The convictions that culture emerged from, and so rightly belonged to, the people, made Scandinavia fertile ground for egalitarian politics, and was a commanding influence on the development of contemporary art which appealed across class barriers. The early collections of folk tales sparked the imagination of Hans Christian Andersen, and for Grieg and Sibelius inspiration came from the folk melodies of their respective countries.

Inevitably there was a reaction against folklore as the first source of artistic endeavour. Too much delving back into the past, it was said, diverted writers from their proper function of making statements about contemporary society and its need to adjust to the challenge of industrialization. In the 1870s the literary movement known as naturalism reached northern Europe. It was made fashionable by a young Danish critic, Georg Brandes, who argued that political and social controversy was the life force of literature. The unashamedly radical edge Brandes gave to his lectures and writing was sharpened by the election to the Folketing of his brother Edvard, an outspoken atheist who started a controversial career by refusing to take the oath. For the old guard Brandes represented a dangerous influence on young people and a threat to accepted standards of decency in public life. When Georg was nominated as by far the best qualified candidate to fill the chair of literature at Copenhagen, the establishment blocked his appointment.

The prospect of turning away from the cosy security of the folk heritage to face the uncertain and in many ways disagreeable present might have inhibited the latest generations of writers; instead it acted as a liberating force. It was as if the folk tradition was a form of cultural apprenticeship, preparing the way for something more exacting. If Strindberg and Ibsen were often too demanding for audiences still tentatively exploring the borders of theatrical propriety, there were other writers, less well known today but famous in their own time, who contributed to a greater sense of realism on the literary scene and invited questions about public affairs which the politicians and Church leaders were too cautious to raise. One such was the Norwegian Bjørnstjerne Bjørnson, first director of the national theatre and winner of the 1903 Nobel prize.

The 'modern breakthrough', as it was known in all the Nordic countries, was identified with the challenge to constraints on middle-class society – established religious beliefs and sexual morality, republicanism and, specifically, the 'decency controversy' which revolved on the question of women's status in the home and the community. But beyond the world of Ibsen, Strindberg and Bjørnson there were writers who responded to the challenges of industrialization and its impact on ordinary people. Martin Andersen Nexø, who was born in the Copenhagen slums, vividly portrayed working-class conditions in *Pelle the Conqueror*, an epic sequence of novels which inspired a generation of proletarian authors. There was a move here away from naturalism with its preoccupation with ideas towards a more imaginative form of social realism which tried to get closer to man's inner feelings. Knut Hamsun who, next to Ibsen, ranks as the most influential Norwegian writer of modern times, sought to capture the 'whisper of the blood, the entreaty of the home, all the unconscious life of the mind', in his depiction of the individual caught up in the degeneracy of industrialization and urban life.

Literary realism was not unique to Scandinavia. But in few other western countries was the movement as powerful as in northern Europe, where books containing a strong social message were the most widely read type of literature amongst all classes in the period up to the Second World War. But while it was taken for granted that a comfortable home and a decent education were the first priorities, it was accepted that culture followed in the wake of economic progress. At the same time the actual process of making society richer was seen as a partly cultural activity.

Nowhere was this more apparent than in building and design. The functionalist concept, inspired by the aim of the Deutsche Werklund to create 'more beautiful things for everyday use', made its first impact on Scandinavia in 1917 when the Swedish Society for Industrial Design organized a Home Exhibition in Stockholm. The purpose was to show how working-class homes could be structured and furnished in a way that was attractive, practical and inexpensive. If there was no immediate follow-up it was because many of the best designers were making a good living turning out exclusively high-price items and were not yet ready to put their talents to wider use. But there was a groundswell of support from those who saw themselves as part of the peasant handicraft tradition and who wanted to carry over the values of individual craftsmanship to the era of industrialization and mass production. It was not long before they found a leader. In 1919 Walter Gropius founded the Bauhaus school of functional design. First in Weimar and later in Dessau he gathered a staff of highly gifted architects, painters, sculptors and technicians whose varied imaginative skills were brought to bear on the problem of combining efficiency with beauty in manufacturing and construction. By the time Gropius left Germany to escape the Nazis his movement had attracted disciples in all European countries. But without doubt the strongest concentration of support for domestic functionalism was to be found in Scandinavia, where young designers vied to create new forms for household products – clean, smooth lines in furniture, colourful and easily manageable kitchenware, unfussy ornaments. Support for the movement among opinion leaders was overwhelming, and aroused envy among modernists abroad who had to fight off a strong rearguard action from sections of the cultural elite who were appalled at the association of art with the manufacture of household implements.

The lead in promoting what was soon recognized everywhere in the world as Scandinavian design was quickly taken by Finland, where functionalism had the added attraction of symbolizing the release from Soviet political and cultural hegemony. It was in architecture where Finnish influence was pre-eminent, with the work of

Alvar Aalto arousing as much interest and controversy as that of Le Corbusier. Aalto had started to make a name for himself with conventional classical-style buildings when, in Norway and Sweden, he detected signs of a change in architectural fashion. By 1927, when the first Scandinavian functionalist building, the Skansen restaurant in Oslo, was completed, he was travelling widely in Europe absorbing the radical ideology of Le Corbusier and Gropius. Aalto himself was established as one of the masters of the modern movement with the construction of the Paimio Sanatorium, memorable for the long tiers of balconies – emphasizing the dominant role of light and air – rising like decks of a ship out of a forest setting. Though functionalism became respectable for residential buildings, and even stirred social-democrat visionaries to advocate collective housing units as part of a grand design for egalitarian living, Aalto and his contemporaries put their best efforts into the construction of factories and various public institutions. The 'mighty goal', as Aalto put it, 'was to bring industrialization step by step to the position, which it will no doubt one day achieve, of being a factor for cultural harmony'.

This concept of 'harmony' which remains dominant in all Nordic design led Aalto to set his imagination to work on the contents of his buildings. He and the Danish architect Arne Jacobsen were chiefly instrumental in popularizing the elegant lightweight furnishings which soon became standard in ordinary homes. One of the wonders of Scandinavia was the widespread regard for improving the domestic environment. 'Nowhere in the world,' wrote an English writer, 'can one find such uniformly charming taste in every household, where the commonplace object is treated more pleasingly by designer and workman, and where that object is so appreciated by the average purchaser.' What made this discovery all the more interesting was that it really was popular taste which the writer had encountered – not standards imposed by an administrative or class elite.

DENMARK

Kongeriget Danmark
(Kingdom of Denmark)

Capital: Copenhagen

Area: 43,096 sq. km

Population estimate, 2000: 5·33m.

Head of State: Queen Margrethe II

Head of Government: Poul Nyrup Rasmussen

TERRITORY AND POPULATION

Denmark is bounded in the west by the North Sea, northwest and
north by the Skagerrak and Kattegat straits (separating it from
Norway and Sweden), and south by Germany. A fixed link with
Sweden will be created during 2000 when the Öresund motorway
and railway bridge between Copenhagen and Malmö is completed.

Administrative divisions		Area (sq. km) 1999	Population Census 1970	Population 1 Jan. 1999	Population per sq. km 1999
København (Copenhagen)	(city)	88	622,773	491,082	5,564·7
Frederiksberg	(borough)	9	101,874	90,227	10,288·1
Københavns	(county)	526	615,343	612,053	1,163·7
Frederiksborg	,,	1,347	259,442	363,098	269·5
Roskilde	,,	891	153,199	229,794	257·8
Vestsjælland	,,	2,984	259,057	293,709	98·4
Storstrøm	,,	3,398	252,363	258,761	76·2
Bornholm	,,	588	47,239	44,529	75·7
Fyn	,,	3,486	432,699	471,732	135·3
Sønderjylland	,,	3,939	238,062	253,771	64·4
Ribe	,,	3,132	197,843	224,348	71·6
Vejle	,,	2,997	306,263	346,182	115·5
Ringkøbing	,,	4,854	241,327	272,644	56·2
Aarhus	,,	4,561	533,190	634,435	139·1
Viborg	,,	4,122	220,734	233,396	56·6
Nordjylland	,,	6,173	456,171	493,816	80·0
Total		43,096	4,937,579	5,313,577	123·3

The projected population for 2000 is 5·33m.

In 1999 an estimated 85·0% of the population lived in urban areas.
In 1999, 93·7% of the inhabitants were born in Denmark, including
the Faroe Islands and Greenland.

On 1 Jan. 1999 the population of the capital, Copenhagen (comprising Copenhagen, Frederiksberg and Gentofte municipalities), was 649,018; Aarhus, 216,564; Odense, 144,940; Aalborg, 119,431; Esbjerg, 73,350; Randers, 55,949; Kolding, 53,216; Horsens, 48,590; Vejle, 47,976; Roskilde, 42,739.

The official language is Danish.

Time Zone
Denmark is 1 hour ahead of GMT

POLITICAL AND SOCIAL CHRONOLOGY OF THE 20TH CENTURY

1906	Frederik VIII crowned King
1912	Christian X crowned King
1914	Denmark remains neutral for World War I
1915	Women are given the right to vote
1918	First female members of parliament
1920	North Slesvig returned to Denmark after plebiscite
	Denmark joins the League of Nations
1924	First Social Democratic government formed
1930	Death penalty abolished
1933	Welfare State initiated
	Danish sovereignty over Greenland confirmed by International court of appeal
1936	New Constitution passed in parliament
1940	Occupation by Germany on 9 April
1944	Iceland declares its independence
1945	German forces surrender to the British on 4–5 May
1947	Frederik IX crowned King

1948   Faroe Islands granted partial autonomy

1949   Denmark joins NATO

1951   Nordic Council established with Norway, Sweden, Finland
       and Iceland

1953   New Constitution passed in parliament
       Female succession to the throne introduced
       Upper chamber of parliament abolished
       Greenland given status of county

1960   Denmark joins EFTA

1967   Danish Krone devalued

1972   Margrethe II crowned queen

1973   Denmark joins EEC after referendum

1978   Voting age lowered to 18

1979   Greenland granted home rule

1982   Poul Schlüter becomes Prime Minister

1985   Greenland leaves the EEC

1992   Maastricht treaty rejected in a referendum

1993   Poul Schlüter resigns
       Poul Nyrup Rasmussen becomes Prime Minister
       Maastricht treaty accepted with some exceptions in a
       referendum

CULTURAL BRIEFING

Danish art is little known outside of Denmark, especially that
produced prior to Denmark's golden age in the nineteenth century.
The Danish Academy of Fine Arts was not founded until 1738; prior to
this Danish art was influenced heavily by German and Dutch artists.
The Romantic painters, including Eckersberg and his pupils, were
the first renowned Danish painters, although the classical sculptor

Bertel Thorvaldsen had caught Canova's attention and thus that of a wider audience in Italy at the end of the 18th century. Christen Købke continued Eckersberg's tradition with a large number of paintings of Copenhagen in the romantic style. By the end of the century, however, Danish painting had lost its distinctive edge and was once again merely part of a larger European movement. At the beginning of the 20th century abstraction took hold in Denmark, the most famous Danish painter of the time perhaps being Vilhelm Lundstrøm.

Danish design is renowned for being simple, attractive, practical and of good quality. This is in part due to the combination of skills traditionally involved in the Danish design process. Artists, architects and industrial designers have all worked together to create innovative ideas. The famous silversmith Georg Jensen, for instance, was trained as a sculptor and some of the simplest yet best known chair designs were dreamt up by the architect Arne Jacobsen. The Royal Copenhagen Porcelain Manufactory was perhaps the first important centre of Danish design, founded in 1775. Artists were employed to decorate the china and porcelain produced and the company is especially know for its blue fluted dinner services that remain in production today. Georg Jensen's silverware and jewellery have been world famous since the founding of his factory in 1904, which employed conventional artists as well as trained jewellers. Equally famous is the Danish tradition of furniture making, developed from the Copenhagen Cabinetmakers' Guild's annual exhibitions and the reputation of architect Kaare Klimt as director of the furniture school at the Academy of Fine Arts. Functionality, comfort and simplicity of design were ideals learned and expanded upon by Hans Wegner and Arne Jacobsen. Jacobsen was a designer in every sense of the word, as shown by the Royal Hotel in Copenhagen, where not only the building, but every fitting and even the place settings in the restaurant were carefully considered in conjunction with each other. One of the world's best recognized structures, the Sydney Opera

House, was also designed by the Dane Jørn Utzon. The legacy of 20th century Danish design is perhaps illustrated best by the stunning functionality and simplicity of Bang & Olufsen's hi-fi equipment which is unrivalled in its success of beautifying normally ugly technology.

Literature in Denmark originated with Viking sagas and myths, much of which has been lost or never recorded, and floundered somewhat with the triumph of Christianity. It was the satirical writing of Ludvig Holberg during the early 18th century that first gave Danish literature a style of its own, but the best known Danish authors all lived and wrote in the 19th century. Hans Christian Andersen and Søren Kierkegaard will remain household names for some time to come. It was, however, Georg Brandes who moved literature in Denmark into a truly modern sphere in the late 19th century, focusing on contentious issues during Denmark's most rapid period of social change. In the 20th century, Denmark's most prominent writer is probably Karen Blixen, author of Out of Africa and Babette's Feast, later filmed by Gabriel Axel.

LEADING CULTURAL FIGURES

Hans Christian Andersen

Hans Christian Andersen was born in Odense in 1805 to poor parents. His father died in 1816 and he received little formal schooling. In 1819 Andersen travelled alone to Copenhagen to seek his fortune and spent a number of years in poverty seeking jobs at the Royal Theatre. Eventually the Theatre director became his guardian and he was sent to school, first in Slagelse, then Helsingør. In 1828 when he joined the University in Copenhagen his writings – poetry, prose and drama – were first published. Andersen travelled extensively, visiting much of

Europe, making acquaintances such as Charles Dickens and staying in an artists' colony in Rome for some time. His first novel, *The Improvisatore*, was published in 1835, as were the first two volumes of *Fairy Tales, Told for Children*. A poem written whilst still at school *The Dying Child*, was published in the Revue de Paris in 1837 and translated into other languages and by this time Andersen's name was well known in European literary circles. A year later he was awarded a grant by the Danish government, the first of many honours bestowed upon him during his own lifetime. His later Fairy Tales lost their 'for children' subtitle and subsequently were described as stories, as Andersen believed they were just as suitable for adults. His last stories were published in 1872, by which time he was known as a successful novelist, travel writer and playwright. He died in 1875.

Søren Kierkegaard

Kierkegaard was born in Copenhagen in 1813 to a dominant Christian father and loving, understanding mother, both of whom did much to shape their son's career. His father was a theologian, bishop and eventually government minister who encouraged a devout belief in God. Thus his son studied psychology and philosophy in Copenhagen from 1831 and was preparing for a theology degree in 1834 when his mother died and he lost his faith. The death of his father propelled him to finish his degree, review his religious beliefs and settle down, but after proposing to Regine Olsen in 1840 he broke off the engagement a year later, shortly before receiving his masters. In 1843 *Either-Or* and *Two Edifying Discourses* were published, two of a number of works that characterized his earlier philosophical writings. His later work became more religious, but Kierkegaard's career was cut short in 1855 when he collapsed in the street and died five weeks later. His work was most closely examined in the early 20th century when he became a focus for existential philosophers and theologians.

Arne Jacobsen

Arne Jacobsen, Denmark's most famous designer and architect, was born in Copenhagen in 1902. He was educated at the architecture school of the Royal Academy of Fine Arts in Copenhagen, where he received his diploma in 1927 and returned as professor from 1956 to 1965. A year after finishing his studies, he won a gold medal for his work on a project for a National Museum. Jacobsen was not merely an architect, however, and as early as 1925 had designed a chair that won a silver medal in the World Exhibition in Paris. In 1952 he designed a stacking chair called the Ant, which is still in production today. The Egg and Swan chairs were equally successful designs. Jacobsen was so prolific that his legacy includes chairs and buildings (such as St. Catherine's College Oxford, Mainz City Hall and the Hamburg Power Company HQ, to name but a few outside Denmark), but also cutlery, lamps, clocks – in fact anything attractive and functional. He was honoured by architects' associations, art academies and universities throughout the world and died in Copenhagen in 1971.

MAJOR CITIES

The international code for telephoning or faxing Denmark is the code required to dial out of your own country followed by 45.

Copenhagen (København)

Population 1,400,000

Copenhagen is Scandinavia's largest and most cosmopolitan city. Water surrounds Copenhagen and the historic centre is built on two islands, Christianshavn and Slotsholmen, which are connected by bridges. Canals weave their way through the rest of the city.

Archaeological finds have placed the earliest settlement of the area at around 5000 BC, but the modern city was founded in 1167 and there are still remnants of 12th century buildings left in the city, which became the capital of Denmark some three hundred years later. Originally, Copenhagen was in the centre of Denmark, for the country at this time consisted of southern Sweden and Norway and was therefore strategically located. The small town was given by King Waldemar the great to Absalon, the Bishop of Roskilde in 1160, who built his castle seven years later. It was then that the town came to be known as København (merchant's town). Copenhagen grew quickly due to its position and was raided many times by the Hanseatic League until in 1416 King Erik of Pomerania finally reclaimed the city for the Danish crown. In 1596 Christian IV came to the throne and made the now wealthy city his capital. This was also a time of great expansion and Christianshavn was built under Christian IV, modelled on Amsterdam. Almost constant wars followed and as a result fortifications were added before and after a number of attempts by Sweden to take the Danish capital. The Amalienborg palace was built in 1749 and became the Royal Palace at the end of the century following a fire at the older Christiansborg, which also engulfed the town hall and large parts of the city. Rebuilding then took place in a classical style, before partial destruction again by the English at the beginning of the nineteenth century. Copenhagen was the centre of Denmark's democratic revolution which started with a city council in 1840 and was followed in 1848 by the proclamation of a free constitution. During this era the Tivoli gardens were planned, the railway station built and the city expanded quickly beyond its fortifications with the new dominance of traders and merchants. A new town hall and its square were laid out at the beginning of the 20th century and apart from the economic downturn in the 1930s, Copenhagen flourished until its occupation by the Germans. The war did not damage the city greatly, though, and the post war period has seen innovative urban planning, new suburbs and restoration of the city's historical monuments. Much of the central area today is pedestrianized; the area between the Town Hall Square (Rådhuspladsen) and Kongens Nytorv is called Strøget and is made up of a number of interlinking pedestrian streets where many of Copenhagen's more upmarket shops can now be found.

Copenhagen Information Service

Rådhuspladsen 7, 1550 Copenhagen V

Tel: 33-66-66-33 Fax: 33-66-70-32

Web: www.copenhagencity.dk

Emergencies

Call 112, or contact the most central hospital (with a 24 hour accident and emergency department) on 35-45-35-45. Rigshospitalet, Blegdamsvej 9.

Steno Apotek is a 24 hour pharmacy on Vesterbrogade, opposite the station.

Transport

Copenhagen's public transport service is efficient and quick, although most of the city centre can be seen or reached on foot. Copenhagen city transport organization:

Hovestadsområdets Trafikselskab

Toftegårds Plads

Gl. Køge Landevej 3

2500 Valby

Tel: 36-13-14-15 Fax: 36-13-20-97

E-mail: ht@ht.dk

Landmarks

The **Amalienborg Palace** has been the seat of the Royal Family since 1794. The changing of the guard happens each day at 12.00 and parts of the palace can be visited by tourists. Northeast of the palace by the water is the statue of the **Little Mermaid**. The **Tivoli Gardens** are perhaps Copenhagen's best known attractions. The amusement park is only open in the summer and at Christmas and features a host of shows, rides, parks and secluded buildings. There are fireworks each Wednesday evening. The **Rådhus**, or Town Hall, is an impressive building merely to look at, but one can also climb the tower for an impressive view over the centre of the city.

Museums

The National Museum in Copenhagen is open every day except Mondays and houses artefacts from Denmark's early history to modern times as well as international exhibits. The museum is housed in an eighteenth century palace in the centre of the city and there are three permanent exhibitions on Danish history (prehistory, the middle ages and renaissance Denmark and seventeenth century Denmark), the Royal collection of coins and medals, the collection of Egyptian and classical artefacts and an ethnographic collection as well as a children's museum, a permanent Greenland exhibition and numerous temporary exhibitions. There are also three other branches of the National Museum outside Copenhagen; an open air museum depicting village life during Denmark's early history, an industrial museum and a resistance museum. Admission is free on Wednesdays.
Ny Vestergade 10, Copenhagen
Web site: www.natmus.dk

History and information on Copenhagen can be found at the city museum
Copenhagen City Museum
Vesterbrogade 59, 1620 Copenhagen V
Tel: 33-21-07-72

One of Denmark's finest museums, the Ny Carlsberg Glyptotek was founded by the brewing family and the collection contains classical sculptures and artefacts as well as an extensive modern art collection including paintings by Van Gogh and Monet.

Ny Carlsberg Glyptotek

Dantes Plads 7, 11556 Copenhagen V

Tel: 33-41-81-41 Fax: 33-91-20-58

Art Galleries

The National Gallery has recently been refurbished and contains works by both Danish and internationally renowned artists from early European art to the twentieth century. There are paintings by Danish masters such as Jens Juel and Eckersberg and modern European artists such as Picasso and Munch, with every artistic style catered for amongst the 9,000 paintings and sculptures and a further 300,000 drawings and sketches.

Statens Museum for Kunst

Sølvgade 48

1307 Copenhagen

Tel: 33-74-84-94

Web: www.smk.dk

The Louisiana Museum of Modern Art was founded in 1958 by Knud Jensen as an independent public institution. Situated on the north Zealand coast (35 minutes from Copenhagen by train) in its own park, the museum has an extensive collection of international modern art and a sculpture garden. There are a number of temporary exhibitions each year as well as the impressive permanent collection including works by Bacon, Ernst, Moore, Picasso and Warhol.

Louisiana Museum of Modern Art

Gl. Strandvej 13

3050 Humlebæk

Tel: 49-19-07-91 Fax: 49-19-35-05

Web: www.louisiana.dk

Theatres

The Royal National Theatre was founded in 1748 and has been the centre of Denmark's theatrical, ballet and operatic scenes since then. There has been a ballet school since 1756 and both the Royal Ballet and Opera companies perform here. The building dates from 1874, replacing the smaller theatre on the same site. The 250th anniversary of the theatre company was celebrated in 1998. For current listings, check *Copenhagen this Week*.

Det Kongelige Teater
Kongens Nytorv, Copenhagen
Tel: 33-69-69-69
Web: www.jgl-teater.dk

Århus

Aarhus (Århus)
Population 265,000

Aarhus is Denmark's second largest city and was settled in Viking times. The town really began to grow at the turn of the 20th century, however, when industry began to grow but the city remains relatively small. The Vikings called the town Aros, meaning river mouth, and the harbour built in the 15th century marked the beginning of Aarhus' prosperity. There are two 15th century cathedrals and Den Gamle By (the Old Town) is part old town and partly a reconstruction of old buildings moved from other parts of the country. Aarhus is considered to be the cultural capital of Denmark and today its university has more than 40,000 students.

Landmarks

The gothic **Domkirke** was originally built in the 12th century but had to be largely rebuilt after a fire. It is Denmark's largest, with a nave stretching some 100 metres. The **Vor Frue Kirke** was restored in the 1950s and the remains of a crypt dating from c.1060 was discovered which can be visited in the basement of the main church. **Den Gamle By** is an interesting open air museum depicting Danish life in Viking times and many of the buildings are used for their original purposes.

Travellers Information
Tourist Århus
Rådhuset, 8000 Århus C
Tel: 89-40-67-00 Fax: 86-12-95-90
Web: www.aarhus-tourist.dk

Emergencies
For a doctor outside of normal working hours, phone 86-20-10-22.
Århus Løve Apotek is a 24 hour chemist on Store Torv 5
(tel: 86-12-00-22).
For the local police station, call 87-31-14-48.

Museums
Aarhus' art museum was founded in 1859 and is the oldest art collection in Denmark outside Copenhagen. It has a collection of 19th and 20th century Danish art and some international work.
Århus Kunst Museum
Vennelystparken
8000 Århus C
Tel: 86-13-52-55
Web: www.aarhuskunstmuseum.dk

The City museum traces the history of Aarhus from its Viking past to the present day.
Århus Bymuseum
Carl Blochs Gade 28
8000 Århus C
Tel: 86-13-28-62
Web: www.bymuseet.dk

SOCIAL STATISTICS

Statistics for calendar years:

	Live births	Still births	Marriages	Divorces	Deaths	Emigration	Immigration
1996	67,638	324	35,953	12,776	61,085	37,312	54,445
1997	67,636	. . .	34,244	12,774	59,925	38,393	50,105
1998	66,170	. . .	34,733	13,141	58,442	40,340	51,372

1998 rates per 1,000 population: birth, 12·5; death, 11·0. Single-parent births: 1995, 46·5%; 1996, 46·3%; 1997, 45·1%; 1998, 44·8%. Annual growth rate, 1990–98, 0·4%. Suicide rate, 1990–97 (per 100,000 population) was 20·0 (men, 27·1; women, 13·1). Life expectancy at birth, 1997–98, was 73·7 years for males and 78·7 years for females. In 1998 the most popular age range for marrying was 25–29 for both males and females. Infant mortality, 1998, 4·7 per 1,000 live births. Fertility rate, 1998, 1·7 births per woman. In 1998 Denmark received 5,700 asylum applications, equivalent to 1·09 per 1,000 inhabitants.

Statistics Denmark
Sejrøgade 11, 2100 København Ø
Tel: 39-17-39-17 Fax: 39-17-39-99
E-mail: dst@dst.dk Web site: www.dst.dk

Statistics Denmark Library
Sankt Kjelds Plads 11, 2100 København Ø
Tel: 39-17-30-30- Fax: 39-17-30-03
E-mail: bib@dst.dk

CLIMATE

The climate is much modified by marine influences and the effect of the Gulf Stream, to give winters that may be both cold or mild and often cloudy. Summers may be warm and sunny or chilly and rainy. In general, the east is drier than the west. Long periods of calm weather are exceptional and windy conditions are common. Copenhagen, Jan. 33°F (0·5°C), July 63°F (17°C). Annual rainfall 650 mm. Esbjerg, Jan. 33°F (0·5°C), July 61°F (16°C). Annual rainfall 800 mm. 10% of rainfall precipitates as snow.

CONSTITUTION AND GOVERNMENT

The present constitution is founded upon the Basic Law of 5 June 1953. The legislative power lies with the Queen and the *Folketing* (parliament) jointly. The executive power is vested in the monarch, who exercises authority through the ministers.

The reigning Queen is **Margrethe II,** b. 16 April 1940; married 10 June 1967 to Prince Henrik, b. Count de Monpezat. She succeeded to the throne on the death of her father, King Frederik IX, on 14 Jan. 1972. *Offspring:* Crown Prince Frederik, b. 26 May 1968; Prince Joachim, b. 7 June 1969; married 18 Nov. 1995 Alexandra Manley, b. 30 June 1964 (*Offspring:* Prince Nikolai William Alexander Frederik, b. 28 Aug. 1999).

Mother of the Queen; Queen Ingrid, b. Princess of Sweden, 28 March 1910.

Sisters of the Queen; Princess Benedikte, b. 29 April 1944; married 3 Feb. 1968 to Prince Richard of Sayn-Wittgenstein-Berleburg; Princess Anne-Marie, b. 30 Aug. 1946; married 18 Sept. 1964 to King Constantine of Greece.

The crown was elective from the earliest times but became hereditary by right in 1660. The direct male line of the house of Oldenburg became extinct with King Frederik VII on 15 Nov. 1863. In view of the death of the king, without direct heirs, the Great Powers signed a treaty at London on 8 May 1852, by the terms of which the succession to the crown was made over to Prince Christian of Schleswig-Holstein-Sonderburg-Glücksburg, and to the direct male descendants of his union with the Princess Louise of Hesse-Cassel. This became law on 31 July 1853. Linked to the constitution of 5 June 1953, a new law of succession, dated 27 March 1953, has come into force, which restricts the right of succession to the descendants of King Christian X and Queen Alexandrine, and admits the sovereign's daughters to the line of succession, ranking after the sovereign's sons.

The Queen receives a tax-free annual sum of 44·7m. kroner from the state (1998).

The judicial power is with the courts. The monarch must be a member of the Evangelical-Lutheran Church, the official Church of the State, and may not assume major international obligations without the consent of the Folketing. The Folketing consists of one chamber. All men and women of Danish nationality of more than 18 years of age and permanently resident in Denmark possess the franchise, and are eligible for election to the Folketing, which is at present composed of 179 members; 135 members are elected by the method of proportional representation in 17 constituencies. In order to attain an equal representation of the different parties, 40 additional seats are divided among such parties which have not obtained sufficient returns at the constituency elections. 2 members are elected for the Faroe Islands and 2 for Greenland. The term of the legislature is 4 years, but a general election may be called at any time. The Folketing convenes every year on the first Tuesday in Oct. Besides its legislative functions, every 6 years it appoints judges who, together with the ordinary members of the Supreme Court, form the *Rigsret*, a tribunal which can alone try parliamentary impeachments.

National Anthem
'Kong Kristian stod ved højen mast' ('King Christian stood by the lofty mast'); words by J. Ewald, tune by J. E. Hartmann.

RECENT ELECTIONS

Parliamentary elections were held on 11 March 1998. The Social Democratic Party won 63 seats, with 35·9% of the votes cast (62 seats with 34·6% in 1994); the Liberal Party 42 with 24% (42 with 23·3%); the Conservative Party 16 with 8·9% (27 with 15%); the Socialist People's Party 13 with 7·6% (13 with 7·3%); and the Danish People's Party 13 with 7·4% (not in 1994 election). The 28 remaining seats went to the Centre Democratic Party (8); the Social Liberal Party (7); the Christian People's Party (4); the Progress Party (4); the Unity List (5). The coalition government led by Poul Nyrup Rasmussen of the Social Democratic Party remained in office. In Feb. 1999, 37·4% of the seats in parliament were held by women, a rate only exceded in Sweden.

European Parliament. Denmark has 16 representatives. At the June 1999 elections turn-out was 49·9%. The Liberal Party won 5 seats with 23·3% of votes cast (group in European Parliament: Liberal, Democrat and Reform Party); the SD, 3 with 16·5% (Party of European Socialists); the June Movement, 3 with 16·1% (Independents for a Europe of Nations); the Radical Liberal Party, 1 with 9·1% (Liberal, Democrat and Reform Party); the Conservative Party, 1 with 8·6% (European People's Party); the People's Anti-EU Movement, 1 with 7·3% (Independents for a Europe of Nations); the

Socialist People's Party, 1 with 7·1% (Greens); DF (Danish People's Party), 1 with 5·8% (Union for a Europe of Nations Group).

CURRENT ADMINISTRATION

Following the 1998 elections a coalition government of the Social Democratic (S) and Radical Left-Social Liberal (RV) Parties took office in March 1998. In March 2000 the government comprised:

Prime Minister: Poul Nyrup Rasmussen, b. 1943; (S; sworn in 25 Jan. 1993; re-elected 11 March 1998).

Minister of Economic Affairs and Minister for Nordic Co-operation: Marianne Jelved. *Trade and Industry:* Pia Gjellerup. *Finance:* Mogens Lykketoft. *Foreign Affairs:* Niels Helveg Petersen. *Justice:* Frank Jensen. *Environment and Energy:* Svend Auken. *Education and Ecclesiastical Affairs:* Margrethe Vestager. *Developmental Aid:* Jan Trojborg. *Interior:* Karen Jespersen. *Health:* Sonja Mikkelsen. *Labour:* Ove Hygum. *Taxation:* Ole Stavad. *Defence:* Hans Haekkerup. *Culture:* Elsebeth Gerner Nielsen. *Transport:* Jacob Buksti. *Social Affairs:* Henrik Dam Kristensen. *Housing and Building:* Jytte Andersen. *Research and Information Technology:* Birthe Weiss. *Food, Agriculture and Fisheries:* Ritt Bjerregaard.

POLITICAL PROFILES

Poul Nyrup Rasmussen

Rasmussen was born in 1943 in Esbjerg and graduated from Copenhagen University as an economics student in 1971. He was employed as an economist at the Danish Trade Union council from then until 1986, becoming chief economist in 1980. In 1987 he became deputy chairman of the Social Democratic Party and in 1988 entered parliament. Four years later he was promoted to Chairman of his party and on 25 Jan. 1993 Rasmussen was made Prime Minister following Poul Schlüter's resignation. He has been in charge of four different governments since taking office, three of them minority governments, and his party has emerged as the largest in the elections of 1994 and 1998. Rasmussen has essentially continued the economic policies of his conservative predecessor, but has also somewhat overcome the two general problems left to him by the conservatives; a high tax burden and a high level of unemployment.

The Prime Minister's Office Web site: www.stm.dk

Marianne Jelved

Marianne Jelved was born in 1943 just north of Copenhagen and became a teacher in 1967. She taught for over twenty years, becoming involved in teacher' organizations and educational affairs. She has written and edited a number of schoolbooks. She entered local politics in 1982 as a councillor in Gundsø for the Social Liberal Party (Det Radikale Venstre) and was deputy mayor for three years. In 1987 she won a seat in parliament and the following year became chairwoman of her party. In 1993 the Social Liberals and other left of centre parties entered into a coalition with the Social Democrats and Jelved was made Minister for Economic affairs. In 1994 she was also appointed Minister for Nordic Co-operation. Jelved is also the Deputy Prime Minister. The Social Liberals and the Social Democrats are now the only two parties in the coalition and as a minority government rely on support from other parties to stay in office.

LOCAL GOVERNMENT

For administrative purposes Denmark is divided into 275 communes; each of them has a district council of between 7 and 31 members, headed by an elected mayor. The city of Copenhagen forms a district by itself and is governed by a city council of 55 members, elected every 4 years, and an executive, consisting of the chief burgomaster and 6 burgomasters, appointed by the city council for 4 years. There are 14 counties, each of which is administered by a county council of between 13 and 31 members, headed by an elected mayor. All councils are elected directly by universal suffrage and proportional representation for 4-year terms. There are also about 2,100 parishes. Government at this level is administered by parish councils elected for 4 years.

The counties and Copenhagen are superintended by the Ministry of Interior Affairs. The municipalities are superintended by 14 local supervision committees, headed by a state county prefect, who is a civil servant appointed by the Queen.

County and municipal elections were held on 16 Nov. 1993. The Social Democrats won 34·9% of votes cast, the Liberals 28·8% (county elections).

DEFENCE

The overall organization of the Danish Armed Forces comprises the Headquarters Chief of Defence, the Army, the Navy, the Air Force and inter-service authorities and institutions; to this should be added the Home Guard, which is an indispensable part of Danish military defence.

The Constitution of 1849 states that it is the duty of every fit man to contribute to the national defence. This provision is still in force. Selection of conscripts takes place at the age of 18–19 years, and the conscripts are normally called up for service ½–1½ years later. In 1998 defence expenditure totalled US$2,799m. (US$534 per capita), representing 1·6% of GDP.

Army

The army is comprised of field army formations and the local defence forces. In 1999 the peacetime strength of the army numbered 15,300 (including about 6,800 conscripts and 470 women). Army reserves (separate to the Home Guard) totalled 58,000.

Navy

The Navy was some 4,300-strong (570 conscripts and 230 women) in 1999 including the Naval Air Arm and Coastal Defence units. In addition there were 8,400 naval reserves. The fleet included 5 coastal submarines and 3 frigates. The 2 main naval bases are at Frederikshavn and Korsoer.

Air Force

The Air Force numbered some 4,700 in 1999 (including 510 conscripts). It operated 69 combat aircraft (all F-16s) of which 9 are kept in reserve. There were 14,800 Air Force reserves.

Home Guard (Hjemmeværnet)

The personnel of the Home Guard is recruited on a voluntary basis. The personnel of the Home Guard in 1999 numbered 61,500 persons (49,700 in the Army section, 4,300 in the Navy section, 7,500 in the Air Force section).

INTERNATIONAL RELATIONS

In a referendum in June 1992 the electorate voted against ratifying the Maastricht Treaty for closer political union within the EU. Turn-out was 82%. 50·7% of votes were against ratification, 49·3% in favour. However, a second referendum on 18 May 1993 reversed this result, with 56·8% of votes cast in favour of ratification and 43·2% against. Turn-out was 86·2%.

Denmark gave US$1·8bn. in international aid in 1998, which at 0·99% of GDP made it the world's most generous country as a percentage of its gross domestic product.

Denmark is a member of the UN, NATO, OECD, the EU, Council of Europe, OSCE, CERN, Nordic Council, Council of Baltic Sea States, Inter-American Development Bank, Asian Devlopment Bank, IOM and the Antarctic Treaty. On 19 Dec. 1996 Denmark acceded to the Schengen Accord of June 1990 which abolishes border controls between Denmark and Austria, Belgium, Finland, France, Germany, Greece, Iceland, Italy, Luxembourg, the Netherlands, Norway, Portugal, Spain and Sweden.

ECONOMY

The Danish economy, although small, is at present reasonably healthy and Denmark retains a high standard of living and excellent health and social security systems as well as an impressive GNP per capita. This is largely due to the reliance on and continuing success of Denmark's exports, which totalled over 320bn. kroner in 1997, just under 30% of the GDP. Denmark's most important trading partners are within the EU and Scandinavia. Germany takes around 20% of Denmark's exports and accounts for almost a quarter of Danish imports, which totalled 290bn. kroner in 1997. Sweden and the UK are, respectively, the next two most valuable trading partners. The main export market is for manufactured goods and foods (Denmark catches more fish than any other EU country), whereas imports are generally bound for industry and further processing, with goods imported for direct household consumption making up a little over 25% of the total. Denmark remained relatively unharmed by the recession of the early 1990s in comparison to other European countries and its economy continues to grow steadily whilst unemployment is gradually reduced, aided by the government's reform of taxation, education and labour policies. However, the Danish economy has slowed down a little in the last year or so and is expected to show only moderate growth for the next couple of years. This has been due to the economic problems in Asia and Russia as well as government policy that has sought to avoid overheating.

Following the 2·5% growth in GDP in 1998, the forecast for 1999 was 1·6% and it is expected that the growth in employment will follow suit, leading even to a possible increase in unemployment, although this is expected to be slight, remaining at around 6% (according to the Danish method of calculation – using EU standard methods puts unemployment around 5%).

Whatever happens elsewhere in Scandinavia, an economic boom can be confidently predicted for the Öresund region. In July 2000 a new link will open between Copenhagen and Malmö. For the first time, it will be possible to cross the stretch of water between Denmark and Sweden in a matter of ten minutes. The achievement outranks the Channel tunnel as a feat of engineering. The 16-kilometre route consists of a tunnel, an artificial island four kilometres long and a bridge incorporating one high bridge and two lower approach bridges. The acceleration in communication will be all the more impressive for offering road and rail services. Infrastructure improvements on both sides of the water include new motorways and huge building projects. Malmö will have a city tunnel and Copenhagen a state-of-the-art light railway. Leading companies are expected to choose the region for their northern European headquarters.

In 1997 services accounted for 69% of GDP in 1997, industry 27% and agriculture 4%.

According to the Berlin-based organization *Transparency International*, Denmark has the least corruption in business and government of any country in the world. It received 10 out of 10 in a corruption perceptions index published in 1999.

Policy

The government announced tax reform proposals in June 1998, with the corporate income tax rate being lowered from 34 to 26%. This, plus other changes, would help to trim back GDP growth from 2·7% to 2·5% in 1998 and from a projected 2·9% to 1·7% in 1999.

Performance

Real GDP growth averaged 3% in the period 1995–97. For 1998 a growth rate of 2·5% was recorded; for 1999 a rate of 1·6% was forecast, and for 2000, 2·2%.The current account has moved into deficit and is unlikely to return to surplus before 2000. As stated in the *OECD's Economic Survey of Denmark (1998–99)*, assessing recent economic performance as a whole, it is evident that fiscal consolidation, monetary policy credibility and the structural reform programme have together been highly successful in creating the conditions for long-term growth.

Budget

The following shows the actual revenue and expenditure as shown in central government accounts for the calendar years 1997 and 1998, the approved budget figures for 1999 and the budget for 2000 (in 1,000 kroner):

	1997	1998	1999	2000
Revenue[1]	394,013,800	421,342,100	396,120,000	407,400,300
Expenditure[1]	380,107,800	384,173,300	388,289,200	394,917,600

[1]Receipts and expenditures of special government funds and expenditures on public works are included.

The 1999 budget envisaged revenue of 119,749m. kroner from income and property taxes and 202,223m. from consumer taxes. The central government debt on 31 Dec. 1998 amounted to 610,596m. kroner.

VAT is 25%.

Currency

The monetary unit is the *Danish krone* (DKK) of 100 *øre*. Inflation was 2·2% in 1997, 1·9% in 1998 and was forecast to rise to 2·5% in 1999. In Feb. 1998 foreign exchange reserves were US$19,085m. and gold reserves were 1·69m. troy oz. In Feb. 1998 the money supply was 332bn. kroner. While not participating directly in EMU, the Danish krone is pegged to the new currency in ERM-2, the successor to the exchange rate mechanism.

Banking and Finance

Danmarks Nationalbank (the only bank to issue bank notes) was established in 1818 by an act of Parliament, confirmed by the Nationalbank Act of 1936. The Nationalbank is independent of the government and fixes interest rates and sets monetary policy. On 31 Dec. 1998 the accounts of the National Bank (*Governor*, Bodil Nyboe Andersen) balanced at 182,794m. kroner. The assets included official net foreign reserves of 101,427m. kroner. The liabilities included notes and coins totalling 40,530m. kroner. On 31 Dec. 1998 there were 95 commercial banks and savings banks, with deposits of 695,099m. kroner.

Banks

Danmarks Nationalbank

Havngade 5

1093 Copenhagen K

Tel: 33-63-63-63 Fax: 33-63-71-03

Web: www.nationalbanken.dk

E-mail: nationalbanken@nationalbanken.dk

Den Danske Bank was founded in 1871 and in 1990 merged with Københavns Handelsbank and Provinsbanken. It is Denmark's largest financial services group and is represented throughout Scandinavia and Europe. The group has some two million customers and in 1998 shareholders'equity totalled 30·4 bn. kroner.

Den Danske Bank

2–12 Holmens Kanal

1092 Copenhagen K

Tel: 33-44-00-00 Fax: 39-29-01-46

Web: www.danskebank.dk

Unibank is the largest subsidiary of Unidanmark, the second largest financial services provider in Denmark. In 1998 total deposits were 161·5 bn. kroner and total assets were 447 bn. kroner.

Unibank

Torvegade 2

1786 Copenhagen

Tel: 33-33-33-33

Web: www.unibank.dk

Founded in 1990, the Danish Bankers Association looks after the interests of its members with regard to the government and facilitates co-operation with other banks in Denmark and the EU. In Aug. 1999 it had 171 members.

Danish Bankers Association

Amaliengade 7

1256 Copenhagen K

Tel: 33-12-02-00 Fax: 33-93-02-60

Web: www.finansraadet.dk E-mail: f@finansraadet.dk

Stock Exchange

The Copenhagen Stock Exchange was made a limited company in 1996 and at the end of 1997 had an equity capital of 118·5m. kroner. There are an average of 66 employees and the Chairman of the Board of Directors is Hans Ejvind Hansen. On 21 Jan. 1998 the Stock exchanges in Copenhagen and Stockholm signed the NOREX alliance, an agreement which may lead to a common exchange, but at present aims to make business and trading simpler between the two countries.

Copenhagen Stock Exchange A/S

Nikolaj Plads 6

PO Box 1040

1007 Copenhagen K

Tel: 33-93-33-66 Fax: 33-12-86-13

Web: www.xcse.dk E-mail: xcse@xcse.dk

Chambers of Commerce

Det Danske Handelskammer Børsen

1217 Copenhagen K

Tel: 33-95-05-00 Fax: 33-32-52-16

Web: www.commerce.dk

E-mail: handelskammer@commerce.dk

The Danish-UK Chamber of Commerce

55 Sloane Street

London SW1X 9SR

Tel: (0)20 7259-6795 Fax: (0)20 7823-1200

Web: www.dan-uk-chamber.org

Dänische Handelsdelegation Hamburg

Brandstwiete 4

20457 Hamburg

Tel: (0)40 32-20-21 Fax: (0)40 33-87-54

E-mail: dtchamburg@t-online.de

Commercial Department

Consulate General of Denmark in New York

885 Second Ave, 18th Floor

New York, NY 10017-2201

Tel: 212 223-4545 Fax: 212 754-1904

Web: www.denmark.org E-mail: information@denmark.org

Trade Associations

Danish Agency for Trade and Industry

Ministry of Trade and Industry

Dahlerups Pakhus, Langelinie Allé 17, 2100 Copenhagen Ø

Tel: 35-46-63-17 Fax: 35-46-63-01

Web: www.investindk.com E-mail: info@investindk.com

Export Promotion Denmark

Gammeltorv 8, 1457 Copenhagen K

Tel: 33-32-17-11 Fax: 33-32-19-10-

Web: www.ees.dk/expopromo.html

Weights and Measures

The metric system is obligatory.

ENERGY AND NATURAL RESOURCES

Environmental Policies

Denmark places environmental concerns high on its list of priorities.
There has been a ministry dedicated to protecting nature and the

environment since 1971 and a ministry of energy since 1974 (they are now combined). In 1993 it was declared that environmental considerations must be taken into account with regard to all construction and also political initiatives. Recycling is common and over 80% of Denmark's paper production is made from recycled paper. There is a plan to harness wind energy by building 2,000 windmills of the coasts of Denmark by 2008, which will generate the power equivalent to eight conventional coal fired power stations. If successful, it is hoped the project will be expanded and it is estimated that half of Denmark's energy could be produced in this way by 2030. Total government expenditure on environmental policies in 1997 was 11,615m. kroner. and between 1990 and 1997 environmental taxes increased seven fold, whilst energy taxes increased by 50%.

Electricity
Installed capacity is 12·0m. kW. Production (1998), 39,195m. kWh. Consumption per capita in 1997 was 5,541 kWh. In 1998 some 5,208 wind turbines produced 3·9% of output.

Oil and Gas
Oil production was (1998) 11·5m. tonnes. Production of natural gas was (1998) 7·2m. cu. metres.

Agriculture
Agriculture accounted for 28·1% of exports and 15·8% of imports in 1998. Land ownership is widely distributed. In May 1998 there were 59,761 holdings with at least 5 ha of agricultural area (or at least a production equivalent to that from 5 ha of barley). There were 11,541 small holdings (with less than 10 ha), 30,301 medium-sized holdings (10–50 ha) and 17,918 holdings with more than 50 ha. There were 23,257 agricultural workers in 1996.

In 1998 the cultivated area was (in 1,000 ha): grain, 1,494; pulses, 106; root crops, 133; other crops, 212; green fodder and grass, 576; set aside, 151; total cultivated area, 2,672.

Chief crops	Area (1,000 ha)				Production (in 1,000 tonnes)			
	1995	1996	1997	1998	1995	1996	1997	1998
Wheat	607	681	689	680	4,599	4,758	4,965	4,928
Rye	96	72	84	105	500	343	453	538
Barley	714	738	720	686	3,898	3,953	3,887	3,565
Oats	31[1]	32	43	31	158	164	155	161
Potatoes	42	43	39	36	1,441	1,617	1,545	1,456
Other root crops	121	111	106	98	6,320	5,656	5,870	5,606

[1]Including mixed grain.

Livestock, 1998 (in 1,000): cattle, 1,977; horses, 38; pigs, 12,095; poultry, 18,674; sheep, 142.

Production (in 1,000 tonnes) in 1998: milk, 4,468; butter, 49; cheese, 292; beef, 179; pork and bacon, 1,770.

In 1997 tractors numbered 141,293 and combine harvesters 25,418.

Forestry

The area under forests in 1995 was 417,000 ha, or 9·8% of the total land area. 2·29m. cu. metres of roundwood were produced in 1995.

Fisheries

The total value of the fish caught was (in 1m. kroner): 1950, 156; 1955, 252; 1960, 376; 1965, 650; 1970, 854; 1975, 1,442; 1980, 2,888; 1985, 3,542; 1990, 3,439; 1995, 2,939; 1998, 3,352 (provisional figures).

In 1997 the total catch was 1,826,852 tonnes, of which 1,826,620 tonnes were from sea fishing.

INDUSTRY

The following table is of gross value added (in 1m. kroner):

	1996[1]	1997[1]	1998[1]
Agriculture, fishing and quarrying	42,962	45,116	36,509
Agriculture, horticulture and forestry	29,743	28,597	25,006
Fishing	2,362	2,830	2,776
Mining and quarrying	10,857	13,689	8,727

[1]Provisional or estimated figures.

In the following table 'number of employees' refers to 22,949 local activity units including single-proprietor units (Nov. 1997):

Branch of industry	Number of employees
Food, beverages and tobacco	89,161
Textiles, wearing apparel, leather	18,668
Wood and wood products	16,992
Paper products	64,496
Refined petroleum products	815
Chemicals and man-made fibres	28,327
Rubber and plastic products	22,666
Non-metallic mineral products	20,921
Basic metals	57,433
Machinery and equipment	75,021
Electrical and optical equipment	46,856
Transport equipment	21,554
Furniture, other manufactures	36,592
Total manufacturing	499,502

Top five companies

Rank	Company	Market Capital (US$m.)
1.	Tele Danmark	10,529·9
2.	Novo-Nordisk	7,582·1
3.	D/S Svendborg	6,951·5
4.	D/S 1912	6,869·1
5.	Den Danske Bank	5,875·5

Labour

In 1998 the labour force was 2,868,307. In 1998, 34·9% of the working population worked in public and personal services; 18·0% in wholesale and retail trade, hotels and restaurants; 17·7% in manufacturing; 11·4% in financial intermediation, commerce etc.; 6·9% in transport, storage and telecommunications; 6·0% in construction; 4·3% in agriculture, fisheries and quarrying; and 0·7% in electricity, gas and water supply. In 1998, 477,527 persons were employed in manufacturing. Retirement age is 67. In 1998 the unemployment rate was 6·6%, with a forecast of 5·7% for 1999.

Trade Unions

The Danish Confederation of Trade Unions was set up in 1898 and is the umbrella organization for Danish Trade Unions. LO has 23 affiliated member organizations with a total of 1·5m. members, of which around 900,000 work in the private sector. Women make up 50% of all members

Landesorganisationen i Danmark (LO)

Tel: 35-24-60-00

Web: www.lo.dk E-mail: sporglo@lo.dk

The Union of Commercial and Clerical Employees is the largest Trade Union in Denmark with c. 350,000 members.

Handels- og Kontorfunktionærernes Forbund i Danmark

H.C. Andersens Boulevard 50, Postboks 268

1780 Copenhagen V

Tel: 33-30-43-43 Fax: 33-30-40-99

Web: www.hk.dk

Employers Associations

DA is the main employers' union in Denmark

Dansk Arbejdsgiverforening (DA)

Vester Voldgade 113, 1790 Copenhagen V

Tel: 33-38-90-00 Fax: 33-12-29-76

Web: www.da.dk

The Confederation of Danish Industries is an umbrella organization for 56 industrial and employers' associations, with 5,800 member companies and approximately 300,000 affiliated employees from the manufacturing industry.

Dansk Industri (Confederation of Danish Industries)

HC Andersens Boulevard 18, 1787 Copenhagen V

Tel: 33-77-33-77 Fax: 33-77-33-00

Web: www.di.dk E-mail: di@di.dk

INTERNATIONAL TRADE

Imports and Exports

In 1996 imports totalled US$44,495m. (US$45,090m. in 1995) and exports US$50,115m. (US$49,763m. in 1995).

Imports and exports (in 1m. kroner) for calendar years:

Leading commodities	1997[1] Imports	Exports	1998[1] Imports	Exports
Live animals, meat and meat preparations	3,635	28,390	3,181	24,341
Dairy products, eggs	. . .	10,434	. . .	9,961

Fish, crustaceans, etc. and preparations	7,557	13,658	8,214	13,870
Cereals and cereal preparations	2,139	5,611	2,444	4,998
Sugar, sugar preparations and honey	1,454	1,677	1,275	1,544
Coffee, tea, cocoa, spices, etc.	2,650	734	2,241	863
Fodder for animals	5,096	3,878	4,781	4,435
Wood and cork	4,783	1,049	4,676	1,056
Textile fibres, yarns, fabrics, etc.	7,700	6,638	8,332	12,900
Mineral fuels, lubricants, etc.	14,740	10,564	10,469	7,771
Medicine and pharmaceutical products	5,585	15,594	6,070	16,854
Fertilizers, etc.	2,241	1,190	2,150	904
Metals, manufacture of metals	24,174	15,534	25,723	16,281
Machinery, electrical, equipment, etc.	72,549	74,896	76,343	78,528
Transport equipment	27,483	14,174	32,713	14,423

[1]Excluding trade not distributed.

Distribution of foreign trade (in 1,000 kroner) according to countries of origin and destination for 1998:

Countries	Imports[1]	Exports[1]
Australia	914,664	1,844,823
Austria	3,116,033	3,380,073
Belgium/Luxembourg	11,150,274	6,700,938
China	6,396,493	2,111,296
Faroes	908,327	1,349,537
Finland	8,193,053	9,772,944
France	17,405,388	16,702,061
Germany	67,822,510	66,971,141
Greece	544,417	2,651,388
Hong Kong	1,595,272	3,177,358
Iceland	753,794	1,677,777
India	1,327,500	926,328
Ireland	3,361,204	2,352,397

Italy	14,549,118	12,666,005
Japan	5,967,847	9,428,204
Lithuania	1,057,981	1,732,006
Netherlands	23,098,193	14,948,860
Norway	14,545,822	19,875,923
Poland	5,308,319	6,392,275
Portugal	2,852,279	1,552,358
Russia	2,269,973	4,856,856
Saudi Arabia	12,139	1,830,687
Singapore	456,263	2,395,040
South Korea	2,300,755	1,990,744
Spain	4,430,351	7,183,504
Sweden	39,286,254	34,509,912
Switzerland	4,042,213	4,615,871
Taiwan	2,508,313	1,070,906
Thailand	1,613,621	925,427
UK	23,900,233	30,567,163
USA	15,292,858	16,063,901

[1]Excluding trade not distributed.

Trade Fairs

Feb.	Copenhagen International Fashion Fair, Copenhagen (Tel: 32-52-88-11 Fax: 32-51-96-36)
March	Explore IT, Multimedia fair, Copenhagen
Aug.	Copenhagen International Fashion Fair, Copenhagen (Tel: 32-52-88-11 Fax: 32-51-96-36)
Aug.	Formland – international trade fair for giftware and crafts, Herning (Tel: 42-42-57-11 Fax: 42-42-52-45)
Aug.	Scandinavian Furniture Fair, Copenhagen

(Tel: 86-15-81-11 Fax: 87-44-81-10)

Sept.   Trade Fair for the building industry

(Tel: 99-26-99-26 Fax: 99-26-99-00)

Oct.   Auto Teknik – automotive trade fair

COMMUNICATIONS

Roads

Denmark proper had (1 Jan. 1999) 861 km of motorways, 1,619 km of other state roads, 9,961 km of provincial roads and 59,882 km of commercial roads. Motor vehicles registered at 1 Jan. 1999 comprised 1,817,147 passenger cars, 38,264 trucks, 308,872 vans, 15,170 taxi cabs (including 9,234 for private hire), 13,911 buses and 64,013 cycles.

Rules of the road

Driving in Denmark is on the right-hand side of the road. The wearing of seat belts is compulsory in the front seats and, if fitted, in the back. Dipped headlights must be used by all vehicles at all times. Helmets must be worn by motorcycle and moped drivers. A warning triangle should be carried by all motorists. Unless otherwise indicated, speed limits are 110 kph (66 mph) on motorways, 80 kph (48 mph) on other roads and 50 kph (30 mph) in built-up areas. Emergency telephones on motorways will put broken down motorists in contact with Falck, the 24 hour Danish motorists' aid organization who can arrange towing if on the spot repairs are not possible. A green card is not necessary in Denmark.

Rail

In 1998 there were 2,265 km of State railways of 1,435 mm gauge (617 km electrified), which carried 149m. passengers and 8·0m.

tonnes of freight. There were also 495 km of private railways.

There are daily railway links to Germany, mainly via Hamburg, and to Sweden and other parts of Scandinavia via ferries between Helsingør and Helsingborg. The Öresund road and rail bridge between Sweden and Denmark is presently being constructed and will open during 2000.

DSB (Danish State Railways)
Sølvgade 40
1349 Copenhagen K
Tel: 33-14-04-00
Web: www.dsb.dk

Civil Aviation

Denmark's main international airport is Copenhagen's Kastrup Airport, just outside the city. There is a rail link with Central Station that takes 12 minutes and costs 16·50 kroner. There are also international flights from Aalborg, Aarhus, Billund and Esbjerg.

Established in 1946 as a consortium of Norway, Denmark and Sweden's national airlines, Scandinavian Airlines System (SAS) is the biggest airline in Scandinavia and the fourth largest in Europe. SAS flies around 21m. passengers a year and collaborates with Lufthansa and United Airlines amongst others in an integrated network called Star Alliance.

Services were also provided in 1998 by Adria, Aer Lingus, Aeroflot, Air Baltic, Air Canada, Air China, Air France, Air India, Air Lithuania, Air Malta, Alitalia, Atlantic Airways (Faroe Islands), Austrian Airlines, Balkan, Braathens, British Airways, British Midland, Cimber Air, Continental Airlines, Croatia Airlines, Crossair, Czech Airlines, Delta Air Lines, Egyptair, El Al, Estonian Air, Finnair, Go, Greenlandair, Helikopterservice, Iberia, Icelandair, Interimpex-Avioimpex, Iran Air, JAT, KLM, Kenya Airways, Kuwait Airways,

Lithuanian Airlines, LOT, Lufthansa, Luxair, Maersk Air, Malév, Muk Air, Olympic Airways, Pakistan International Airlines, Regional Airlines, Royal Air Maroc, SABENA, Singapore Airlines, Skyways, South African Airways, Spanair, Swissair, TAP, Tarom, Thai Airways International, Transeast Airlines, Tunis Air, Turkish Airlines, United Airlines, Varig, Virgin Express and Wideroe's Flyveselskap.

On 1 Jan. 1998 Denmark had 1,087 aircraft with a capacity of 22,800 seats. In 1997 there were 292,168 take-offs and landings to and from abroad, and 361,885 to and from Danish airports, including local flights. Copenhagen (Kastrup) handled 15,591,000 passengers in 1996 (12,696,000 on international flights).

Kastrup Airport

Lufthavnsboulevarden 6

Box 74

2770 Kastrup

Tel: 32-31-32-31 Fax: 32-31-31-32

Web: www.cph.dk

SAS

Hedegaardsvej 88, Postboks 150, 2770 Kastrup

Tel: 32-32-00-00

Web: www.scandinavian.net

Shipping

On 1 Jan. 1998 the merchant fleet consisted of 785 vessels (above 20 GRT) totalling 5·5m. GRT. In 1998, 42m. tonnes of cargo were unloaded and 31m. tonnes were loaded in Danish ports; traffic by passenger ships and ferries is not included.

Telecommunications

At 31 Dec. 1998 there were 3·5m. telephone subscribers; 1·95m. mobile telephones were in use. There were 1·1m. Internet users in

Nov. 1998. In 1997, 1·9m. PCs were in use (360 per 1,000 persons) and, in 1995, 250,000 fax machines.

For emergencies in Denmark, dial 112. There are no area codes in Denmark and all telephone numbers have 8 figures. For the international operator, dial 141. There are public phones accepting cards and coins, the minimum cost for a coin phone is 2 kroner. Cards costing 30 kroner to 100 kroner can be bought from post offices and kiosks.

Postal Services

Main Post offices in Denmark are generally open on weekdays from 09.00 to 17.30 and on Saturday until 12.00. Smaller post offices may open at 10.00 and close at 17.00. Poste restante can be received at any post office. Letters and postcards (up to 20g) to Europe cost 4·50 kroner, 5·50 kroner outside Europe.

In 1998 there were 1,196 post offices.

Internet Cafes

There is an internet cafe in Copenhagen called Babel on Frederiksborggade 33 in Copenhagen. (Tel: 33-33-93-38)

SOCIAL INSTITUTIONS

Justice

The lowest courts of justice are organized in 82 tribunals *(byretter)*, where minor cases are dealt with by a single judge. The tribunal at Copenhagen has one president and 44 other judges; and Aarhus one president and 13 other judges; the other tribunals have 1 to 11 judges. Cases of greater consequence are dealt with by the 2 High Courts *(Landsretterne)*; these courts are also courts of appeal for the above-named minor cases. The Eastern High Court in Copenhagen has one president and 60 other judges; and the Western in Viborg one president and 36 other judges. From these an appeal lies to the Supreme Court in Copenhagen, composed of a president and at present 18 other judges. Judges under 65 years of age can be removed only by judicial sentence.

In 1998, 14,641 men and 1,759 women were convicted of violations of the criminal code, fines not included. In 1998 the daily average population in penal institutions was 3,422, of whom 893 men and 55 women were on remand.

Religion

There is complete religious liberty. The state church is the Evangelical-Lutheran to which about 90% of the population belong. It is divided into 10 dioceses each with a Bishop. The Bishop together with the Chief Administrative Officer of the county make up the diocesan-governing body, responsible for all matters of ecclesiastical local finance and general administration. Bishops are appointed by the Crown after an election by the clergy and parish council members. Each diocese is divided into a number of deaneries (107 in the whole country), each with its Dean and Deanery Committee, who have certain financial powers.

Education

Education has been compulsory since 1814. The *folkeskole* (public primary and lower secondary school) comprises a pre-school class *(børnehaveklasse)*, a 9-year basic school corresponding to the period of compulsory education and a 1-year voluntary tenth form. Compulsory education may be fulfilled either through attending the *folkeskole* or private schools or through home instruction, on the condition that the instruction given is comparable to that given in the *folkeskole*. The *folkeskole* is mainly a municipal school and no fees are paid. In the year 1997–98, 2,298 primary and lower secondary schools had 602,783 pupils; they employed 56,323 teachers in 1992–93. 19·9% of the total number of schools were private schools and were attended by 11·6% of the total number of pupils. The 9-year basic school is in practice not streamed. However, a certain differentiation may take place in the eighth and ninth forms.

On completion of the eighth and ninth forms the pupils may sit for the leaving examination of the *folkeskole (folkeskolens afgangs-prøve)*. On completion of the tenth form the pupils may sit for either the leaving examination of the *folkeskole (folkeskolens afgangs-prøve)* or the advanced leaving examination of the *folkeskole (folkeskolens udvidede afgangsprøve)*.

For 14–18 year olds there is an alternative of completing compulsory education at continuation schools, with the same leaving examinations as in the folkeskole. In the year 1997–98 there were 244 continuation schools with 20,220 pupils. Under certain conditions the pupils may continue school either in the 3-year gymnasium (upper secondary school) or 2-year studenterkursus (adult upper secondary school), ending with studentereksamen (upper secondary school leaving examination); or in the 2-year or 3-year higher preparatory examination course, ending with the højere forberedelseseksamen. There were (1997–98) 150 of these upper secondary schools with 71,223 pupils.

Another way of continuing school is to attend HHX (*Højere handelseksamen*) which are diploma courses within the field of trade and commerce (26,710 pupils were enrolled in 1997–98), or HTX (*Højere tekniskeksamen*) which are technical diploma courses (6,241 pupils in 1997–98). Vocational education and training consists of a ½-year or 1-year basic course, followed by a second part of 2–4 years. Vocational education and training cover courses in commerce and trade, iron and metal industry, chemical industry, construction industry, graphic industry, service trades, food industry, agriculture, horticulture, forestry and fishery, transport and communication, and health-related auxiliary programmes. In 1997–98, 39,526 students were enrolled within trade and commerce. 82,278 students were enrolled within technical education.

Tertiary education comprises all education after the 12th year of education, regardless of whether the 3 years after the 9th form of the *folkeskole* have been spent on a course preparing for continued studies (*studentereksamen, højere forberedelseseksamen* or *HHX/HTX*), or a course preparing for a vocation (*EUD*). Tertiary education can be divided into 2 main groups; short courses of further education and long courses of higher education. There were a total of 19,737 students at short courses of further education in 1997–98. There were 18 teacher-training colleges with 14,075 students in 1997–98 and 33 institutes for social educators (early childhood and social education) with 18,936 students.

Degree courses in engineering: the Technical University of Denmark had 6,372 students in 1997–98. 8 engineering colleges had 6,126 students. Universities, 1997–98: the University of Copenhagen (founded 1479), 29,389 students; the University of Aarhus (founded in 1928), 17,901 students; the University of Odense (founded in 1964), 9,127 students; the University of Aalborg (founded in 1974), 8,927 students; Roskilde University Centre (founded in 1972), 5,719 students.

Other types of post-secondary education (1996–97): the Royal Veterinary and Agricultural University has 3,054 students; The Danish School of Pharmacy, 1,137 students; 7 colleges of economics, business administration and modern languages, 22,276 students; 2 schools of architecture, 2,065 students; 7 academies of music, 1,291 students; 2 schools of librarianship, 929 students; The Royal Danish School of Educational Studies, 3,024 students; 5 schools of social work, 1,733 students; The Danish School of Journalism, 998 students; 10 colleges of physical therapy, 2,768 students; 2 schools of

Midwifery Education, 255 students; 2 colleges of home economics, 537 students; The School of Visual Arts, 196 students; 27 schools of nursing, 9,402 students; 3 military academies, 601 students.

Of adult education institutions, the best-known are *Folkeskolehøjskoler*, folk high schools (with 47,954 students). Adult education includes: single subjects (since 1978, with 97,374 students); labour market training courses for semi-skilled workers and for skilled workers (188,468 students in 1995); and courses in single subject education at vocational schools (136,457 students).

In 1995 total expenditure on education came to 8·2% of GNP and represented 13·1% of total government expenditure.

The adult literacy rate in 1997 was at least 99%.

Health

In 1994 there were 14,497 doctors (1 per 358 persons), 5,088 dentists, 63,841 nurses and 1,038 midwives. There were 163 hospitals in 1992, with a provision of 35 beds per 10,000 population.

In 1993 an estimated 37% of men and 37% of women smoked. The rate among women is one of the highest in the world.

Welfare

The main body of Danish social welfare legislation is consolidated in 7 acts concerning: (1) public health security, (2) sick-day benefits, (3) social pensions (for early retirement and old age), (4) employment injuries insurance, (5) employment services, unemployment insurance and activation measures, (6) social assistance including assistance to handicapped, rehabilitation, child and juvenile guidance, daycare institutions, care of the aged and sick, and (7) family allowances.

Public health security, covering the entire population, provides free medical care, substantial subsidies for certain essential medicines together with some dental care, and a funeral allowance. Hospitals are primarily municipal and treatment is normally free. All employed workers are granted daily sickness allowances; others can have limited daily sickness allowances. Daily cash benefits are granted in the case of temporary incapacity because of illness, injury or childbirth to all persons in paid employment. The benefit is paid up to the rate of 100% of the average weekly earnings. There is, however, a maximum rate of 2,758 kroner a week.

Social pensions cover the entire population. Entitlement to the old-age pension at the full rate is subject to the condition that the beneficiary has been ordinarily resident in Denmark for 40 years. For a shorter period of residence, the benefits are reduced proportionally. The basic amount of the old-age pension in July 1999 was 138,984 kroner a year to married couples and 95,640 to single persons. Various supplementary allowances, depending on age and income, may be payable with the basic amount. Depending on health and income, persons aged 60–66 may apply for an early retirement pension. Persons over 67 years of age are entitled to the basic amount. The pensions to a married couple are calculated and paid to the husband and the wife separately. Early retirement pension to a disabled person is payable at ages 18–66 years, having regard to the degree of disability (physical as well as otherwise), at a rate of up to 151,248 kroner to a single person. Early retirement pensions may be subject to income regulation. The same applies to the basic amount of the old-age pension to persons aged 67–69.

Employment injuries insurance provides for disability or survivors' pensions and compensations. The scheme covers practically all employees.

Employment services are provided by regional public employment agencies. Insurance against unemployment provides daily allowances and covers about 85% of the unemployed. The unemployment insurance system is based on state subsidized insurance funds linked to the trade unions. The unemployment insurance funds had a membership of 2,186,467 in Aug. 1999.

The *Social Assistance Act* applies to individual benefits in contrast to the other fields of social legislation which apply to fixed benefits. Total social expenditure, including hospital and health services, statutory pensions etc. amounted in the financial year 1997 to 330,125·7m. kroner.

CULTURE

Broadcasting

Danmarks Radio is the government broadcasting station and is financed by household licence fees. Television is broadcast by *Danmarks Radio* and *TV2* with colour programmes by PAL system. Number of licences (1998): TV, 2·12m., including 2·09m. colour sets. Denmark had 1·26m. cable TV subscribers in 1997. There were 6m. radio receivers in 1996.

Television Stations

Danmarks Radio-TV

TV Byen, DK-2860 Søborg

Tel 00 45 35 20 3040; fax 00 45 35 20 3023

Website: www.dr.dk

Founded in 1951. Broadcasts on 2 channels – DR1 and DR2 (satellite channel).

TV-2 Danmark

Rugaardsvej 25, DK-5100 Odense C

Tel 00 45 65 91 1244; fax 00 45 65 91 3322

Website: www.tv2.dk

Commercial television; commenced broadcasting in 1988.

TV-Danmark

Indiakaj 12, DK-2100 Copenhagen Ø

Tel 00 45 35 43 0522; fax 00 45 35 43 0655

Launched in 1997 by the Scandinavian Broadcasting System SA (SBS).

Radio Stations (National)

Danmarks Radio

Radioavisen-NF-03 , Rosenørns Allé 22, DK-1999 Frederiksberg C

Tel 00 45 35 20 5784; fax 00 45 35 20 5781

Website: www.dr.dk/rdk

Broadcasts on 4 channels – P1, P2-musik, P3 and Danmarkskanalen.

Cinema

In 1998 there were 328 auditoria. Total attendance in 1998 was 11·0m.

Press

In 1998 there were 36 daily newspapers with a combined circulation of 1·61m.

Daily circulation of largest national newspapers, in 1,000s (1997 average):

Morgenavisen Jyllands-Posten	176
Ekstra Bladet	169
Berlingske Tidende	155
Politiken	147
BT	138
Jydske Vestkysten	96
Aalborg Stiftstidende	70
Morgenposten Fyens Stiftstidende	66
Aarhus Stiftstidende	63
Dagbladet / Frederiksborg Amts avis	60

Morgenavisen Jyllands-Posten

Grøndalsvej 3, 8260 Viby J

Tel: 87-38-38-38 Fax: 87-38-34-89

Web: www.mjp.dk

Ekstra Bladet

Rådhuspladsen 37, 3. Sal, 1785 Copenhagen V

Tel: 33-11-13-13 Fax: 33-11-25-28

Web: www.eb.dk

Berlingske Tidende

Pilestræde 34, 1147 Copenhagen K

Tel: 33-75-75-00 Fax: 33-75-20-01

Politiken

Rådhuspadsen 37, 1785 Copenhagen V

Tel: 33-11-85-11 Fax: 33-11-59-18

Web: www.pol.dk

BT

Møntergade 19, 1140 Copenhagen K

Tel: 33-75-75-00 Fax: 33-75-20-01

Web: www.bt.dk

English language newspaper:

Copenhagen Post Aps

Skt. Peders Stræde 27b, 1453 Copenhagen K

Tel: 33-36-33-00 Fax: 33-93-13-13

Web: www.cphpost.dk E-mail: info@cphpost.dk

Circulation of largest magazines, in 1,000s (1997):

Seg og Hør	319
Familie Journalen	268
Hjemmet	243
Billed-Bladet	231

Ude og Hjemme	208
Ugebladet Søndag	122
Femina	94
Anders And og Co.	93
Alt for Damerne	85

Book Publishers

Forlaget Apostrof ApS

Founded 1980. Publishes essays, fiction, humor, literature, literary criticism, psychology, psychiatry and general non-fiction.
Postboks 2580, DK–2100 Copenhagen. Tel: 00 45 39 208420.
Fax: 00 45 39 208453.

Aschehoug Dansk Forlag A/S

Founded 1977. Publishes biography, fiction, cookery, health, how-to, maritime and nutrition.
Landemærkt 8, DK–1119 Copenhagen K. Tel: 00 45 33 305522.
Fax: 00 45 33 305822.

Borgens Forlag A/S

Founded 1948. Publishes fiction, literature, literary criticism, general non-fiction, art, crafts, dance, education, environmental studies, essays, games, gay and lesbian, hobbies, health, music, nutrition, philosophy, poetry, psychology, psychiatry and religion.
Valbygardsvej 33, DK–2500 Valby. Tel: 00 45 36 462100.
Fax: 00 45 36 441488.

Egmont Ladermann A/S

Founded 1954. Publishes general non-fiction.
Gerdasgade 37, DK–2500 Valby. Tel: 00 45 361 56600.
Fax: 00 45 361 44162.
Website: www.egmont.com

Egmont Wangel AS

Founded 1946. Publishes fiction and management.

Gerdasgade 37, DK–2500 Valby. Tel: 00 45 36 156600.

Fax: 00 45 36 441162.

Forum Publishers

Founded 1940. Publishes fiction and mysteries.

Snaregade 4, DK–1205 Copenhagen K. Tel: 00 45 33 147714.

Fax: 00 45 33 147791.

GEC Gads Forlags Aktieselskab

Founded 1855. Publishes general non-fiction, biological sciences, cookery, crafts, games, economics, education, English as a second language, environmental studies, gardening, history, mathematics, natural history, physics, plants and travel.

Vimmelskaftet 32, DK–1161 Copenhagen K. Tel: 00 45 33 150558.

Fax: 00 45 33 110800.

Gyldendalske Boghandel-Nordisk Forlag A/S

Founded 1770. Publishes fiction, art, biography, dance, dentistry, education, history, how-to, medicine, music, poetry, nursing, philosophy, psychology, psychiatry, sociology, general and social sciences.

Klareboderne 3, DK–1001, Copenhagen K. Tel: 00 45 33 110775.

Fax: 00 45 33 110323.

Website: www.gyldendal.dk

Hekla Forlag

Founded 1979. Publishes general fiction and non-fiction.

Valbygaardsvej 33, DK–2500 Valby. Tel: 00 45 36 462100.

Fax: 00 45 36 441488.

Høst & Søns Publishers Ltd

Founded 1836. Publishes fiction, crafts, environmental studies, games, hobbies, regional interests and travel.

PO Box 2212, DK–1018 Copenhagen. Tel: 00 45 33 382888.
Fax: 00 45 33 382898.

Lindhardt og Ringhof
Founded 1971. Publishes fiction and general non-fiction.
Kristianiagade 14, DK–2100 Copenhagen. Tel: 00 45 33 695000.
Fax: 00 45 33 436520.

Munksgaard International Publishers & Booksellers Ltd
Founded 1917. Publishes dentistry, medicine, nursing, psychology,
psychiatry and general science.
PO Box 2148, DK–1016 Copenhagen K. Tel: 00 45 77 333333.
Fax: 00 45 77 333377.
Website: www.munksgaard.dk

Nyt Nordisk Forlag Arnold Busck A/S
Founded 1896. Publishes fiction, art, biography, dance, dentistry,
history, how-to, music, philosophy, religion, medicine, nursing,
psychology, psychiatry, sociology, general and social sciences.
Købmagergade 49, DK–1150 Copenhagen K. Tel: 00 45 33 733575.
Fax: 00 45 33 733576.

Politikens Forlag A/S
Founded 1946. Publishes general non-fiction, art, crafts, dance,
history, games, hobbies, how-to, music, natural history, sport and
travel.
Vestergade 26, DK–1456 Copenhagen K. Tel: 00 45 33 470707.
Fax: 00 45 33 470708.
Website: www.polforlag.dk

Samlerens Forlag A/S
Founded 1942. Publishes fiction, essays, government, history,
literature, literary criticism and political science.
Snaregade 4, DK–1205 Copenhagen K. Tel: 00 45 33 131023.
Fax: 00 45 33 144314.

Det Schønbergske Forlag

Founded 1857. Publishes art, biography, fiction, history, humour, philosophy, poetry, psychology, psychiatry and travel.

Landemaerket 5, DK–1119 Copenhagen K. Tel: 00 45 33 113066.

Fax: 00 45 33 330045.

Spektrum Forlagsaktieselskab

Founded 1990. Publishes general non-fiction.

Snaregade 4, DK–1205, Copenhagen K. Tel: 00 45 33 147714.

Fax: 00 45 33 147791.

Tiderne Skifter Forlag A/S

Founded 1979. Publishes fiction, literature and literary criticism, essays, ethnicity, photography and behavioural sciences.

Pilestraede 51/5, DK–1001 Copenhagen K. Tel: 00 45 33 324772.

Fax: 00 45 33 144205.

Tourism

In 1998, 3,482,000 foreign tourists visited Denmark. In 1998 foreign tourists spent some 21,504m. kroner. Foreigners spent 6,084,000 nights in hotels and 3,763,600 nights at camping sites in 1998.

Danish Tourist Board Offices

Web site: www.visitdenmark.dk

UK: 55 Sloane Street, London SW1X 9SY.

Tel: (0)20 7259-5959

E-mail: dtb.london@dtb.dk

USA: PO Box 4649, Grand Central Station, New York, NY 10163.

Tel: 212 885-9700

Germany: Postfach 101329, 20008 Hamburg

Tel: (0)40 320-210

E-mail: daninfo@t-online.de

Visas

Visas are not required by citizens of EU countries, the USA, Canada, Australia or New Zealand for stays of less than 3 months. Residents of other countries should contact the Danish Embassy in their own country for details of entry requirements.

Festivals

The **Copenhagen Jazz Festival**, at the beginning of July, is a large event lasting ten days that takes over many parts of the city, both in bars and cafes and outdoors.

Festival Office

Tel: 33-93-20-13

Web site: www.cjf.dk

The **Aarhus Festival** takes place every Sept. and consists of jazz, classical and folk music along with exhibitions, films, ballet and sport for young and old alike. The first festival took place in 1965 and since 1979 each year's festivities have had a particular theme.

Århus Festuges Sekretariat

Officersbygningen

Vester Allé 3

8000 Århus C

Tel: 89-31-82-70 Fax: 86-19-13-36

Web: www.aarhusfestuge.dk

Public Holidays in 2000

1 Jan.	New Year's Day
20 April	Ash Thursday
21 April	Good Friday
23 April	Easter Sunday
24 April	Easter Monday

19 May	Bank Holiday
1 June	Ascension Day
11 June	Whitsunday
12 June	Whit Monday
24 Dec.	Christmas Eve
25 Dec.	Christmas Day
26 Dec.	Boxing Day

Social Etiquette

Tipping is not always necessary in Denmark as service is included in taxi costs and most restaurant bills, but rounding up is always appreciated and especially good service should be rewarded.

The Danish would perhaps like to think of themselves as the most modern thinking of all the Scandinavians and the wearing of folk costumes and celebrating traditional festivals, although not entirely unusual, especially in the countryside, are less common than in other Nordic countries. Danes are usually open, tolerant and respectful of others. Same-sex marriages are legal in Denmark, for instance, and when during the occupation period the Nazis insisted that Jews wear the Star of David, a large part of Copenhagen's non-Jewish population wore the star too to combat discrimination.

Business Etiquette

English is spoken widely (and competently), but German may be more common near the border. Businesses are generally small and staff will have more say than in companies outside Scandinavia. Dress is likely to be more informal than in other countries but it will be expected that foreigners will dress formally if this is their custom. It is important to shake hands on meeting and parting with business colleagues. Do be punctual and use the 24 hour clock to avoid mistakes. Business and social relationships will almost certainly be kept separate, but if invited into a home be punctual and take a small gift for the hostess. The Danes may seem direct and blunt but are more likely to consider themselves honest and professional in their actions, as should the foreigner. Payments will normally be made promptly and the same will be expected or interest will usually be charged.

DIPLOMATIC REPRESENTATIVES

Of Denmark in Great Britain (55 Sloane St., London, SW1X 9SR)
  Ambassador: Ole Lønsmann Poulsen.
Of Great Britain in Denmark (Kastelsvej 36/38/40, DK-2100, Copenhagen Ø)
  Ambassador: Philip Astley, LVO.
Of Denmark in the USA (3200 Whitehaven St., NW, Washington, D.C., 20008-3683)
  Ambassador: K. Erik Tygesen.
Of the USA in Denmark (Dag Hammarskjölds Allé 24, DK-2100, Copenhagen Ø)
  Ambassador: Edward E. Elson.
Of Denmark to the United Nations
  Ambassador: Jørgen Bøjer.

FURTHER READING

Statistical Information: Danmarks Statistik (Sejrøgade 11, DK-2100
  Copenhagen Ø. *Website:* http://www.dst.dk/) was founded in 1849 and
  reorganized in 1966 as an independent institution; it is administratively
  placed under the Minister of Economic Affairs. Its main publications are:

Statistisk Årbog (Statistical Yearbook). From 1896: *Statistiske Efterretninger* (Statistical News). *Statistiske Månedsoversigt* (Monthly Review of Statistics), *Statistisk tiårsoversigt* (Statistical Ten-Year Review).

Dania polyglotta. Annual Bibliography of Books . . . in Foreign Languages Printed in Denmark. State Library, Copenhagen. Annual

Kongelig Dansk Hof og Statskalender. Copenhagen. Annual

Johansen, H. C., *The Danish Economy in the Twentieth Century.* London, 1987

Miller, K. E., *Denmark.* [Bibliography] ABC-Clio, Oxford and Santa Barbara (CA), 1987. – *Denmark: a Troubled Welfare State.* Boulder (Colo.), 1991

Petersson, O., *The Government and Politics of the Nordic Countries.* Stockholm, 1994

National library: Det kongelige Bibliotek, P.O.B. 2149, DK-1016 Copenhagen K. *Director:* Erland Kolding Nielsen.

THE FAROE ISLANDS

Key historical events

A Norwegian province till the peace treaty of 14 Jan. 1814, the islands have been represented by 2 members in the Danish parliament since 1851. In 1852 they obtained an elected parliament of their own which in 1948 secured a certain degree of home-rule. The islands are not included in the EU but left EFTA together with Denmark on 31 Dec. 1972. Recently, negotiations for independence were given a push by the prospect of exploiting offshore oil and gas.

Territory and population

The archipelago is situated due north of Scotland, 300 km from the Shetland Islands, 675 km from Norway and 450 km from Iceland, with a total land area of 1,399 sq. km (540 sq. miles). There are 17 inhabited islands (the main ones being Streymoy, Eysturoy, Vágoy, Suðuroy, Sandoy and Borðoy) and numerous islets, all mountainous and of volcanic origin. Population in 1995 was 43,678; density, 31 per sq. km. In 1995 an estimated 67·9% of the population lived in rural areas. The capital is Tórshavn (15,000 residents in 1995) on Streymoy.

The official languages are Faroese and Danish.

Social statistics

Birth rate per 1,000 inhabitants (1996 est.), 13·91; death rate, 8·69. Life expectancy at birth for total population (1996 est.), 77·83.

Constitution and government

The parliament comprises 32 members elected by proportional representation by universal suffrage at age 18. Parliament elects a government of at least 3 members which administers home rule. Denmark is represented in parliament by the chief administrator.

Recent elections

In parliamentary elections held on 30 April 1998 the People's Party (FF) and the Party for People's Government (TF) each won 8 seats with 21·3% and 23·8% respectively, the Equality Party (JF) 7 seats with 21·9%, the Union Party (SF) 6 seats with 18%, the Self-Government Party (SSF) 2 seats with 7·7%, and the Centre Party (MF) 1 seat with 4·1%.

Current administration

Prime Minister: Anfinn Kallsberg (FF).

Following the 1998 elections, a coalition government was formed comprising FF, TF and SSF members.

Local Government

Local government is vested in the 50 *kommunur,* of 29 or more inhabitants, which raise their own income taxes.

Economy
Budget

The 1995 budget balanced at 2,805m. kr. As a result of an economic crash in the early 1990s, Denmark restructured the banks and lent money to the government to meet its international obligations. Since then the economy has improved, but 5·5bn. Danish krone (£480m.) is still owed to the Danish state. Meanwhile, subsidies from Copenhagen are worth at least 1bn. Danish kreone a year.

Currency

Since 1940 the currency has been the Faroese *króna* (kr.) which remains freely interchangeable with the Danish krone.

Banking and Finance

The largest bank is the state-owned Føroya Banki.

Energy and natural resources
Electricity

Installed capacity is 91,000 kW. Total production in 1996 was 170m. kWh, of which hydro-electric 80m. kWh. There are 5 hydro-electric stations at Vestmanna on Streymoy and one at Eiði on Eysturoy. Consumption per capita was 4,043 kWh in 1995.

Agriculture

Only 2% of the surface is cultivated; it is chiefly used for sheep and cattle grazing. Potatoes are grown for home consumption. Livestock (1996): sheep, 68,000; cattle, 2,000.

Fisheries

Deep-sea fishing now forms the most important sector (90%) of the economy, primarily in the 200-mile exclusive zone, but also off Greenland, Iceland, Svalbard and Newfoundland and in the Barents Sea. Total catch (1997) 329,736 tonnes, primarily cod, coalfish, redfish, mackerel, blue whiting, capelin, prawns and herring.

International trade
Imports and Exports

Exports, mainly fresh, frozen, filleted and salted fish, amounted to 2,026m. kr. in 1995; imports to 1,776m. kr. In 1995 Denmark supplied 35% of imports, Norway 16% and UK 8%; exports were mainly to UK (26%), Denmark (22%), Germany (10%), France (8%) and Spain (5%).

Communications
Roads

In 1995 there were 458 km of highways, 11,528 passenger cars and 2,901 commercial vehicles.

Civil Aviation

The airport is on Vágoy, from which there are regular services to Aberdeen, Billund, Copenhagen, Reykjavík and Glasgow (in summer), with Atlantic Airways (Faroe Islands) and Maersk Air.

Shipping

The chief port is Tórshavn, with smaller ports at Klaksvik, Vestmanna, Skálafjørður, Tvøroyri, Vágur and Fuglafjørður. In 1995 merchant shipping totalled 104,000 GRT, including oil tankers, 230,000 GRT.

Telecommunications

In 1997 there were 23,600 telephone main lines in use (538 for every 1,000 inhabitants). There were 4,700 mobile phone subscribers in 1997.

Social institutions
Religion

About 80% are Evangelical Lutherans and 20% are Plymouth Brethren, or belong to small communities of Roman Catholics, Pentecostal, Adventists, Jehovah Witnesses and Bahai.

Education

In 1994–95 there were 4,898 primary and 3,041 secondary school pupils with 554 teachers.

Health

In 1994 there were 90 doctors, 38 dentists, 10 pharmacists, 17 midwives and 355 nursing personnel. In 1994 there were 3 hospitals with 297 beds.

Culture

Broadcasting

Radio and TV broadcasting (colour by PAL) are provided by Utvarp Føroya and Sjónvarp Føroya respectively. In 1994 there were 24,000 radio and 14,000 TV receivers registered.

Further reading

Árbók fyri Føroyar. Annual.

Rutherford, G. K., (ed.) *The Physical Environment of the Færoe Islands.* The Hague, 1982

West, J. F., *Faroe.* London, 1973

Wylie, J., *The Faroe Islands: Interpretations of History.* Lexington, 1987

GREENLAND

Key Historical Events

A Danish possession since 1380, Greenland became an integral part of the Danish kingdom on 5 June 1953. Following a referendum in Jan. 1979, home rule was introduced from 1 May 1979.

Territory and Population

Area, 2,166,086 sq. km (840,000 sq. miles), made up of 1,755,437 sq. km of ice cap and 410,449 sq. km of ice-free land. The population, 1 Jan. 1999, numbered 56,087. In 1999, 45,523 persons were urban (81%); 49,281 were born in Greenland and 6,806 were born outside Greenland. 1999 population of West Greenland, 51,045; East Greenland, 3,471; North Greenland (Thule/Qaanaaq), 857; and 714 not belonging to any specific municipality. The capital is Nuuk (Godthåb), with a population in 1999 of 13,169.

The predominant language is Greenlandic. Danish is widely used in matters relating to teaching, administration and business.

Social Statistics

Registered live births (1998), 986. Number of abortions (1998): 913. Death rate per 1,000 population (1998), 8·3. In 1998 suicide was the cause of death in 12% of all deaths. Annual growth rate (1997), 0·2%. Density, 0·03 sq. km.

Constitution and Government

There is a 31-member Home Rule Parliament, which is elected for 4-year terms and meets 2 to 3 times a year. The 7-member cabinet is elected by parliament. Ministers need not be members of parliament. In accordance with the Home Rule Act, the Greenland Home Rule government is constituted by an elected parliament, *Landstinget* (The Greenland Parliament), and an administration headed by a local government, *Landsstyret* (The Cabinet).

Recent Elections

At the elections of 16 Feb. 1999 Siumut (Social-Democratic Forward Party) gained 11 seats and 35·2% of votes cast, Atássut (Liberal Feeling of Community Party) 8 with 25·2%, Inuit Ataqatigiit (Left-wing Inuit Party) 7 with 22·1%, Katusseqatigiit (independents) 5 with 17·3%.

Current Administration

In Dec. 1998 the cabinet comprised 5 SDP and 2 LP ministers. Greenland elects 2 representatives to the Danish parliament (*Folketing*). Denmark is represented by an appointed High Commissioner.

The *Prime Minister* is Jonathan Motzfeldt (Siumut).

Local Government

Administratively, Greenland is divided into 3 regions (North, East and West Greenland), and subdivided into 18 municipalities (1 in North, 2 in East and 15 in West Greenland). Town councils are elected for 4-year terms. The last elections were in April 1997.

International Relations

Greenland has 2 representatives, appointed by the Greenland Parliament, in the Council for European Politics.

Economy

Policy

(The statistical data is too fragmentary to draw up detailed national accounts showing the flow of money between the individual sectors of Greenland's economy. However, by using the assessment material from the Greenland tax authority, it is possible to compute some crude totals for certain central national account figures.) All figures are in m. kroner.

	1994	1995	1996	1997
GNP at factor cost	6,289	6,762	6,891	7,060
GNP at market prices	6,399	6,773	6,945	7,080
Transfers from the Danish state	2,924	2,974	3,031	3,128
(of which block grants[1])	*2,375*	*2,393*	*2,441*	*2,512*
Gross National Disposable				
Income at market prices	8,973	9,472	9,776	10,008

Real GNP growth	5·9	3·7	1·5	1·4
Real GNDI growth	4·5	3·5	2·2	1·9

[1]Other transfers include (amongst others): defence, fisheries inspection, the judicial system (including the police), which are financed directly by the Danish state.

The figures show that the transfers from the Danish state were 31·3% of gross national disposable income in 1997. There is an ongoing debate regarding the size of the secondary effect of the transfers from the Danish state. According to one estimate, these effects amount to 55% of GNP at market prices.

Performance

Following a period of recession between 1990–93, the economy has been growing since 1994, although at a rate well below the OECD average in recent years. Only in 1997 did GNP achieve its pre-1990 level.

Budget

The budget (*finanslovsforslag*) for the following year must be approved by the Home Rule Parliament (*Landstinget*) no later than 31 Oct.

The following table shows the actual revenue and expenditure as shown in Home Rule government accounts for the calendar years 1997–98, the approved budget figures for 1999 and forecasts for 2000 and 2001. Figures are in 1,000 kroner:

	1997	1998	1999	2000	2001
Revenue[1]	4,178	4,304	4,359	4,344	4,342
Expenditure[1]	4,089	4,366	4,359	4,344	4,342

[1]Receipts and expenditures of special government funds and expenditures on public works are included.

Currency

The Danish krone is the legal currency.

Banking and Finance

There is 1 private bank, Grønlandsbanken.

Weights and Measures

The metric system in use.

Energy and Natural Resources

Electricity

Installed capacity is 92,500 kW. Production in 1998 was 281m. GWh. Consumption was 157·7 GWh in 1996–97.

Oil and Gas

Imports of fuel and fuel oil (1998), 194,484 tonnes worth 271m. kroner.

Water

Production of water in tonnes (1998), 5·5m. cu. metres, of which 2·8m. cu. metres were for industry.

Minerals

Exploitation of minerals (1998): number of licences, 42; area, 27,000 sq. km.

Agriculture

Livestock, 1998: sheep, 21,195; reindeer, 2,600. There are approximately 60 sheep-breeding farms in southwest Greenland. A quota hunt for 2,000 caribous per year has been introduced.

Fisheries

Fishing and product-processing are the principal industry. Total catch in 1997 was 120,596 tonnes. In 1997 prawns accounted for 64·8% of the country's economic output. Greenland Halibut and other fish made up 25%.

In 1998, 184 whales were caught (subject to the International Whaling Commission's regulations) and in 1997, 159,939 seals. Around 75,000 of these were traded, the rest used in domestic households.

Industry

6 shipyards repair and maintain ships and produce industrial tanks, containers and steel constructions for building.

Labour

At 1 Jan. 1998 the labour force born in Greenland was 30,540.

International Trade

Imports and Exports

Principal commodities (in 1m. kroner):

Imports, 1998 provisional figures (c.i.f.), 2,740·3, including: food and live animals, 378·6 (meat and meat preparations 98·3); beverages and tobacco, 104·3 (beverages 75·8); minerals, fuels, lubricants, etc., 232·5 (petroleum products 232·3); chemicals, 110·3; basic manufactures, 458·5; machinery and transport equipment, 655·2 (machinery, 483·2; transport equipment, 172·0); miscellaneous manufactured articles, 326·8.

Exports, 1998 provisional figures (f.o.b.), 1,702·1: prawns, 1,146·6; Greenland halibut, 310·4; cod, 18·8; other fish products, 112·5; other products, 113·8.

Principal trading partners (provisional, 1m. kroner, 1997): imports (c.i.f.): Denmark, 1,712·1; Norway, 315·4; Japan, 74·5; Others, 522·8. Exports (f.o.b.): Denmark, 1,697·9; UK, 67·7; Japan, 65·5; Others, 105·6.

Communications

Roads

There are no roads between towns. Registered vehicles (1998): passenger cars, 2,003; lorries and trucks, 1,391; total (including others), 3,874.

Rail

There is no railway system.

Civil Aviation

Number of passengers to/from Greenland (1998): 95,973. Domestic flights – number of passengers (1998): aeroplanes, 125,843; helicopters, 92,270. Greenland Air operates services to Denmark, Iceland and Frobisher Bay (Canada). Icelandair and SAS also serve Greenland. There are international airports at Kangerlussuaq (Søndre Srømfjord) and Narsarsuaq; and 18 local airports/heliports with scheduled services. There are cargo services to Denmark, Iceland and St John's (Canada).

Shipping

There are no overseas passenger services. In 1998, 100,969 passengers were carried on coastal services. There are cargo services to Denmark, Iceland and St John's (Canada).

Telecommunications

In 1998 there were 24,600 telephone main lines (491 per 1,000 persons) and 12,729 Internet dial-ups. There were 6,400 mobile phone subscribers in 1997.

Social Institutions

Justice

The High Court in Nuuk comprises one professional judge and 2 lay magistrates, while there are 18 district courts under lay assessors.

Religion

About 99% of the population are Evangelical Lutherans. In 1998 there were 17 parishes with 81 churches and chapels, and 22 ministers.

Education

Education is compulsory from 6 to 15 years. A further 3 years of schooling are optional. Pre-primary and primary schools (1998–99):

11,087 pupils and 1,047 teachers; secondary schools: 3 with 512 pupils.

Health

The medical service is free to all citizens. There is a central hospital in Nuuk and 15 smaller district hospitals. In 1998 there were 84 doctors.

Non-natural death occurred in approximately one-quarter of all deaths in 1998. Suicide is the most dominant non-natural cause of death. There were 57 reported cases of tuberculosis in 1998 and 567 cases of venereal disease. Reported cases of syphilis had decreased from 37 in 1991 to 4 in 1998. In 1997, 12 cases of HIV were reported while a total of 17 new HIV-positive cases were reported in 1998.

Welfare

Old-age pension is granted to persons who are 63 or above. The right to maternity leave has been extended to 2 weeks before the expected birth and up to 19 weeks after birth against a total of 20 weeks in earlier regulations. The father's right to 1 week's paternity leave in connection with the birth has been extended to 2 weeks as from 1 Jan. 1998. Unemployment and illness: wage earners who are members of SIK (The National Workers' Union) receive financial assistance (unemployment benefit) according to fixed rates, in case of unemployment or illness.

Culture

Broadcasting

The government Kalaallit Nunaata Radioa provides broadcasting services, and there are also local services. In 1996 there were estimated to be 30,000 radio and 21,000 TV sets (colour by PAL). Several towns have local television stations.

Cinema

There is 1 cinema in Nuuk at the Cultural Centre Katuaq. Video is
widely used.

Press

There are 3 national newspapers.

Tourism

In 1998 visitors stayed 200,573 nights in hotels (including 112,317
Greenlandic visitors) at 28 hotels.

Libraries

There are 17 municipal libraries and the National Library, Nunatta
Atuagaateqarfia, which is administered by the Home Rule authorities.

Museums and Galleries

There are museums in most towns. The Greenland National Museum
is in Nuuk. 14,555 persons visited the museum in 1997.

Further Reading

Greenland 19xx: Statistical Yearbook has been published annually since 1989
    by Statistics Greenland.

Gad, F., A History of Greenland. 2 vols. London, 1970–73

Miller, K. E., Greenland. [Bibliography] ABC-Clio, Oxford and Santa Barbara
    (CA), 1991

Greenland National Library, P.O. Box 1011, DK-3900 Nuuk

National statistical office: Statistics Greenland, PO Box 1025, DK-3900 Nuuk.

Website: http://www.statgreen.gl/

FINLAND

Suomen Tasavalta–
Republiken Finland

Capital: Helsinki

Area: 338,144 sq. km

Population estimate, 2000: 5·18m.

Head of State: Tarja Halonen

Head of Government: Paavo Lipponen

TERRITORY AND POPULATION

Finland, a country of lakes and forests, is bounded in the northwest and north by Norway, east by Russia, south by the Baltic Sea and west by the Gulf of Bothnia and Sweden. The area and the population of Finland on 31 Dec. 1996 (Swedish names in brackets):

Province	Area (sq. km)[1]	Population	Population per sq. km
Uusimaa (Nyland)	6,366	1,257,702	197·6
Itä–Uusimaa (Östra Nyland)	2,747	87,287	31·8
Varsinais–Suomi (Egentliga Finland)	10,624	439,973	41·4
Satakunta	8,290	242,021	29·2
Kanta–Häme (Egentliga Tavastland)	5,204	165,026	31·7
Pirkanmaa (Birkaland)	12,605	442,053	35·1
Päijät–Häme (Päijänne–Tavastland)	5,133	197,710	38·5
Kymenlaakso (Kymmenedalen)	5,106	190,570	37·3
Etelä–Karjala (Södra Karelen)	5,674	138,852	24·5
Etelä–Savo (Södra Savolax)	14,436	171,827	11·9
Pohjois–Savo (Norra Savolax)	16,510	256,760	15·6
Pohjois–Karjala (Norra Karelen)	17,782	175,137	9·8
Keski–Suomi (Mellersta Finland)	16,248	259,839	16·0
Etelä–Pohjanmaa (Södra Österbotten)	13,458	198,641	14·8
Pohjanmaa (Österbotten)	7,675	174,230	22·7
Keski–Pohjanmaa (Mellersta Österbotten)	5,286	72,336	13·7
Pohjois–Pohjanmaa (Norra Österbotten)	35,291	359,724	10·2
Kainuu (Kajanaland)	21,567	93,218	4·3
Lappi (Lappland)	93,003	199,051	2·1
Ahvenanmaa (Åland)	1,527	25,392	16·6
Total	*304,529*	*5,147,349*	*16·9*

[1]Excluding inland water area which totals 33,615 sq. km.

The growth of the population, which was 421,500 in 1750, has been:

End of year	Urban[1]	Semi-urban[2]	Rural	Total	Percentage urban
1800	46,600	. . .	786,100	832,700	5·6
1900	333,300	. . .	2,322,600	2,655,900	12·5
1950	1,302,400	. . .	2,727,400	4,029,800	32·3
1970	2,340,300	. . .	2,258,000	4,598,300	50·9
1980	2,865,100	. . .	1,922,700	4,787,800	59·8
1990	2,846,220	803,224	1,349,034	4,998,500	56·9
1995	2,978,170	896,775	1,241,881	5,116,826	58·2
1996	3,004,850	895,526	1,231,944	5,132,320	58·5
1997	3,077,050	854,015	1,216,284	5,147,349	59·8

The classification urban/rural has been revised as follows:

[1]Urban – at least 90% of the population lives in urban settlements, or in which the population of the largest settlement is at least 15,000.

[2]Semi-urban – at least 60% but less than 90% live in urban settlements, or the population of the largest settlement is more than 4,000 but less than 15,000.

The population on 31 Dec. 1997 by language spoken: Finnish, 4,773,576; Swedish, 293,691; other languages, 78,366; Lappish, 1,716.

The UN gives a projected population for 2000 of 5·18m.

The principal towns with resident population, 31 Dec. 1997, are (Swedish names in brackets):

Helsinki (Helsingfors)–capital	539,363	Lahti	95,854
Espoo (Esbo)	200,834	Kuopio	85,862
Tampere (Tammerfors)	188,726	Pori (Björneborg)	76,566
Vantaa (Vanda)	171,297	Jyväskylä	76,194
Turku (Åbo)	168,772	Lappeenranta (Villmanstrand)	57,196
Oulu (Uleåborg)	113,567	Vaasa (Vasa)	56,277

Kotka	55,769	Imatra	31,508
Joensuu	50,980	Kerava	29,830
Hämeenlinna (Tavastehus)	45,380	Seinäjoki	29,417
Porvoo (Borgå)	43,791	Savonlinna (Nyslott)	28,682
Hyvinkää (Hyvinge)	41,685	Nokia	26,476
Rauma (Raumo)	37,654	Riihimäki	25,975
Kajaani	36,541	Kemi	24,485
Rovaniemi	35,718	Varkaus	23,893
Kokkola (Karleby)	35,513	Iisalmi	23,772
Järvenpää	34,768	Salo	23,561
Lohja (Lojo)	34,172	Tornio	23,116
Mikkeli (St Michel)	32,847	Raisio	22,854
Kouvola	31,884	Kuusankoski	21,713

Nearly 60% of the population live in urban areas. About one-fifth of the total population lives in the Helsinki metropolitan region.

Finnish and Swedish are the official languages. Sami is spoken in Lapland.

Time Zone
Finland is 2 hours ahead of GMT.

POLITICAL AND SOCIAL CHRONOLOGY OF THE 20TH CENTURY

1906   New Legislative body created to replace old estates system

1917   Independence declared from Russia

1918   Left wing Coup forces government to flee

       Civil War ends in victory for government troops

1919   Republic of Finland declared

1921   Aaland Islands accept Finnish sovereignty after League of
        Nations decision

1926   First Social Democratic government (minority rule)

1930   Communist activities banned

1932   Non aggression pact signed with USSR
        Abortive right wing revolt by Lapua movement

1935   Parliament approves new Scandinavian orientation in
        Finnish foreign policy

1939   Non aggression pact between Germany and USSR places
        Finland in Soviet sphere of control
        Invasion by Soviet forces (the Winter War)

1940   South-eastern Finland ceded to USSR

1941   Hostilities with USSR resumed (The Continuation War)

1944   Armistice signed ending Finnish participation in the war
        Petsamo ceded to USSR

1945   Communists enter government

1947   Paris Treaty confirms terms of armistice

1948   Treaty of Friendship, Co-operation and Mutual Assistance
        signed with USSR

1952   Olympics held in Helsinki

1955   Finland joins UN
        Finland joins Nordic Council

1986   Finland joins EFTA

1989   Finland joins Council of Europe

1990   Military limitations stipulated in Treaty of Paris declared
        obsolete by government

1992   1948 Treaty with USSR declared void by Finland and
        Russia

1994   Finns approve EU membership in a referendum

1995   Parliament approves EU membership

CULTURAL BRIEFING

Finnish culture prior to 1809 is generally seen as a part of the
Swedish cultural heritage, and although there was a translation of the
New Testament into Finnish in the mid-16th century, there was little
writing in Finnish until the 1800s. It was then that a wave of nationalism and desire for a national character became important,
encouraged especially by H. G. Porthan and A. I. Arwidsson at Aabo
University. It was Elias Lönnrot's Kalevala compilation of Finnish folk
songs and stories that inspired a domestic literary interest. The end
of the century saw novelists such as Aleksis Kivi take up that mantle
and Finnish theatre was given a boost in 1872 with the foundation of
a national theatre company. Juhani Aho and Aino Kallas were the
most important realist novelists at the turn of the century, but it was
with independence that Finnish literature really came into its own.
Eemil Sillanpää, Mika Waltari and Väinö Linna were the most
important writers of the inter and immediate post war years, whilst
Paavo Rintala and Veijo Meri took the Finnish novel into the modern
era. The dramatist Hella Wuolijoki is also well known, partly due to
her collaboration with Bertolt Brecht.

Similarly, art and architecture in Finland was very much
associated with Swedish traditions until the founding of Helsinki,
when an individual style became more apparent. Engel's plan for
Helsinki is still apparent today and Finnish design has become an
important symbol of nationality. C. E. Sjöstrand interpreted many of
the images from Kalevala in his designs and a national style in
romantic painting, also associated with the Kalevala tradition, was
led by Axel Gallen-Kallela at the end of the 19th century. With the
decline in popularity of romanticism in the 20th century came an
architectural golden age, spearheaded by Alvar Aalto. This was
mirrored in other spheres of the arts and the sculptor Wäinö Aaltonen
achieved a blend of classicism and Finnish cultural history. Painting

in Finland has for the last 100 years followed the main European trends, with impressionism and expressionism especially important before the first world war, but a national enthusiasm for aesthetic art has held sway in the works of Per Stenius, for instance.

Finnish, and especially Lapp, traditions are more obvious in early history when we consider the country's musical heritage. Church song books have been discovered that date from around 1100 and folk songs remain important. It was not until 1882, however, that Finland had an orchestra of its own and Martin Wegelius founded a musical institute. It was of course Sibelius that brought Finnish music onto the world scene, but he owes little to the traditional folk ballads that are perhaps more characteristically Finnish. Since Sibelius, many of Finland's most important composers and conductors have been classically trained in Russia, but little of their work is heard outside Finland.

LEADING CULTURAL FIGURES

Sibelius

Jean Sibelius was born in 1865 and studied music in Berlin and Vienna before returning to Finland to become a theory teacher in Helsinki in the 1890s. It was a state grant that enabled him to turn completely to composing and his works immediately displayed a romantic element. Sibelius was particularly influenced by the nationalistic Karelianist movement which had sprung up around the folk songs collected by Elias Lönnrot earlier in the century. Sibelius' music was often based around folk stories, such as Kullervo (1892), about a mythical Kalevalian hero, and legends and myths continued to be a source of inspiration in the composer's work throughout his career. The Kalevala is now seen as a national masterpiece, but

Sibelius will probably be best remembered for his symphonic poem Finlandia, composed at the turn of the century. His fame was by this point secured and his works were being performed all across Europe and in America. In the twentieth century Sibelius' compositions took on a more classical tone and in 1929 he stopped writing, having composed 7 symphonies and numerous other pieces. In 1939 the musical academy in Helsinki was renamed the Sibelius academy and in 1949 the museum of musical history in Aabo was also dedicated in the composer's honour. Sibelius died in 1957, probably as Finland's most famous son.

Alvar Aalto

Alvar Aalto was born in Kuortane in 1898 and studied as an architect, graduating in 1921. His career was interwoven with that of his wife Aino Marsio, the architect whom he married in 1924, but it is not only for his architectural design that he will be remembered. Aalto established his own architectual practice in 1923 in Jyväskylä, near his home town, which he moved to Turku in 1927 and then to Helsinki in 1933, and he continued to practice as an architect after his immense success as an industrial designer. Aalto was a pioneer of Modernism and his own house in Turku, built in 1927, is one of the first examples of the Scandinavian Modernist movement that has come to characterize the region's design ethic in the twentieth century. The Viipuri Library, completed in 1935, was famed not only for its architectural design, but showed Aalto's prowess as a furniture designer, for it was here that the simple 3-legged stacking stool first made its appearance. Functionality and attractive simple design rule in Aalto's works, and it was his use of wood, especially birch, that was so innovative. The Paimio chair, designed in the early thirties, is now a classic, combining comfort and attractive simplicity. Aalto's success as a furniture designer led him to start the Artek manufacturing company with his wife in 1935, that produced many of his 'organic' designs. The Savoy vase, recognized by almost all Finns as an Aalto classic, was apparently derived from the Fjord coastlines of his native country and Aalto firmly believed in the use of natural forms and materials. The successful reception to his Finnish Pavilion for the New York World's Fair in 1939 also ensured that Aalto achieved recognition abroad, and he continued to work until his death in 1976, collaborating with his second wife Elissa Mäkiniemi after their marriage in 1952, to ensure that Modernism and Scandinavian design became world renowned.

CITY PROFILE

Helsinki

Population 546,000

Helsinki was founded in 1550 by King Gustavus Wasa of Sweden and is still called Helsingfors in Swedish today. The city's original purpose was to compete as a port with Tallin on the other side of the Gulf of Finland and in order to speed up its growth, Gustavus Wasa ordered that all inhabitants of 4 neighbouring towns move to his new city.

The city has been devastated by warfare on a number of occasions and was occupied by Russian troops twice in the 1700s. Until the beginning of the nineteenth century, Helsinki remained a small city and in 1808 a large proportion of its buildings were destroyed in a fire. This coincided with the separation from Sweden and the establishment of an autonomous Grand Duchy within the Russian empire. Helsinki was entirely replanned by Johan Albrecht Ehrenström and built by Carl Ludvig Engel over the next thirty years. In 1812 it had replaced Turku as the Finnish capital and continued to expand over the islands surrounding the peninsula on which the historical city was focused. During the 20th century Helsinki was once again torn apart by war, first in 1918 and then in 1939–40 and 1941–4, when it suffered heavy bombing by Russian forces. As a result, much of Finland's military force is located around the city and the main naval bases are located here. The port also remains important to Finnish trade, handling a large share of imports and exports, and is kept open in winter by ice breakers. A minimum of 30% of Helsinki's area is reserved for open spaces, but there is little further space for the city to expand, as the islands are now inhabited and to the north there is an almost constant urban sprawl to the cities of Esbo and Vantaa.

Helsinki Tourist Office
Pohjoisepanadi 19
00100 Helsinki
Tel: (0)9 169-3757 Fax: (0)9 169-3839
Web: www.hel.fi

Helsinki Tourist Association
Lönnrotinkatu 7B
00120 Helsinki
Tel: (0)9 2288-1333 Fax: (0)9 2288-1399

Hotel Booking Centre
Central Railway Station
00100 Helsinki
Tel: (0)9 2288-1400 Fax: (0)9 2288-1499

Landmarks
Senaatintori
The Senate Square is Helsinki's central square, largely constructed by Engel in the nineteenth century, except for the Sederholm residence (now the Helsinki city museum), built in the mid-eighteenth century. The square's buildings are in the neo-classical style and the

intention was to mimic St. Petersburg's grandeur. On the north side of the square is the Lutheran Cathedral (Tuomiokirkko) and to the west is the University.

Museums

The National Museum is currently being renovated and was expected to open in the spring of 2000. The exhibits are largely historical, starting with the first human habitation of Finland and including all aspects of the history and culture of the country. There is some art from the 16th century and later and there are examples of Finnish furniture as well as a section on minority (including Lapp) culture and history. Temporary exhibitions are also held regularly.

Kansallismuseo – National Museum of Finland
Mannerheimintie 34
00101 Helsinki
Tel: (0)9 40-501 Fax: (0)9 405-0400

Art Galleries

The National Gallery holds largely Finnish art from the past three centuries up to 1960 and is the largest collection in Finland. There is also a collection of foreign art from the nineteenth century to 1960. Closed Mondays.

Ateneum – The Finnish National Gallery
Kaivokatu 2, 00100 Helsinki
Tel: (0)9 173-361
A new modern art gallery was opened in 1998 to allow more space for exhibits in the Ateneum and to show a larger proportion of contemporary art. The collection contains exhibits from 1960 to the present day and is constantly being added to. All forms of visual art are represented. The building (designed by Stephen Holl) alone is worth a visit. Closed Mondays.

Kiasma – The National Museum of Contemporary Art

Mannerheiminaukio 2, Helsinki

Opera Houses

The National Opera has a constantly changing repertoire which can
be checked in Helsinki This Week. There is also a restaurant and
shop in the Opera House and guided tours can be arranged.

Finnish National Opera

Helsinginkatu 58, 00251 Helsinki

Tel: (0)9 4030-2352

www.operafin.fi

SOCIAL STATISTICS

Statistics in calendar years:

	Living births	Of which outside marriage	Still-born	Marriages	Deaths (exclusive of still-born)	Emigration
1991	65,395	17,896	306	24,732	49,294	5,984
1992	66,731	19,257	288	23,560	49,844	6,055
1993	64,826	19,665	271	24,660	50,988	6,405
1994	65,231	20,439	249	24,898	48,000	8,672
1995	63,067	20,886	293	23,737	49,280	8,957
1996	60,723	21,484	231	24,464	49,167	10,587
1997	59,329	21,659	221	23,444	49,108	9,854

In 1997 the rate per 1,000 population was: births, 12; marriages, 5;
deaths, 10; infant deaths (per 1,000 live births), 3·7. Annual growth
rate, 1990–95, 0·5%. Over 1990–95 the suicide rate per 100,000
population was 29·8 (men, 48·9; women, 11·7). Finland has the

highest suicide rate in the European Union. Life expectancy at birth, 1997, 73·0 years for males and 80·6 years for females. In 1995 the most popular age range for marrying was 25–29 for both males and females. Fertility rate, 1997, 1·7 births per woman. In 1998 Finland received 1,200 asylum applications, equivalent to 0·23 per 1,000 inhabitants.

Statistics Finland

Työpajankatu 13, 00580 Helsinki
Tel: (0)9 17341 Fax: (0)9 1734-2750
Web site: www.stat.fi E-mail: tiedotus.tilastokeskus@stat.fi

CLIMATE

A quarter of Finland lies north of the Arctic Circle. The climate is severe in winter, which lasts about 6 months, but mean temperatures in the south and southwest are less harsh, 21°F (–6°C). In the north, mean temperatures may fall to 8·5°F (–13°C). Snow covers the ground for three months in the south and for over six months in the far north. Summers are short but quite warm, with occasional very hot days. Precipitation is light throughout the country, with one third falling as snow, the remainder mainly as rain in summer and autumn. Helsinki (Helsingfors), Jan. 21°F (–6°C), July 62°F (16·5°C). Annual rainfall 24·7" (618 mm).

CONSTITUTION AND GOVERNMENT

Finland is a republic governed by the Constitution of 17 July 1919. Parliament consists of one chamber of 200 members chosen by direct and proportional election by all citizens of 18 or over. The country is divided into 15 electoral districts, with a representation proportional to their population. Every citizen over the age of 18 is eligible for Parliament, which is elected for 4 years, but can be dissolved sooner by the President.

The *President* is elected for 6 years by direct popular vote. In the event of no candidate winning an absolute majority, a second round is held between the 2 most successful candidates.

National Anthem

'Maamme'/'Vårt land' ('Our land'); words by J. L. Runeberg, tune by F. Pacius (same as Estonia).

RECENT ELECTIONS

Presidential elections were held on 16 Jan. 2000. SDP candidate Tarja Halonen came first with 40·0%, followed by Esko Aho (KESK) with 34·4%. There were 5 other candidates. In the run-off Halonen won with 51·6% against 48·4% for Aho.

At the elections for the 200-member parliament on 21 March 1999, turn-out was 68%. The Social Democratic Party (SDP) won 51 seats with 22·9% of votes cast (63 seats and 28·3% in 1995); Centre Party (KESK), 48 with 22·4%; National Coalition Party, 46 with 21·0%; Left Wing League, 20 with 10·9%; Greens, 11 with 7·3%; Swedish People's Party in Finland (SPP), 11 with 5·1%; Finnish Christian League, 10 with 4·2%. 3 other parties each obtained 1 seat.

European Parliament. Finland has 16 representatives. At the June 1999 elections turn-out was 30·1%. The National Rally won 4 seats with 25·3% of votes cast (political affiliation in European Parliament: European Liberal, Democrat and Reform Party);

Centre Party, 4 with 21·3% (European People's Party); Social Democratic Party, 3 with 17·8% (Party of European Socialists); Green League, 2 with 13·4% (Greens); Left Wing League, 1 with 9·1% (Confederal Group of the European United Left/Nordic Green Left); Swedish People's Party in Finland, 1 with 6·8% (European Liberal, Democrat and Reform Party); Christian League of Finland, 1 with 2·4% (European People's Party).

CURRENT ADMINISTRATION

President: Tarja Halonen (b. 1943; Social Democrat).

The Council of State (Cabinet) is composed of a 'rainbow' coalition, spanning the former Communist Left Wing Alliance at one end and the conservative National Coalition party at the other. In March 2000 it comprised:

Prime Minister: Paavo Lipponen (b. 1941; SDP).

Minister of Finance: Sauli Niinistö. *Foreign Affairs:* Erkki Tuomioja. *Justice:* Johannes Koskinen. *Education:* Maija Rask. *Culture:* Suvi Linden. *Interior (Police Affairs):* Kari Hakamies. *Trade and Industry:* Sinikka Mönkäre. *Transport and Communications:* Olli-Pekka Heinonen. *Social Affairs and Health:* Maija Perho. *Labour:* Tarja Filatov. *Defence:* Jan Erik Enestam. *Environment:* Satu Hassi. *Basic Services:* Eva Biaudet. *Local and Regional Affairs:* Martti Korhonen. *Foreign Trade:* Kimmo Sasi. *Agriculture and Forestry:* Kalevi Hemilä.

The *Speaker* is Riitta Uosukainen.

POLITICAL PROFILES

Tarja Halonen

Tarja Halonen won the Finnish Presidential election on 6 Feb. 2000.

Born in 1943 in Helsinki she became secretary of the National Union of Finnish Students in 1969. A trained lawyer, she represented the Central Organisation of Finnish Trade Unions (SAK) from 1970 until she became the Prime Minister's parliamentary secretary in 1974. Since becoming an MP in 1979 she has held numerous positions including Minister of Foreign Affairs (1995–2000). She has been a member of the board of several organizations and has been a member of Helsinki City Council since 1977.

Paavo Lipponen

Paavo Lipponen has been the Prime Minister of Finland since April 1995.

Born in 1941 in Turtola, Finland he editied the student newspaper Ylioppilaslehti before working as a freelance reporter for the Finnish Broadcasting Company YLE from 1965–67. A Social Democrat, he was their research and international affairs secretary and planning chief of the political section from 1967–79. He was a member of parliament from 1983–87 and again from 1991. He is a member of Helsinki City Council and the Chairman of the SDP. He married Päivi Hiltunen in 1998.

LOCAL GOVERNMENT

Finland is divided into 6 provinces (*lääni*, Sw.: *län*). The administration of each province is entrusted to a governor (*maaherra*, Sw.: *landshövding*) appointed by the President. The governor directs the activities of the provincial office (*lääninhallitus*, Sw.: *länsstyrelse*) and of local districts (*kihlakunta*, Sw.: *härad*). In 1997 the number of local districts was 88.

The unit of local government is the municipality (*kunta*, Sw.: *kommun*). Main fields of municipal activities are local planning, roads and harbours, sanitary services, education, health services and social aid. The municipalities raise taxes independent from state taxation. Two categories of municipalities are distinguished by names: Towns (*kaupunki*, Sw.: *stad*), and other municipalities. In 1997 there were altogether 452 municipalities of which 107 were towns. In all municipalities, municipal councils are elected for terms of 4 years; all inhabitants (men and women) of the municipality who have reached their 18th year are entitled to vote and eligible. The executive power is in each municipality vested in a board which consists of members elected by the council. Several municipalities regularly form associations for the administration of common institutions, *e.g.*, a hospital or a vocational school, as well as for regional development and planning. Elections were held on 20 Oct. 1996. The SDP gained 24·5% of votes cast, the Centre Party, 21·8%.

The semi-autonomous province of **Åland Islands** occupies a special position as a demilitarized area. **Åland** elects a 30-member Legislature (*Lagting*), which in turn elects the provincial Executive Board. The capital is Mariehamn (Maarianhamina). It is 95% Swedish-speaking. At a referendum on 20 Nov. 1994 Åland voted to join the EU along with the rest of Finland.

DEFENCE

Conscript service is 6–12 months. Total strength of trained and equipped reserves is about 540,000 (to be 430,000).

Defence expenditure in 1998 totalled US$1,855m. (US$360 per capita), representing 1·5% of GDP.

Army

The country is divided into 3 military commands which include 12 military provinces. Total strength of 24,000 (19,000 conscripts).

Frontier Guard

This comes under the purview of the Ministry of the Interior, but is militarily organized to participate in the defence of the country. It is in charge of border surveillance and border controls. It is also responsible for conducting maritime search and rescue operations. Personnel, 1999, 3,400 (professional) with a potential mobilizational force of 23,000.

Navy

The organization of the Navy was changed on 1 July 1998. The Coastal Defence, comprising the coast artillery and naval infantry, was merged into the navy.

About 50% of the combatant units are kept manned, with the others on short-notice reserve and re-activated on a regular basis. Naval bases exist at Upinniemi (near Helsinki), Turku and Kotka. Naval Infantry mobile troops are trained at Tammisaari. Total personnel strength (1999) was 5,000, of whom 2,600 were conscripts.

Air Force

Personnel (1999), 2,700 (1,500 conscripts). There were 85 combat aircraft including F-18 Hornets and SAABSK-35s.

INTERNATIONAL RELATIONS

Finland is a member of the UN, NATO Partnership for Peace, OECD, EU, Council of Europe, OSCE, CERN, Nordic Council, Council of Baltic Sea States, Inter-American Development Bank, Asian

Development Bank, IOM and the Antarctic Treaty. Finland has acceded to the Schengen Accord, which abolishes border controls between Finland and Austria, Belgium, Denmark, France, Germany, Greece, Iceland, Italy, Luxembourg, the Netherlands, Norway, Portugal, Spain and Sweden.

ECONOMY

Services accounted for 63% of GDP in 1997, industry 32% and agriculture 5%.

According to the Berlin-based organization *Transparency International*, Finland ranks second behind Denmark in having the least corruption in business and government of any country. It received 9·8 out of 10 in a corruption perceptions index published in 1999.

Policy

The Finnish economy not only saw rapid growth in the late 1990s but also redressed a number of imbalances in the economy. Owing to these developments, employment has risen substantially, aided by reductions in taxes and indirect labour costs as well as by structural reforms that have improved the functioning of the labour markets. Finnish public finances have been brought into balance and state debt into decline, as targeted by the government.

Performance

The general European recession of the early 1990s and the collapse of the USSR meant that Finland was particularly hard hit and by 1994 unemployment was at 18%. 1997–98 were good years for the Finnish economy, however, and the focus for trade is now firmly centred on

Western Europe, after joining the EU in 1995 and signing up to the Euro. Over half of Finland's exports go to Europe and almost 60% of its imports come from the EU. There is no longer the enormous budget deficit that plagued the mid-1990s, but unemployment does remain high, at around 11% in early 1999. GDP is steadily increasing, although growth is now a little down on around 5% of 1997–98. Finland's industry is dominated by timber, paper and pulp, engineering and technology, mobile phones especially, and investment into industries and R & D is impressive. Nokia is Finland's success story and the electronics industry as a whole saw a rise of almost 40% in production in 1998. Most Finnish businesses are small (99·5% have less than 200 employees) and taxes are high for businesses and individuals, but these have been reduced over the past years and are set to go down further. Inflation is very low, predicted at 1% for 1999 and the only problem for the Finnish economy now is a fear of overheating in the next few years.

   The OECD reported in 1999 that 'Finland's recent economic performance has been admirable in most respects and the economy is projected to do well in 2000. The monetary conditions may become too easy in 2000, however, and excessive wage rises due to labour market bottlenecks are a major risk, despite the still high unemployment. Sound macroeconomic fundamentals, a strong competitive position and the existence of a pole of excellence in the electronic equipment sector may not be sufficient to achieve a satisfactory labour market performance in the coming years. The new government has identified the need to reduce taxes and to proceed with labour and product market reforms, but the envisaged income tax cuts are fairly timid whilst most reform measures, such as the reform of the early retirement scheme, still have to be specified. Wide-ranging and timely reform measures would help to alleviate obstacles to the continuation of strong, non-inflationary growth in the medium term and increase the chances of further reducing unemployment significantly. Some labour market reforms, especially of the early retirement scheme, could have an immediate effect on labour supply. In the absence of such reforms, a tight fiscal policy stance will be all the more needed to prevent overheating. Concerning sustainable development, both a more systematic economic assessment of environmental policy measures and a further integration of environmental matters in sectoral policies are needed.'

Budget

Revenue and expenditure for the calendar years 1995–99 in 1m. marks:

	1995	1996	1997	1998	1999
Revenue	201,372	198,390	184,668	188,621	187,111
Expenditure	198,332	199,426	187,378	188,619	187,111

Of the total revenue, 1997, 25% derived from value added tax, 27% from income and property tax, 13% from excise duties, 8% from other taxes and similar revenue, 7% from loans and 20% from miscellaneous sources. Reductions in income tax between 1996 and 1999 have reduced the total tax burden from 48·1% of GDP to 45·8%. Of the total expenditure, 1998, 14% went to education and culture, 4% to transport, 23% to health and social security, 6% to agriculture and forestry, 5% to defence and 48% to other expenditure.

VAT is 22% (reduced rates, 12% and 8%).

At the end of Dec. 1997 the central government debt totalled 418,184m. marks. Domestic debt amounted to 262,045m. marks; foreign debt (1996), 175,008m. marks.

Currency

On 1 Jan. 1999 the euro (EUR) became the legal currency in Finland and the *markka* became a subdivision of it; irrevocable conversion rate 5·94573 marks to 1 euro. The euro, which consists of 100 cents, will not be in circulation until 1 Jan. 2002. Even though notes and coins will not be introduced until 1 Jan. 2002 the euro can be used in banking; by means of cheques, travellers' cheques, bank transfers, credit cards and electronic purses. Banking will be possible in both euros and marks until the markka is withdrawn from circulation – which must be by 1 July 2002.

The *markka* (FIM) or mark consists of 100 *pennis*. The mark was pegged to the ecu in June 1991 with a 3% margin of fluctuation. It was devalued by 12·3% in Nov. 1991, and unpegged from the ecu in Sept. 1992. Inflation in 1997 was running at 1·2%. In Feb. 1998 foreign exchange reserves were US$7,064m. and gold reserves were 1·6m. troy oz. Total money supply in Feb. 1998 was 210,276m. marks. Notes in circulation at the end of 1997 amounted to 17,817m. marks.

Banking and Finance

The central bank is the Bank of Finland (founded in 1811), owned by the State and under the guarantee and supervision of Parliament. Its *Governor* is Matti Vanhala. It is the only bank of issue, and the limit of its right to issue notes is fixed equal to the value of its assets of gold and foreign holdings plus 1,500m. marks.

At the end of 1997 the deposits in banking institutions totalled 303,711m. marks and the loans granted by them 291,989m. marks.

The most important groups of banking institutions in 1997 were:

	Number of institutions	Number of offices	Deposits (1m. marks)	Loans (1m. marks)
Commercial banks	9	930	188,325	190,944
Savings banks	40	233	21,648	15,968
Co-operative banks	294	670	91,727	78,932
Foreign banks	6	12	2,011	6,145

The 3 largest banks are MeritaNordbanken (formed in 1997 when Nordbanken of Sweden merged with Merita of Finland), the state-owned Leonia (formerly Postipankki) and Okobank.

There is a stock exchange in Helsinki.

In 1998 Finland received US$11bn. worth of foreign direct investment, equivalent to 8·9% of GDP. No other country received foreign investment totalling such a high proportion of its GDP.

Banks

Bank of Finland
PO Box 160, 00101 Helsinki
Tel: (0)9 1831
Web: www.bof.fi

Commercial Banks and Bankers' Associations

Merita Nordbanken
The Merita Nordbanken group was formed with the merger of the Finnish bank Merita and Swedish Nordbanken and has more than 6·5m. private customers and 400,000 commercial customers. Merita Nordbanken has over 1m. Internet Banking users and is the largest banking group in the Nordic area.
Web: www.meritanordbanken.com

Nordic Investment Bank
Pohjoismaiden Investointipankki
Fabianinkatu 34, PO Box 249, 00171 Helsinki
Tel: (0)9 18001 Fax: (0)9 1800210

Finnish Bankers' Association
Suomen Pannkiydistys
Museokatu 8a, PO Box 1009, 00101 Helsinki
Tel: (0)9 405-6120 Fax: (0)9 4056-1291

FINLAND

NORWAY

SWEDEN

RUSSIA

Arctic Circle
Rovaniemi
Tornio
Oulu
Kajaani
G U L F   O F   B O T H N I A
Vaasa
FINLAND
Kuopio
Jyäskylä
Joensuu
Lake Ladoga
Savonlinna
Tampere
Åland
Turku
Porvoo
GULF OF
HELSINKI FINLAND
St Petersburg
0   200 km

Stockholm ▽   ▽ Tallinn

N

NORWAY

Main bus routes

Nordkapp
Honningsvåg
Hammerfest
Berlevåg
Båtsfjord
Vadsø
Vardø
Tana bru
Kirkenes
Lakselv
Alta
Karasjok
RUSSIA
Tromsø
Gryllfjord
Andenes
Harstad
Kautokeino
Stokmarknes
Lofoten Islands
Lødingen
Narvik
Leknes
Stamsund
Reine
Værøy
Røst
Bodø
Fauske

NORWEGIAN
SEA

Arctic Circle

Mo-i-Rana

FINLAND

SWEDEN

Mosjøen

Hurtigrute
coastal steamer

Namsos

Steinkjer

Trondheim

GULF OF BOTHNIA

Kristiansund

Ålesund
Åndalsnes
Oppdal
Røros
HWY 15
Stryn
Lom
Dombås
Flora
Skei
Otta
Førde
Sogndal
Trysil
Lillehammer
Flåm
Fagernes
Gol
Gjøvik
Bergen
Gelio
Kongsvinger
Kinsarvik
Odda
Hanefoss
Haugesund
Drammen
Kongsberg
OSLO
Horten
Tønsberg
Fredrikstad
Stavanger
Larvik
Halden
Arendal
Mandal
Kristiansand

Helsinki

Stockholm

SWEDEN

ESTONIA

0   200km

NORTH SEA

DENMARK

SWEDEN

0   200 km

N

Arctic Circle

Kiruna

Gällivare

Pajala

Jokkmokk

LAPPLAND

NORR-BOTTEN

Haparanda

Arvidsjaur

Luleå

Sorsele

Piteå

Storuman

Skellefteå

Vilhelmina

Dorotea

Strömsund

VÄSTER-BOTTEN

Umeå

JÄMTLAND

Storlien

Östersund

Sollefteå

Örnsköldsvik

FINLAND

Åsarna

MEDELPAD

Härnösand

HÄRJE-DALEN

Sundsvall

Sveg

HALSING-LAND

GULF OF

Hudiksvall

BOTHNIA

Söderhamn

Mora

DALARNA

Gävle

GÄSTRIK-LAND

Oslo

Uppsala

UPPLAND

VÄRMLAND

VÄSTMAN-LAND

Örebro

STOCKHOLM

NÄRKE

SÖDERMAN-LAND

DALS-LAND

BOHUS-LÄN

Linköping

Norrköping

ESTONIA

VÄSTER-GÖTLAND

ÖSTER-GÖTLAND

Gothenburg

Jönköping

GOTLAND

Varberg

SMÅLAND

Falkenberg

HALLAND

Halmstad

Kalmar

ÖLAND

Ängelholm

LITHUANIA

Helsingborg

BLEKINGE

SKÅNE

BALTIC

Lund

Kristianstad

SEA

Malmö

Trelleborg

Ystad

DENMARK

NORWAY

© Rough Guides, 2000

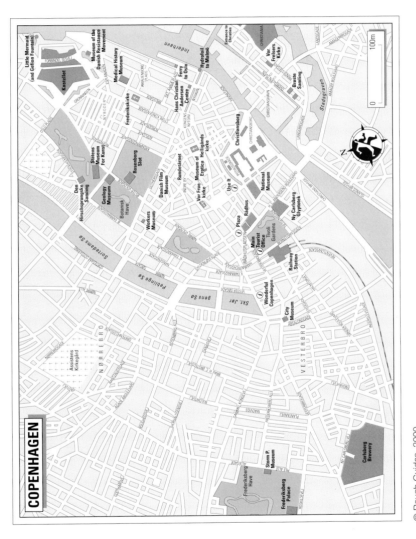

© Rough Guides, 2000

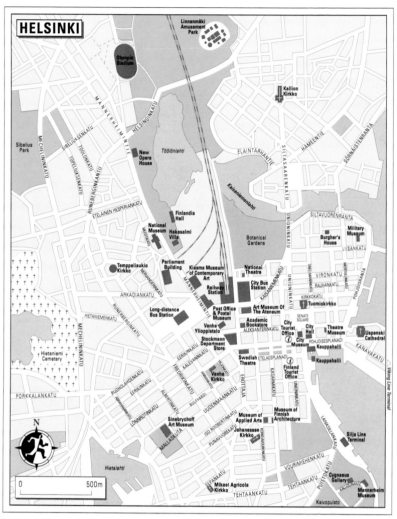

HELSINKI

Linnanmäki Amusement Park

Olympic Stadium

Kallion Kirkko

Sibelius Park

MANNERHEIMINTIE

HELSINGINKATU

MECHELININKATU

SIBELIUKSENKATU

TÖÖLÖNKATU

TOPELIUKSENKATU

RUNEBERGINKATU

New Opera House

Töölönlahti

ELAINTARHANTIE

SILTASAARENKATU

HAMEENTIE

SÖRNÄISTENRANTA

Finlandia Hall

National Museum

Hakasalmi Villa

Etelainen Hesperiankatu

Kaisaniemenlahti

UNIONINKATU

Botanical Gardens

SILTAVUORENRANTA

Burgher's House

Military Museum

LIISANKATU

Temppeliaukio Kirkko

Parliament Building

Kiasma Museum of Contemporary Art

National Theatre

VIRONKATU

ARKADIANKATU

KEINUKAMPENKATU

MANNERHEIMINTIE

Railway Station

City Bus Station

KAISANIEMENKATU

RAUHANKATU

POHJOISRANTA

MEROKATU

RUNEBERGINKATU

HIETANIEMENKATU

Long-distance Bus Station

Post Office & Postal Museum

Art Museum Of The Ateneum

KIRKKOKATU

Tuomiokirkko

MECHELININKATU

Hietaniemi Cemetery

Vanha Ylioppistalo

Stockmann Department Store

Academic Bookstore

ALEKSANTERINKATU

City Tourist Office

City Hall

SENATE SQUARE

Theatre Museum

Uspenski Cathedral

EERIKINKATU

KALEVANKATU

FREDRIKINKATU

ANNANKATU

Swedish Theatre

ETELAESPLANADI

City Museum

POHJOISESPLANADI

Finland Tourist Office

Kauppahalli

KANAVAKATU

Viking Line Terminal

PORKKALANKATU

RUOHOLAHDENKATU

EERIKINKATU

ALBERTINKATU

LÖNNROTINKATU

Vanha Kirkko

BULEVARDI

UUDENMAANKATU

EROTTAJA

KASARMIKATU

UNIONINKATU

Hietalahti

ISO ROOBERTINKATU

PUNAVUORENKATU

MALLASLITA

Sinebrychoff Art Museum

Museum of Applied Arts

Museum of Finnish Architecture

Johanessen Kirkko

LAIVASILLANKATU

Silja Line Terminal

SEPANKATU

VUORIMIEHENKATU

PUISTOKATU

TEHTAANKATU

Mikael Agricola Kirkko

TEHTAANKATU

Cygnaeus Gallery

KALLIOLINNA

Mannerheim Museum

Kaivopuisto

N

0   500m

© Rough Guides, 2000

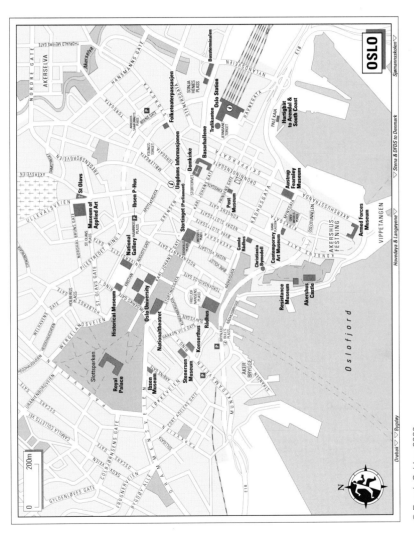

OSLO

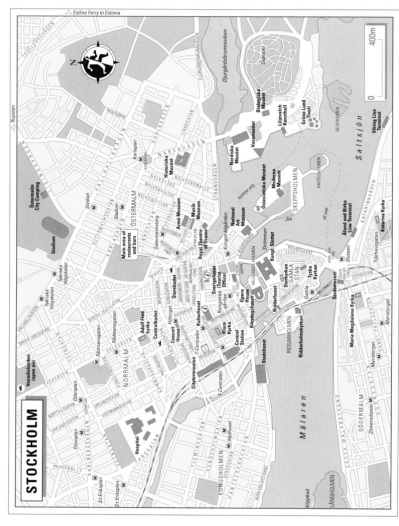

STOCKHOLM

Estline Ferry to Estonia

Ropsten

NORRMALM

ÖSTERMALM

GAMLA STAN

SKEPPSHOLMEN

RIDDARHOLMEN

SÖDERMALM

KUNGSHOLMEN

LÅNGHOLMEN

Saltsjön

Mälaren

Östermalm
City Camping

Stadium

Stadion

Vasastan
(open air)

Hospital

Tekniska
Högskolan

Karlaplan

Historiska
Museet

Armé Museum

Musik
Museum

Royal Theatre
of Drama

Kungsträdgården

National
Art
Museum

Nordiska
Museet

Vasamuseet

Biologiska
Museet

Liljevalch
Konsthall

Gröna Lund
Tivoli

Skansen

Viking Line
Terminal

Östasiatiska Museet

Moderna
Museet

Åland and Birka
Line Terminal

Katarina Kyrka

Kungl.
Slottet

Storkyrkan

Tyska
Kyrkan

Stadsmuseet

Maria Magdalena Kyrka

Strömmen

Riddarholmskyrkan

Stadshuset

Riddarhuset

Riksdagshuset

Opera
House

Kungsträd-
gården

Sverigehuset
(Tourist
Office)

Kulturhuset

Klara
Kyrka

Central
Station

Concert
House

Strömbadet

Hötorget

T-Centralen

Cityterminalen

Adolf Fred.
kyrka

Centralbadet

Main area of
restaurants
and bars

Arné Museum

Östermalmstorg

Stadion

400m

0

© Rough Guides, 2000

Finnish Savings Banks' Association

Säästöpankkiliitto

Mannerhiemintie 14a, 00100 Helsinki

Tel: (0)9 133-986 Fax: (0)9 133-4077

Stock Exchange

Hex Ltd was formed in 1997 when the old Helsinki Stock Exchange and SOM Ltd., the securities and derivatives exchange, merged. In Dec. 1998 Hex formed an agreement with Eurex AG and Deutsche Börse AG after considering either an alliance with Frankfurt or closer Scandinavian co-operation. Hex Ltd. is partly owned by some of Finland's largest private banks.

Hex Ltd. Helsinki Securities and Derivatives Exchange

Clearing House, Fabianinkatu 14, 00131 Helsinki

Tel: (0)9 616-671 Fax: (0)9 6166-7366

Chambers of Commerce

Central Chamber of Commerce

Keskuskauppakamari

World Trade Centre, Aleksanterinkatu 17, PO Box 1000, 00101 Helsinki

Tel: (0)9 696-969 Fax: (0)9 650-303

Web: www.keskuskauppakamari.fi

There are organizations in place to serve as Finnish Chambers of Commerce, but these do not necessarily have a physical presence in foreign countries. For assistance, contact the Finnish Foreign Trade Association (see below).

Trade Associations

Finnish Foreign Trade Association

Arkadiankatu 2, PO Box 908, 00101 Helsinki

Tel: (0)9 204-6951 Fax: (0)9 2046-95535
Web: www.finpro.fi or www.trade-finland.com

Finland Trade Centre
30-35 Pall Mall, London SW1Y 5LP
Tel: (0)20 7747-3000 Fax: (0)20 7747-3007

Weights and Measures
The metric system is in use.

ENERGY AND NATURAL RESOURCES

Electricity
Installed capacity was 15·70m. kW in 1997. Production was (in 1m. kWh) 66,357 in 1996 (17·6% hydro-electric) and 66,149 in 1997 (18·1%). Consumption per capita in 1997 was an estimated 14,338 kWh. In 1998 there were 4 nuclear power stations, which contributed 30·3% of production in 1997. Parliament has rejected the construction of a fifth. Supply: 220 volts; 50 Hz.

Oil and Gas
There is no oil and gas production.

Water
Finland has abundant surface water and groundwater resources relative to its population and level of consumption. The total ground-water yield is estimated to be 10–30bn. cu. metres a day, of which some 6m. is suitable for water supplies. Approximately 15% of this latter figure is made use of at the present time. A total of 2–4% of Finland's exploitable water resources are utilized each year.

Minerals

Notable of the mines are Pyhäsalmi (zinc–copper), Orivesi (gold ore), Vammala (nickel) and Keminmaa (chromium). In 1996 the metal content (in tonnes) of the output of copper ore was 9,261; of zinc ore, 26,924; of nickel ore, 2,136; and of chromium, 228,100.

Agriculture

The cultivated area covers only 7% of the land, and of the economically active population 7% were employed in agriculture and forestry in 1997. The arable area was divided in 1996 into 155,337 farms, and the distribution of this area by the size of the farms was: less than 5 ha cultivated, 48,484 farms; 5–20 ha, 64,248 farms; 20–50 ha, 35,319 farms; 50–100 ha, 6,355 farms; over 100 ha, 931 farms.

Agriculture accounted for 7·8% of exports and 8·6% of imports in 1997.

The principal crops (area in 1,000 ha, yield in 1,000 tonnes) were in 1997:

Crop	Area	Yield	Crop	Area	Yield
Rye	22·8	47·3	Oats	369·2	1,243·4
Barley	582·8	2,003·5	Potatoes	33·2	754·1
Wheat	124·8	464·1	Hay	219·8	862·5

In 1997 there were 2·13m. ha of arable land and 3,000 ha of permanent crops. Production of dairy butter in 1997 was 56,598 tonnes, and of cheese, 82,946 tonnes.

Livestock (1997): horses, 53,100 (including trotting and riding horses, and ponies); cattle, 1,142,400; pigs, 1,467,000; poultry, 5,439,300; reindeer (1995), 333,000.

Forestry

The total forest land amounts to 23·0m. ha. The productive forest land covered 20·1m. ha in 1995. Timber production in 1997 was 51·28m. cu. metres. Finland is one of the largest producers of roundwood in Europe, but in 1997 it was the second largest importer of industrial roundwood in the world after Japan. Finland's per capita consumption of roundwood is the highest in the world, at 11·6m. cu. metres per person in 1995.

Fisheries

The catch in 1997 was 180,087 tonnes, of which 132,496 tonnes came from sea fishing. In 1997 there were 287 food fish production farms in operation, of which 87 were freshwater farms. Their total production amounted to 16,426 tonnes. In addition there were 134 fry-farms and 322 natural food rearers, most of these in freshwater.

INDUSTRY

Finland originally became industrialized by harnessing its forest resources. Over a century later, forests are still Finland's most crucial raw material resource, although the metal and engineering industry has long been Finland's leading branch of manufacturing, both in terms of value added and as an employer. Today Finland is a typical advanced industrial economy: two-thirds of its total output is generated in the service sector.

In 1996 there were 26,375 establishments in industry (of which 25,095 were manufacturing concerns) with 415,708 personnel (of whom 397,398 were in manufacturing). Gross value of industrial production in 1996 was 436,319m. marks, of which manufacturing accounted for 397,514m. marks.

Top Ten Finnish Companies:

Company	Sales (m. FIM)
Nokia	79,231
Stora Enso	62,369
Fortum	50,501
UPM Kymmene	49,735
Merita Nordbanken	38,283
Kesko	35,629
Metsäliitto	28,509
Tamro	17,955
Outokumpu	17,176
Varma-Sampo	16,500

Labour

In 1996 the labour force was 2,603,000 (52% males). In 1995, 32% of the economically active population worked in community, social and personal services, and 21% in manufacturing. In 1998 unemployment was 10·5%, against 3·5% in 1990, but down from 20·0% in 1993.

Trade Unions

According to an incomes policy agreement reached by the central labour market organizations in Dec. 1997, which was in force until Jan. 2000, wages and salaries were raised by 1·6% in Jan. 1998 and by 1·6% in Jan. 1999. The government has undertaken to cut taxes on wages and salaries to support moderate pay increases.

SAK is the largest Trade Union umbrella organization with over 1·1m. members and 25 member unions. 46% of members are women.

SAK
PO Box 157, 00531 Helsinki
Tel: (0)9 77211 Fax: (0)9 772-1223
Web: www.sak.fi

STTK is the next largest organization, with 650,000 members, of whom 67% are female. 26 unions are affiliated to STTK.
Confederation of Salaried Employees (STTK)
Web: www.sttk.fi

INTERNATIONAL TRADE

At the start of the 1990s a collapse in trade with Russia led to the worst recession in the country's recent history. Today, exports to Russia are less than 7% of the total.

The product pattern of exports has also changed dramatically over the last 40 years. In 1960 wood and paper industry dominated exports with their 69% contribution. By 1995 the metal and engineering industry was the largest export sector. But as capital goods for the forest industry form a large proportion of machinery exports, 'the forest cluster' can still be considered the dominant exporter.

Region	Exports 1997	Imports 1997
European Union	53%	59%
Other Europe	16%	12%
Developing Countries	13%	7%
EFTA	4%	6%
Other Countries	15%	16%

Industry	Exports 1997
Metal, Engineering, Electronics	51%
Forest Industry	31%
Chemical Industry	10%
Other	8%

Use of Goods	Imports 1997
Raw materials, production necessities	57%
Consumer goods	22%
Investment goods	15%
Fuels	4%
Other	2%

Imports and Exports

Imports and exports for calendar years, in 1m. marks:

	1996	1997
Imports	140,996	159,192
Exports	185,798	211,695

Trade with principal partners in 1997 was as follows (in 1,000 marks):

	Imports	Exports
Australia	1,020,255	2,666,167
Austria	1,702,373	2,002,910
Belgium-Luxembourg	4,048,400	4,889,737
Canada	1,033,203	2,047,582
China	2,844,379	3,814,419

Denmark	5,458,525	6,493,814
Estonia	2,187,842	6,719,499
France	7,734,021	8,862,287
Germany	23,147,212	23,225,939
Hong Kong	633,397	3,944,248
Indonesia	596,569	2,550,801
Ireland	1,241,789	1,681,572
Italy	6,460,827	6,289,541
Japan	8,586,256	4,025,495
Malaysia	594,947	1,462,729
Netherlands	6,437,308	8,675,449
Norway	5,898,532	6,345,361
Poland	1,794,233	3,755,726
Portugal	1,167,060	1,192,160
Republic of Korea	701,237	2,455,701
Russia	12,521,700	15,462,534
Singapore	544,194	2,003,446
Spain	2,274,836	4,594,396
Sweden	19,088,295	20,830,192
Switzerland	2,668,542	2,080,337
Taiwan	1,298,820	1,057,601
Thailand	632,130	1,987,607
Turkey	389,237	1,672,645
UK	12,163,669	21,107,835
USA	11,719,088	14,732,762

COMMUNICATIONS

Roads

In Jan. 1998 there were 77,796 km of public roads, of which 49,919 km were paved. At the end of 1997 there were 1,948,126 registered cars, 54,217 lorries, 212,727 vans and pick-ups, 8,450 buses and coaches, and 18,798 special automobiles.

Rules of the road

Driving in Finland is on the right-hand side of the road. The wearing of seatbelts is compulsory in the front seats and, if fitted, in the back. Dipped headlights must be used by all vehicles at all times. Helmets must be worn by motorcycle and moped drivers. Strict drink-drive laws are enforced with fines or imprisonment for those over the limit of 0·5% alcohol in the bloodstream. There are no road tolls in Finland. Service stations are often open 24 hours and mostly accept credit cards. Petrol on sale is generally unleaded. Studded or snow tyres may be needed in winter although they are not compulsory. Accidents involving foreign vehicles in Finland should be reported to:

Finnish Motor Insurer's Centre, Green Card Bureau and Guarantee Fund, Liikennevakuutuskeskus, Bulevardi 28, 00120 Helsinki. Tel: (0)9 680-401 Fax: (0)9 6804-0368.

Rail

On 31 Dec. 1997 the total length of the line operated was 5,865 km (2,061 km electrified), of which all was owned by the State. The gauge is 1,524 mm. In 1997, 50m. passengers and 40·3m. tonnes of freight were carried. There is a metro (17 km) and tram/light rail network (75 km) in Helsinki.

In 1995 the Finnish State Railways was transformed into a joint-stock company. Operations continue under the VR Group, the largest transport services group in Finland.

There are international services to Moscow (daily) and St. Petersburg (twice daily) as well as an extensive national rail service. Seat reservations are recommended for most journeys within Finland and are compulsory on Intercity services.

VR (Finnish Railways)
Vilhonkatu 13, PO Box 488, 00100 Helsinki
Tel: (0)9 707-3519 Fax: (0)9 707-3500
Web: www.vr.fi

Civil Aviation

The main international airport is at Helsinki (Vantaa), and there are
also international airports at Turku, Tampere, Rovaniemi and Oulu.
The national carrier is Finnair. Its scheduled traffic covered 92·0m.
km in 1997. The number of passengers was 6·9m. and the number of
passenger-km 11,924,000 in 1997; the air transport of freight and
mail amounted to 312·6m. tonne-km. In 1998 services were also
provided by Aer Lingus, Aeroflot, Air Baltic, Air Botnia, Air Canada,
Air China, Air Express, Air France, Alitalia, Austrian Airlines, Balkan,
British Airways, Continental Airlines, Czech Airlines, Delta Air Lines,
Deutsche BA, El Al, Estonian Air, Iberia, Icelandair, KLM, Lithuanian
Airlines, LOT, Lufthansa, Malév, SABENA, SAS, Skyways, Swissair,
Thai Airways International, Tyrolean Airways and United Airlines.
Helsinki-Vantaa handled 7,689,218 passengers in 1996 (5,423,408
on international flights) and 82,813 tonnes of freight.

　　Helsinki-Vantaa is 20 km from the centre of the city. Bus 615
(15Mk) or the Finnair bus (25Mk) will take you to the Railway station,
a taxi costs approximately 120Mk or there is a shared taxi system
with a flat fare of 70Mk.

Finnair

Finland's national airline flies to most major European cities daily and
has connections.
Asema-aukio 3, 00100 Helsinki
Tel: (0)9 828-7750

Shipping

The total registered mercantile marine on 31 Dec. 1997 was 605 vessels of 1,616,000 GRT. In 1997 the total number of vessels arriving in Finland from abroad was 25,203 and the goods discharged amounted to 39m. tonnes. The goods loaded for export from Finnish ports amounted to 36·1m. tonnes.

The lakes, rivers and canals are navigable for about 6,300 km. Timber floating has some importance, and there are about 9,650 km of floatable inland waterways. In 1997 bundle floating was about 2·4m. tonnes.

Telecommunications

In 1997 there were 2,861,000 telephone main lines in use. 2,162,574 mobile telephones were in use in 1997. The sales of mobile phones are increasing rapidly; in March 1999 more than 3m. Finns (58% of the population) owned a mobile phone, the highest density of users in the world. The rate among 18- and 19-year-olds is almost 100%. Mobile subscribers account for 51% of all telephone subscribers–a percentage only exceeded in Cambodia. In mid-1999 approximately 19% of Finnish households only had a mobile phone and did not have a fixed-line phone at all. The Finnish company Nokia is the world's biggest manufacturer of mobile phones, making 41m. of the 163m. phones sold in 1998. It is by far the biggest company in Finland, accounting for more than 10% of the country's GDP and more than half the value of its stock exchange. The biggest operator is Sonera (formerly Telecom Finland). Approximately 50% of all voice and data traffic streams through the company's networks, and around 70% of all mobile users are Sonera customers. In 1997 there were 1·6m. PCs in use (311 per 1,000 persons) and 198,000 fax machines. There were 1·43m. Internet users in Aug. 1998.

The emergency number is 112. The international code for telephoning or faxing Finland is the code required to dial out of your own country followed by 358. For directory enquiries, dial 020202, for international directory enquiries 020208. To make an international call from Finland, dial 00 first. Finland's area codes were changed on 12 Oct. 1996 and all codes (including mobile numbers) begin with 0. Numbers beginning with 9 are no longer valid – contact directory enquiries for the new code.

Postal Services

In 1997 there were 585 primary post offices and 1,034 agents providing postal services in Finland. Finland Post Group is now exposed to competition in its business operations, with the exception of addressed letter mail for which it holds a licence for nationwide delivery.

Most Post offices are open 09.00-17.00 Monday to Friday. Post Restante can be collected in Helsinki at:

Main Post Office

Mannerheimaukio 1, 00100 Helsinki
Open 08.00-21.00 Monday to Friday, 09.00-18.00 Saturday and 11.00-21.00 Sunday.

Post boxes are yellow and collections are made daily. Stamps are available at post offices, book shops, newsagents, R-kiosks, stations and hotels.

Internet Cafes

Because the Finns now use the internet so widely and public libraries offer free internet access for those that do not have it at home, school or work, there are few internet cafes in Finland and none in Helsinki. It should however, be possible to use a computer relatively easily – ask at your hotel. If all else fails, the Lasipalatsi Multimedia Centre on Mannerheimintie 22–24 has a library with a number of terminals.

SOCIAL INSTITUTIONS

Justice

The lowest court of justice is the District Court. In most civil cases a District Court has a quorum with 3 legally qualified members present. In criminal cases as well as in some cases related to family law the District Court has a quorum with a chair and 3 lay judges present. In the preliminary preparation of a civil case and in a criminal case concerning a minor offence, a District Court is composed of the chair only. From the District Court an appeal lies to the courts of appeal in Turku, Vaasa, Kuopio, Helsinki, Kouvola and Rovaniemi. The Supreme Court sits in Helsinki. Appeals from the decisions of administrative authorities are in the final instance decided by the Supreme Administrative Court, also in Helsinki. Judges can be removed only by judicial sentence.

Two functionaries, the Chancellor of Justice and the Ombudsman or Solicitor-General, exercise control over the administration of justice. The former acts also as counsel and public prosecutor for the government; the latter is appointed by Parliament.

At the end of 1997 the prison population numbered 2,830 men and 144 women; the number of convictions in 1997 was 307,314, of which 249,460 were for minor offences with a maximum penalty of fines, and 22,448 with penalty of imprisonment. 9,501 of the prison sentences were unconditional.

Religion

Liberty of conscience is guaranteed to members of all religions. National churches are the Lutheran National Church and the Greek Orthodox Church of Finland. The Lutheran Church is divided into 8 bishoprics (Turku being the archiepiscopal see), 80 provostships and 595 parishes. The Greek Orthodox Church is divided into 3 bishoprics (Kuopio being the archiepiscopal see) and 27 parishes, in addition to which there are a monastery and a convent.

Percentage of the total population at the end of 1997: Lutherans, 85·6; Greek Orthodox, 1·1; others, 1·0; not members of any religion, 12·3.

Education

Number of institutions, teachers and pupils (1997).

Primary and Secondary Education:

	Number of institutions	Teachers[1]	Students
First-level Education			387,598
(Lower sections of the comprehensive schools, grades I–VI)			
Second-level Education	4,793	45,732	333,053
General education			
(Upper sections of the comprehensive schools, grades VII–IX, and senior secondary schools)			
Vocational Education	350[2]	15,063[2]	153,656

[1]Data for teachers refers to 1996.

[2]Numbers of institutions and teachers at vocational and professional education institutions refer to second and third level education.

Higher Education. Education at vocational and professional education institutions at third level was provided for 34,232 students in 1997. Education at AMK-institutions (polytechnics) was provided at 16 permanent and 15 experimental AMK institutions with 1,019 teachers and 62,258 students.

University Education. Universities and university-type institutions with the number of teachers and students in 1997:

	Founded[1]	Teachers	Students Total	Women
Universities				
Helsinki	1640	1,712	33,452	20,691
Turku (Swedish)	1918	345	5,901	3,514
Turku (Finnish)	1922	758	13,047	8,093
Tampere	1925	577	13,293	8,502
Jyväskylä	1934	575	11,127	7,170
Oulu	1958	840	12,641	6,034
Vaasa	1968	165	3,473	1,902
Joensuu	1969	348	6,127	3,812
Kuopio	1972	310	4,315	2,902
Lapland	1979	177	2,958	1,862
Universities of Technology				
Helsinki	1849	554	13,035	2,481
Tampere	1965	308	8,289	1,466
Lappeenranta	1969	193	3,930	846
Schools of Economics and Business Administration				
Helsinki (Swedish)	1909	111	2,170	881
Helsinki (Finnish)	1911	152	3,789	1,660
Turku (Finnish)	1950	91	1,978	1,021
Universities of Art				
Academy of Fine Arts	1848	19	228	147
University of Art and Design	1871	134	1,465	879
Sibelius Academy	1882	283	1,415	773
Theatre Academy	1943	54	329	179
Total		7,706	142,962	74,815

[1]Year when the institution was founded regardless of university level at the time or not.

There were a total of 2·85m. participants in adult education within the formal education system in 1997 (1,870,800 at general education institutions, 711,800 at vocational and professional education institutions, 158,200 at universities, 71,800 at summer universities and 34,400 at AMK-institutions/polytechnics).

In 1995 total expenditure on education came to 7·6% of GNP and represented 12·2% of total government expenditure.

The adult literacy rate in 1997 was at least 99%.

Health

In 1996 there were 15,192 physicians, 4,839 dentists and (in 1995) 46,362 hospital beds. The average Finnish adult smokes 2·2 cigarettes a day, compared to a European Union average of 4·5, and drinks 8·4 litres of alcohol a year, compared to a European Union average of 11·1 litres.

Medical Services

Note that chemists (kemikaalikauppa) only sell cosmetics; medicines are sold at pharmacies (apteekki). There is a 24-hour pharmacy in Helsinki at: Mannerheimintie 96, Tel: (0)9 02032-0200, Fax: (0)9 4178-0350.

EU citizens with a valid E111 form and Scandinavians will be charged 50Mk to visit a doctor, 100Mk at an hospital outpatient clinic and 125Mk per day for hospitalisation. For those without these documents or citizens from other countries without health insurance full payment will be required. Information on health care and doctors who will make house calls can be obtained by telephoning 10023. For information on dental services call 736-166. For 24-hour emergency hospital treatment in Helsinki:

Helsinki University Central Hospital

Töölö Hospital (serious accidents), Topeliuksenkatu 5.
Meilahti Hospital (medicine and surgery), Haartmaninkatu 7
Tel: (0)9 4711

No vaccinations are required for entry into Finland.

Welfare

The Social Insurance Institution administers general systems of old-age pensions (to all persons over 65 years of age and disabled younger persons) and of health insurance. An additional system of compulsory old-age pensions paid for by the employers is in force and works through the Central Pension Security Institute. Systems for other public aid are administered by the communes and supervised by the National Social Board and the Ministry of Social Affairs and Health.

The total cost of social security amounted to 185,385m. marks in 1996. Out of this 38,422m. (20·7%) was spent on health, 25,031m. (13·5%) on unemployment, 80,318m. (43·3%) on old-age and disability, 31,731m. (17·1%) on family allowances and child welfare, and 9,883m. (5·4%) on general welfare purposes and administration. Out of the total expenditure, 28·5% was financed by the State, 16·2% by local authorities, 35·5% by employers, 13% by the insured and 6·7% by property income.

CULTURE

Helsinki is one of nine European Cities of Culture in the year 2000, with the theme of 'Knowledge, Technology and the Future'. 2000 also marks the 450th anniversary of the founding of Helsinki. The other Cities of Culture are Avignon (France), Bergen (Norway), Bologna (Italy), Brussels (Belgium), Kraków (Poland), Prague (Czech Republic), Reykjavík (Iceland) and Santiago de Compostela (Spain). The title attracts large European Union grants.

Broadcasting

The Finnish Broadcasting Company, YLE, is the biggest national radio and television service provider. YLE operates two television channels (colour by PAL) with full national coverage. The second biggest television broadcaster, the privately owned Commercial MTV3, has one nationwide channel. A new private TV channel, Ruutunelonen, started in 1997. Television programmes from TV Sweden are transmitted over YLE's channel 4. There are some 30 local TV stations that mainly relay foreign and domestic programmes over cable and radio waves, in addition to locally produced material. The only radio broadcaster with full nationwide coverage is YLE. It transmits 3 national channels in Finnish and one in Swedish, as well as various regional channels, including 1 in Sami in Lapland. In 1997 there were 58 local radio stations. Two of them, the news and music stations Nova and Classic, cover almost 60% of the population. There were 7·1m. radio receivers in 1996. On 31 Dec. 1997 the number of television licences was 1,947,400.

National Television Stations

Yleisradio Oy (YLE)

PO Box 00024, Yleisradio, SF-00240 Helsinki

Tel 00 358 9 14801; fax 00 358 9 14803391

Website: www.yle.fi

Founded in 1926, the Finnish Broadcasting Company transmits public service television in Finnish and Swedish on 2 channels – TV1 and TV2. FST is Swedish-language television programming, TV Finland broadcasts via satellite and SVT Europe caters for the Swedish-speaking population along the Finnish coastal regions.

MTV3 Finland

Ilmalantori 2, SF-00240 Helsinki

Tel 00 358 9 15001; fax 00 358 9 1500707

Website: www.mtv3.fi

Private television company, broadcasting since 1957.

National Radio Stations
Yleisradio Oy (YLE)
PO Box 00024, Yleisradio, SF-00240 Helsinki
Tel 00 358 9 14801; fax 00 358 9 14803391
Website: www.yle.fi
   Broadcasts 5 national channels – R1 (Radio Ylen Ykkönen), R2
(Radiomafia), R3 (Radio Suomi), R4 (Radio Extrem) and R5 (Radio
Vega). Radio Peili, Ylen Klassinen and Radio Aino are digital
channels, Sámi Radio covers northern Lapland, Radio Finland is the
external service of YLE and Capital FM is a foreign language service
for Helsinki.

Cinema

In Dec. 1997 there were 321 cinema halls with a seating capacity of
55,532. In 1995 total attendance was 5·3m.

Press

Finland has 56 newspapers that are published 4 to 7 times a week, 9
of which are in Swedish, and 167 with 1 to 3 issues per week. The
total daily circulation of all newspapers is 3·4m. In terms of total
circulation of dailies relative to population, Finland ranks second in
Europe after Norway. Most newspapers are bought on subscription
rather than from newsstands. Only 2 newspapers depend entirely on
newsstand sales.
   Largest national newspapers with place of publication and
weekday circulation for first part of 1999:

Helsingin Sanomat	Helsinki	454,707
Ilta-Sanomat	Helsinki	218,010
Aamulehti	Tampere	134,047
Iltalehti	Helsinki	119,907
Turun Sanomat	Turku	114,739

Kaleva	Oulu	84,292
Kauppalehti	Helsinki	81,764
Keskisuomalainen	Jyväskylä	76,315
Savon Sanomat	Kuopio	72,757
In Swedish:		
Hufvudstadsbladet	Helsinki	58,876

Book Publishers

Gummerus Publishers

Founded 1872. Publishes fiction and general non-fiction.

PO Box 2, SF–Helsinki. Tel: 00 358 9 584301.

Fax: 00 358 9 58430200.

Karisto Oy

Founded 1900. Publishes fiction and general non-fiction.

PO Box 102, SF–13101 Hämeenlinna. Tel: 00 358 3 6161551.

00 358 3 6161565.

Kirjayhtymä Oy

Founded 1958. Publishes fiction and general non-fiction.

PO Box 409, SF–00100 Helsinki.

Tel: 00 358 9 6937641. Fax: 00 358 9 69376366.

Otava Kustannusosakeyhtiö

Founded 1890. Publishes fiction, general non-fiction and how-to.

PO Box 134, 00121 Helsinki. Tel: 00 358 9 19961.

Fax: 00 358 9 643136.

Werner Söderström Osakeyhtiö (WSOY)

Founded 1878. Publishes fiction, general non-fiction and education.

PO Box 222, 00121 Helsinki. Tel: 00 358 9 61681.

Fax: 00 358 9 6168405.

Tami Publishers
Founded 1943. Publishes fiction and general non-fiction.
PO Box 410, 00101 Helsinki. Tel: 00 358 9 6937621.
Fax: 00 358 9 69376266.

Libraries

The Helsinki University Library doubles as a National Library. The
collections of the university libraries and major research libraries
include altogether 43·1m. volumes (of which the university libraries
have 19·0m.). They issued 8·6m. loans in total (university libraries
7·6m.).

The revised Public Library Act, which came into force on 1 Jan.
1999, requires each municipality to provide basic library services
free of charge. The public library network is comprehensive with 992
libraries altogether. These are complemented by 210 mobile units
with over 18,000 service stops. The Helsinki City Library doubles as
a Central Library in this sector. Additionally the country is divided into
19 regions with a Regional Central Library providing supplementary
services. In 1997 there were over 2·5m. registered borrowers, who
represent 49·3% of the population. The number of loans issued
totalled 102·3m.

Theatre and Opera

A new Opera House and a new 14,000-seat Arena Show Hall opened
in 1999 in Helsinki. The city hosts both the National Theatre and the
National Opera. All major cities have theatres and showhalls. In the
summer season open air theatres are very popular. In 1997 there
were 12,690 performances in total with over 2·5m. tickets sold.

Museums and Galleries

The National Museum as well as the National Gallery (the Atheneum)
are located in Helsinki. The new Museum of Modern Art (Kiasma) was

opened in Helsinki in 1998 and a new Ethnographic Museum opened in 1999. A Media Centre is also scheduled to open. Major cities all host their own art galleries and local museums. The Alvar Aalto Museum is located in Jyväskylä in Central Finland. In 1997 there were 145 museums with full-time personnel. The number of exhibitions was 1,081 in 1997, and there were 4m. visitors.

Tourism

There were 1,828,000 foreign tourists in 1997. In 1997 the income from tourism was US$1·66bn.

Major international tourist attractions include Santa Park on the Polar Circle, the Kemi Snow Castle, and the Bomba House and Carelian Village in Nurmes.

Finnish Tourist Offices

Central Office
Töölönkatu 11, PL 625, 00101 Helsinki.
Tel: (0)9 417-6911 Fax: (0)9 4176-9333.
E-mail: etunimi.sukunimi@mek.fi Web site: www.mek.fi

UK
30-35 Pall Mall, London SW1Y 5LP.
Tel: (0)20 7839-4048 Fax: (0)20 7321 0696.
E-mail: mek.lon@mek.fi

USA
655 Third Avenue, New York, NY 10017.
Tel: 212 885-9700 Fax: 212 885-9739.

Germany
Lessingstr. 5, 60325 Frankfurt.
Tel: (0)69 719-1980 Fax: (0)69 724-1725.

France
13 rue Auber, 75009 Paris.
Tel: (0)1 42-66-40-13 Fax:(0)1 47-42-87-22.

Visas

Citizens from EU countries, the USA and many other countries need only a valid passport to enter Finland. Citizens of Denmark, Iceland, Sweden and Norway do not need a passport, visa or residence permit to enter or reside in Finland. Valid identity cards are accepted in place of a passport for citizens of all EU countries (except Greece), Liechtenstein, San Marino and Switzerland. For further information and to check visa requirements for countries not mentioned here contact the following address or your local Finnish embassy or consulate:

Ministry for Foreign Affairs, Unit for Passports and Visas, PO Box 176, 00161 Helsinki.
Tel: (0)9 134-151

Festivals

Helsinki's Festival of Light will have spectacular displays for 2000. Other major festivals include: the Helsinki Festival Week, the Savonlinna Opera Festival, the Kuhmo Chamber Music Festival, Pori Jazz, Kaustinen Folk Music Festival, Tampere Theatre Festival, Kuopio Dance Festival and the Sodankylä Film Festival.

Public Holidays

	2000	2001
New Year's Day	1 Jan.	1 Jan.
Epiphany	6 Jan.	6 Jan.
Good Friday	21 April	13 April
Easter	23–24 April	15–16 April
May Day Eve	30 April	30 April

May Day	1 May	1 May
Ascension Day	1 June	24 May
Whitsun	11 June	3 June
Midsummer	23–24 June	22–23 June
All Saints Day	4 Nov.	3 Nov.
Independence Day	6 Dec.	6 Dec.
Christmas Eve	24 Dec.	24 Dec.
Christmas Day	25 Dec.	25 Dec.
Boxing Day	26 Dec.	26 Dec.

Millennium Events

Helsinki is one of the European Cities of Culture in 2000. For more information on special events to be held during the year look at the Web site: www.2000.hel.fi

Business Etiquette

As a language, English ranks after Finnish and Swedish although many Finns may have learnt Russian at school instead. Languages are important to Finns, so communication should not be a problem. The use of technology is widespread, with more mobile telephones than land lines and a high level of internet use. Finnish businesses are generally small and staff will have more say than in companies outside Scandinavia. Dress is likely to be more informal than in other countries but it will be expected that foreigners will dress formally if this is their custom. It is important to shake hands on meeting and parting with business colleagues. Payments will normally be made promptly and the same will be expected or interest will usually be charged. Finns will generally be direct and honest, but do not make meaningless chatter if they have nothing to say. Do be punctual and use the 24 hour clock to avoid mistakes. Business and social relationships will almost certainly be kept separate, but if invited into a home be punctual and take a small gift for the hostess.

DIPLOMATIC REPRESENTATIVES

Of Finland in Great Britain (38 Chesham Pl., London, SW1X 8HW)
  Ambassador: Pertti Salolainen.
Of Great Britain in Finland (Itäinen Puistotie, 17, 00140 Helsinki)
  Ambassador: Gavin Hewitt, CMG.
Of Finland in the USA (3301 Massachusetts Ave., NW, Washington,
D.C., 20008)
  Ambassador: Jaakko Laajava.
Of the USA in Finland (Itäinen Puistotie 14A, Helsinki 00140)
  Ambassador: Eric S. Edelman.
Of Finland to the United Nations
  Ambassador: Marjatta Rasi.

FURTHER READING

Statistics Finland. *Statistical Yearbook of Finland* (from 1879). – *Bulletin of
    Statistics* (monthly, from 1924).
Constitution Act and Parliament Act of Finland. Helsinki, 1984
Suomen valtiokalenteri – Finlands statskalender (State Calendar of Finland).
    Helsinki. Annual
Facts About Finland. Helsinki. Annual (Union Bank of Finland)
Finland in Figures. Helsinki, Annual
Arter, D., *Politics and Policy-Making in Finland.* Brighton, 1987
Jakobson, M., *Myth and Reality.* Helsinki, 1987
Jutikkala, E. and Pirinen, K., *A History of Finland.* 3rd ed. New York, 1979
Kekkonen, U., *President's View.* London, 1982
Kirby, D. G., *Finland in the Twentieth Century.* 2nd ed. London, 1984
Klinge, M., *A Brief History of Finland.* Helsinki, 1987
Mead, W. R., *Experience of Finland.* Farnborough, 1993

Petersson, O., *The Government and Politics of the Nordic Countries.* Stockholm, 1994

Screen, J. E. O., *Finland.* [Bibliography] 2nd ed. ABC-Clio, Oxford and Santa Barbara (CA), 1997

Singleton, F., *The Economy of Finland in the Twentieth Century.* Univ. of Bradford Press, 1987. – *A Short History of Finland*, 2nd edition. Cambridge University Press, 1998

Tillotson, H. M., *Finland at Peace and War, 1918–1993.* London, 1993

National statistical office: Statistics Finland, Tilastokeskus, FIN-00022.

Website: http://www.stat.fi/

ICELAND

Lyðveldið Ísland
(Republic of Iceland)

Capital: Reykjavík

Area: 103,000 sq. km

Population estimate, 2000: 282,000

Head of State: Ólafur Ragnar Grímsson

Head of Government: Davíð Oddsson

TERRITORY AND POPULATION

Iceland is an island in the North Atlantic, close to the Arctic Circle. Area, 103,000 sq. km (39,758 sq. miles).

There are 8 regions:

Region	Inhabited land (sq. km)	Mountain pasture (sq. km)	Waste- land (sq. km)	Total area (sq. km)	Popula- tion (1 Dec. 1998)
Capital area	1,266	716	–	1,982	167,959
Southwest Peninsula					15,823
West	5,011	3,415	275	8,711	13,950
Western Peninsula	4,130	3,698	1,652	9,470	8,601
Northland West	4,867	5,278	2,948	13,093	9,581
Northland East	9,890	6,727	5,751	22,368	26,501
East	16,921	17,929	12,555	21,991	12,285
South				25,214	20,564
Iceland	42,085	37,553	23,181	102,819	275,264

The population (1980), according to the National Register of Persons, was 229,187. In 1998 the population was 275,264, of whom 21,424 were domiciled in rural districts and 253,840 (92·2%) in towns and villages (of over 200 inhabitants). Population density (1998), 2·7 per sq. km.

The UN gives a projected population for 2000 of 282,000.

The population is almost entirely Icelandic. In 1998 foreigners numbered 6,521 (1,038 Polish, 936 Danish, 584 US, 348 British, 297 Norwegian, 315 German).

The capital, Reykjavík, had on 1 Dec. 1998, a population of 107,753; other towns were: Akranes, 5,188; Akureyri, 15,102; Bolungarvík, 1,023; Dalvík, 1,503; Eskifjörður, 1,022; Garðabær, 7,895; Grindavík, 2,172; Hafnarfjörður, 18,600; Húsavík, 2,480; Ísafjörður, 2,943; Keflavík, 7,574; Kópavogur, 21,370;

Neskaupstaður, 1,523; Njarðvík, 2,739; Ólafsfjörður, 1,091;
Sauðárkrókur, 2,598; Selfoss, 4,339; Seltjarnarnes, 4,691;
Seyðisfjörður, 805; Siglufjörður, 1,605; Vestmannaeyjar, 4,594.
    The official language is Icelandic.

Time Zone

Iceland has no daylight saving time in summer, but operates on GMT
the whole year round.

POLITICAL AND SOCIAL CHRONOLOGY OF THE 20TH CENTURY

1904	Iceland gains home rule from Denmark
1905	First Icelandic trawler revolutionizes fishing industry
1911	University of Iceland established
1918	Iceland made independent under Act of Crown Union. King of Denmark remains head of state
1925	Population reaches 100,000
1930	Icelandic Althingi Parliament celebrates its millennium
1940	Occupation by British troops to defend Iceland
1941	British forces replaced by US troops
1944	Republic of Iceland formally proclaimed following a referendum
1946	Iceland joins the United Nations
1947	Iceland is a founding member of OEEC
1949	Iceland joins NATO
1950	Iceland joins Council of Europe
1951	Defence agreement signed with USA
1952	Iceland joins the Nordic Council
1970	Iceland joins EFTA

CULTURAL BRIEFING

Iceland's literary history starts with the epic poems and sagas that characterize Nordic culture. Due to the isolation of Iceland, much of this tradition has remained and influences from the rest of Europe have not been so important until the 20th century. Egill Skallagrimsson's works (c. 900) are perhaps the most important of this early period, but until the middle ages many writers remained anonymous, either because there is no record of them, or because the sagas they wrote were not original in themselves, having possibly been previously passed own by word of mouth. After the reformation, many tales took on a religious edge, but it was not until the romantic period that Icelandic literature really flourished. Bjarni Thorarensen was the first exponent and Grimur Thomsen, a businessman in Copenhagen before settling down in Iceland, translated many Greek classical works into Icelandic in the late 19th century. Halldór Laxness transformed Icelandic literature in the 20th century and although there was competition from traditionalists like Gudmundur Hagalin, a new generation of modern European authors established itself with original writers like Thor Vilhjalmsson.

Art in Iceland was generally associated with religion until the 20th century, with the arrival of Christianity especially giving opportunities for book illustrations and church decorations. The pre-20th century era was a dark one for Icelandic art, and apart from Bertel Thorvaldsen, the sculptor who lived and worked in Denmark, there were few notable artists until the 1900s, when there was a new appreciation of the domestic landscape. Asgrimir Jonsson and Jon Stefansson were amongst this first generation of painters and sculpture too became important with the works of Einar Jonsson, but the surrealist Johannes Kjarval was to become Iceland's most famous artist. Expressionism found favour with many artists, including Gunnlaugur Scheving, whose paintings of fishing towns retained an Icelandic essence in their subject. There are now a host of Icelandic painters and sculptors working in a variety of styles reflecting all major European influences.

The Tvisöngur is the oldest style of music known in Iceland, using two voices in harmony to sing folk ballards and it was the folk music tradition that reigned until the end of the 1800s. Sveinbjörn Sveinbjörnsson was the first composer to achieve any recognition, and is the writer of the national hymn. Folk influences began to be reintroduced in the 20th century and in 1930 the Conservatory was founded in Reykjavík. Modern Icelandic composers have enjoyed some success, including Altu Heimir Sveinsson, who won the Nordic Council's music prize in 1976. In the 1990s, however, the pop group the Sugarcubes emerged from Iceland and their lead singer Björk went on to achieve worldwide fame as a solo artist.

CULTURAL PROFILE

Halldór Laxness

Halldór Laxness, Iceland's most famous writer, was born in 1902. He travelled widely whilst still relatively young, and was influenced by a variety of cultures. At the age of 21 he converted to Catholicism in Luxembourg and in the 1920s became influenced by socialist ideas whist in America. At this time he rejected his religion and, in an effort to collate his experiences, wrote *The Great Weaver of Cashmere* in 1927. His works were radical in tone and politically involved whilst retaining the essence of the Icelandic story telling tradition. The epics *Salka Valka* and *Independent People* were openly socialistic at a time when political diversity was not widespread in Iceland and Laxness' fame was assured in 1955 when he received the Nobel Prize for Literature. He also translated Hemmingway's *Farewell to*

Arms and Voltaire's *Candide*, amongst other works, into Icelandic and has written numerous other novels, plays and memoirs, although his later work has less of a political tone. He died in 1998.

CITY PROFILE

Reykjavík
Population 164,000

Reykjavík is the site of the first Icelandic settlement, where Ingolfur Arnarson landed in 874 and built his home. It is the northernmost capital city in the world and for many seems unexciting and small, but is home to over half of Iceland's population. Reykjavík means 'smoky bay' and was so named by Arnarson because of the steam rising from the hot springs in the area that in fact help to heat many of the houses in the city today. The city did not grow until relatively late although there was a trading centre there in the 1700s. The old city and the heart of the present capital lies between Tjörnin (a small lake) and the harbour, centred around Austurvöllur, the central square which Arnarson was reputed to have used as farmland. It was in the late 18th century that Reykjavík began to grow and in 1818 the national library was constructed, followed by the National Museum (1863) and the University (1911). Reykjavík is the cultural and economic centre of Iceland and remains an important port. During the Second World War the port was important as a harbour for American ships crossing the Atlantic and it was partly for this reason that Iceland was occupied by Allied forces.

Upplysingamidstöd Ferdamala (Central Tourist Office)
Bankastræti 2
Tel: 1 562-3045

Transport

Reykjavík is small enough for one to be able to walk between most central destinations, but the bus service (for enquiries telephone 551 2700) is efficient. Bus stops are indicated by the letters SVR.

Taxis are reasonably priced and tipping is not usual. They can be found in the centre of the city or ordered by telephone (561 0000).

Landmarks

Reykjavík's most imposing monument is **Hallgrimskirkja**, designed by Gudjon Samuelsson and started in 1945. 30 years later, only the tower had been built, but the entire church, originally designed to seat 1,200 people, is now complete. The tower is 75 metres high and commands excellent views over the city. In front of the church is a statue of Leif Erikson, who set sail from Iceland to first discover Vinland (America). It was donated by the USA in 1930, on the 1,000 year anniversary of the Althing.

The oldest building in Reykjavík is **Fogetinn** on Adalstræti, now a pub, but originally a weaving shed built in 1764.

Museums

The National Museum will reopen in late 2000 after renovation and houses an excellent collection of artefacts from early Norse and Icelandic history. Closed Mondays and limited opening in winter.
National Museum of Iceland, Sudurgata 41, 101 Reykjavík
Tel: 530-2200

Art Galleries

Iceland's national gallery has works by all of Iceland's major artists and a collection of international work, both of which are weighted in favour of the 19th and 20th centuries. Open 11.00-17.00 daily except Mondays.
Listasafn Íslands (National Gallery of Iceland), Fríkirkjuvegur 7, PO Box 668, 121 Reykjavík.

Tel: 562-1000 Fax: 563-1312
Web: www.ismennt.is

Opera House
The Icelandic Opera, Ingólfsstaræti, 101 Reykjavík.
Tel: 551-1475 Fax: 552-7384

Theatre
The National Theatre, Hverfisgoetu 19, 101 Reykjavík
Tel: 551-1200 Fax: 561-1200

SOCIAL STATISTICS

Statistics for calendar years:

	Living births	Still-born	Marriages	Divorces	Deaths	Infant deaths	Net immi-gration
1995	4,280	8	1,238	472	1,923	26	1,418
1996	4,329	20	1,371 (21 same sex)	530	1,879	16	−444
1997	4,151	13	1,481 (12 same sex)	514	1,844	23	69
1998	4,178	9	1,529 (12 same sex)	484	1,821	11	880

1998 rates per 1,000 population: births, 15·3; deaths, 6·7. 65% of births are to unmarried mothers. Annual growth rate, 1990–95, 1·1%. In 1998 the most popular age range for marrying was 25–29 for both males and females. Life expectancy (1997–98): males, 77·0 years; females, 81·5. Infant mortality, 1997, 5·5 per 1,000 live births; fertility rate, 1997, 2·1 births per woman.

Statistics Iceland
Skuggasund 3, 150 Reykjavík

Tel: 560-9800 Fax: 562-8865
E-mail: hagstofa@statice.is Web site: www.statice.is

CLIMATE

The climate is cool temperate oceanic and rather changeable, but mild for its latitude because of the Gulf Stream and prevailing S.W. winds. Precipitation is high in upland areas, mainly in the form of snow. Reykjavík, Jan. 34°F (1°C), July 52°F (11°C). Annual rainfall 34" (860 mm).

CONSTITUTION AND GOVERNMENT

The President is elected by direct, popular vote for a period of 4 years. Presidential elections were held on 29 June 1996. The electorate was 195,000. Ólafur Ragnar Grímsson (b. 1943) was elected against 3 opponents and sworn in 1 Aug 1996.

An electoral law of 1984 provides for an *Althingi* (parliament) of 63 members. Of these, 54 seats are distributed among the 8 constituencies as follows: 14 seats are allotted to Reykjavík, 8 to Reykjanes (i.e. the South-west excluding Reykjavík) and 5 or 6 to each of the remaining 6. From the 9 seats then left, 8 are divided beforehand among the constituencies according to the number of registered voters in the preceding elections. Finally, one seat is given to a constituency after the elections, to compensate the party with the fewest seats as compared to its number of votes.

National Anthem

'Ó Guð vors lands' ('Oh God of Our Country'); words by M. Jochumsson, tune by S. Sveinbjörnsson.

RECENT ELECTIONS

In the presidential election of 29 June 1996 Ólafur Ragnar Grímsson won with 40·9% against 3 other candidates.

In the parliamentary election held on 8 May 1999, the conservative Independence Party of Prime Minister Davíð Oddsson won 26 of the 63 seats with 40·7% of the votes cast, the Alliance (consisting of the People's Alliance, the People's Party and the Alliance of the Women's List) 17 with 26·8%, the Progressive Party 12 with 18·4%, the Left-Green Alliance 6 with 9·1% and the Liberal Party 2 with 4·2%.

CURRENT ADMINISTRATION

President: Ólafur Ragnar Grímsson (b. 1943; sworn in 1 Aug 1996.)
  In March 2000 the government comprised:
  Prime Minister, Minister for Statistics Iceland: Davíð Oddsson (IP).
Minister of Foreign Affairs and Foreign Trade: Halldór Ásgrímsson.
Finance: Geir H. Haarde. *Social Affairs:* Páll Pétursson. *Fisheries:*
Árni Matthiesen. *Justice and Church:* Sólveig Pétursdóttir.
Agriculture: Guðni Ágústsson. *Environment:* Siv Friðleifsdóttir. *Health and Social Security:* Ingibjörg Pálmádottir. *Education and Culture:*
Björn Bjarnason. *Trade and Industry:* Valgerdur Sverrisdóttir.
Transport and Communications: Sturla Bóðvarsson.

POLITICAL PROFILES

Ólafur Ragnar Grímsson

Ólafur Ragnar Grímsson was born in 1943 in Ísafjörður, northwest Iceland and finished his schooling in Reykjavík in 1962. He then studied economics and political science at Manchester University, taking his BA in 1965 and completing a doctorate in 1970 on Smaller European Democracies. He then returned to Iceland and became a lecturer at the University before being made a professor in 1973. Grímsson first stood for election to the Althingi in 1974 for the Liberal and Left Alliance and sat as an alternate member on a number of occasions before he joined the People's Alliance party and won a seat in 1978 which he held for 5 years. He then served as an alternate member until 1991 when he again won a permanent seat. In 1987 he was elected leader of the People's Alliance Party and the following year was made Minister of Finance, a post he held until 1991. He stepped down as party leader in 1995 and was elected President the following year. Grímsson has been a member of a large number of public bodies in Iceland and international organizations. He has been active in European initiatives and travelled widely in Europe, America and further afield.

Davíð Oddsson (PM)

Oddsson is chairman of the Independence party and formed a coalition government in 1995 with the Progressive Party, chaired by the Minister for Foreign Affairs and External trade, Halldór Ásgrímsson. Following elections in April 1999, the government renewed its coalition agreement.

LOCAL GOVERNMENT

On 1 Dec. 1999 Iceland was divided into 124 communes, of which 30 had the status of a town. The commune councils are elected by universal suffrage, in towns and other urban communes by proportional representation, in rural communes by simple majority.

For general co-operation the communes are free to form district councils. All the communes except 10 towns are members in 20 district councils. The communes appoint one or more representatives to the district councils according to their population size. The commune councils are supervised by the Ministry of Social Affairs. In 1992 the government administration and the jurisdictional system at local level were fundamentally reformed, so that the jurisdictional power was totally separated from the executive power, resulting in a new division of responsibilities and functions between the magistrates and the district courts. For national government there are 27 divisions exercised by the magistrates.

Municipal elections were held on 31 May 1998.

DEFENCE

Iceland possesses no armed forces. Under the North Atlantic Treaty, US forces are stationed in Iceland as the Iceland Defence Force.

Navy
There is a paramilitary coastguard of 120.

INTERNATIONAL RELATIONS

Iceland is a member of the UN, NATO, OECD, EFTA, OSCE, the Council of Europe, the Nordic Council and the Council of Baltic Sea States, and is an Associate Member of the WEU. Iceland has acceded to the Schengen Accord, which abolishes border controls between Iceland and Austria, Belgium, Denmark, Finland, France, Germany, Greece, Italy, Luxembourg, Norway, Portugal, Spain and Sweden.

ECONOMY

The Icelandic economy is centred around a fishing industry that is the 15th largest in the world. Fish makes up 70% of all exports and the industry employs some 10% of the workforce. Aluminium products are the next biggest Icelandic export. Tourism is important with as many foreign visitors per year as inhabitants on the island. Iceland is heavily reliant on imports of consumer goods and there has been a trade deficit for years, but this is not seen as a major problem. Unemployment was low at under 2% in mid 1999 and inflation too is low. Foreign trade makes up a large proportion of GNP, yet manufacturing is a far smaller sector than in other European countries. The Icelandic economy is in good shape, however, and has been growing at a rate of just under 5% for the last years of the millennium.

Services contributed 63% of GDP in 1997, industry 24% and agriculture 13%.

According to the anti-corruption organization *Transparency International*, Iceland ranked 5th in the world in a survey of the countries with the least corruption in business and government. It received 9·2 out of 10 in the annual index published in 1999.

Performance

GDP in 1998 totalled US$8·3bn.

Budget

Total central government revenue and expenditure for calendar years (in 1m. kr.):

	1995	1996	1997	1998	1999	2000
Revenue	130,454	143,590	150,056	169,169	183,569	192,586
Expenditure	142,015	150,929	147,308	159,978	173,114	180,062

Central government debt was, on 31 Dec. 1998, 233,035m. kr, of which the foreign debt amounted to 111,928m. kr.

Currency

The unit of currency is the *króna* (ISK) of 100 *aurar*, (singular: *eyrir*). Foreign exchange markets were deregulated on 1 Jan. 1992. The krona was devalued 7·5% in June 1993. Inflation was 1·7% in 1998 with a forecast for 2000 of 4·5%; the average annual rate during the period 1990–96 was 3·1%. Foreign exchange reserves were US$348m. in Feb. 1998 and gold reserves were 50,000 troy oz. Note and coin circulation at 31 Dec. 1998 was 6,322m. kr.

Banking and Finance

The Central Bank of Iceland is the sole issuing bank in Iceland and was established in 1961. The bank also controls monetary policy and manages the nation's foreign exchange reserves. The board of directors is elected by parliament for terms of four years. The current chairman is Mr. Birgir Ísleifur Gunnarsson. The governors of the bank, currently Mr. Finnur Ingólfsson and Mr. Eiríkur Guðnason, are appointed by the Minister of Commerce.

On 31 Dec. 1998 the accounts of the Central Bank balanced at 74,974m. kr. Commercial bank deposits were 169,642m. kr. and deposits in the 29 savings banks, 51,869m. kr.

Central Bank of Iceland (Sedlabanki Islands)
Kalkofnsvegi, 150 Reykjavík.
Tel: 569-9600. Fax: 569-9605
E-mail: webmaster@sedlabanki.is Web site: www.sedlabanki.is

There are four commercial banks in Iceland, the largest being the National Bank of Iceland which, like the Agricultural Bank Ltd., was partly privatized in 1998. Icebank Ltd. is owned by the 27 savings bank in Iceland and Islandsbanki Ltd. is privately owned, having been formed in 1990 by the merger of four older banks.

Banking is being deregulated in stages and by 1999 the State was in the process of selling off shares to the public.

Islandsbanki

Kirkjusandur, 155 Reykjavík

Tel: 560-8000 Fax: 560-8522

Web: www.isbank.is E-mail: upplysingar@isbank.is

Stock exchange

The ISE was founded in 1985 and trading began the following year in T-bonds only. Companies were first listed on the exchange in 1992 and the exchange was made an independent institution in 1993. In 1998 Parliament altered this status and forced the exchange to become a limited company with shareholders and removed its monopoly on trading. This came into force at the beginning of 1999.

Iceland Stock Exchange

Engjateigur 3, 105 Reykjavík

Tel: 525-2800 Fax: 525-2888

Web: www.vi.is E-mail: www.vi@vi.is

Chambers of Commerce

The Icelandic American Chamber of Commerce

800 Third Avenue, 36th Floor, New York, NY 10022

Tel: 212 593-2700 Fax: 212 593-6269

Trade Associations

Trade Council of Iceland

Web site: www.icetrade.is or www.invest.is

PO Box 1000, 121 Reykjavík

Tel: 511-4000 Fax: 511-4040

E-mail: tradecouncil@icetrade.is

800 Third Avenue, 36th Floor, New York, NY 10022, USA
Tel: 212 593-2700 Fax: 212 593-6269

Weights and Measures
The metric system is obligatory.

ENERGY AND NATURAL RESOURCES

Electricity
The installed capacity of public electrical power plants at the end of
1998 totalled 1,212,722 kW; installed capacity of hydro-electric
plants was 951,534 kW. Total electricity production in public-owned
plants in 1998 amounted to 6,276m. kWh; in privately owned plants,
5m. kWh. Consumption per capita was estimated in 1998 to be
22,922 kWh – the second highest in the world after Norway.

Agriculture
Of the total area, about six-sevenths is unproductive, but only about
1·3% is under cultivation, which is largely confined to hay, potatoes
and turnips. Arable land totalled 6,000 ha in 1997. In 1998 the total
hay crop was 2,338,732 cu. metres; the crop of potatoes, 11,544
tonnes, and of turnips, 627 tonnes. Livestock (end of 1998): horses,
78,400; cattle, 75,500 (milch cows, 29,219); sheep, 490,000; pigs,
3,987; poultry, 166,911. Livestock products (1998, in tonnes): milk,
108,900; butter and dairy margarines, 1,575; cheese, 3,710; lamb,
8,176.

Forestry
In 1995 forests covered 11,000 ha, or approximately 0·1% of the total
land area.

Fisheries

Fishing is of vital importance to the economy. Fishing vessels at the end of 1998 numbered 799 with a gross tonnage of 184,728. Total catch in 1995, 1,605,127 tonnes; 1996, 2,055,244 tonnes; 1997, 2,199,111 tonnes; 1998, 1,678,696 tonnes. Virtually all the fish caught is from marine waters.

Fishery limits were extended from 12 to 50 nautical miles in 1972 and to 200 nautical miles in 1975.

INDUSTRY

Production, 1998, in 1,000 tonnes: aluminium, 150·1; diatomite, 27·1; fertilizer (1995), 50·6; ferro-silicon, 61·1; sales of cement, 117·7.

Labour

In 1998 the economically active population was 152,100, of which 2·7% were unemployed. In 1999 the rate declined to 2%.

Trade Unions

In 1995 trade union membership was 85% of the workforce.

INTERNATIONAL TRADE

The economy is heavily trade-dependent.

Imports and Exports

Total value of imports (c.i.f.) and exports (f.o.b.) in 1,000 kr.:

	1994	1995	1996	1997	1998
Imports	102,571,300	113,613,600	135,994,500	143,226,581	176,072,107
Exports	112,653,800	116,606,700	125,689,800	131,213,200	136,591,964

Main exports, 1998 (in 1m. kr.): fish, crustaceans, molluscs and preparations thereof, 85,292; non-ferrous metals, 18,422; fodder for animals (excluding unmilled cereals), 11,954; iron and steel, 3,241. Main imports: road vehicles, 16,881; petroleum and products, 8,391; other transport equipment, 8,299.

Value of trade with principal countries for 3 years (in 1,000 kr.):

	1996		1997		1998	
	Imports (c.i.f.)	Exports (f.o.b.)	Imports (c.i.f.)	Exports (f.o.b.)	Imports (c.i.f.)	Exports (f.o.b.)
Austria	836,600	124,700	859,000	130,900	1,058,900	150,800
Belgium	2,581,500	1,552,500	2,860,000	1,426,800	3,226,800	1,716,400
Brazil	184,900	674,900	175,000	781,900	184,800	618,900
Canada	1,240,000	1,462,100	1,484,300	1,586,100	1,487,800	2,111,300
China	1,774,200	69,000	1,959,200	526,200	2,418,300	516,400
Czech Republic	483,700	74,300	486,800	48,800	757,400	27,500
Denmark	11,357,800	9,094,100	12,365,800	7,430,700	13,519,800	7,449,000
Faroe Islands	191,300	529,400	367,300	1,467,600	975,800	691,500
Finland	2,240,700	1,206,700	2,332,800	1,507,900	2,823,300	1,012,000
France	4,457,100	8,442,500	4,741,500	8,317,000	6,343,400	9,226,800
Germany	14,801,500	16,229,200	16,847,400	17,154,800	20,175,800	20,487,300
Greece	75,200	840,000	84,700	791,900	102,800	633,000
Hungary	135,400	26,900	127,500	19,800	232,900	7,400
India	375,300	55,000	392,200	46,000	483,300	10,400
Ireland	1,383,500	167,700	1,680,500	240,600	2,603,700	565,600
Israel	102,100	80,400	130,500	131,900	211,300	130,400
Italy	4,374,000	2,402,700	4,635,500	2,310,600	5,668,500	2,367,400
Japan	5,455,500	12,369,600	7,036,700	8,696,300	8,933,300	6,544,800

Korea, Rep. of	1,514,100	471,400	1,577,200	253,800	2,123,200	146,300
Netherlands	8,116,600	4,522,300	9,262,400	4,392,200	10,477,100	5,548,000
Nigeria	5,700	577,600	3,800	904,900	300	993,200
Norway	18,396,300	4,687,000	16,500,600	7,294,900	16,178,600	6,574,400
Poland	2,660,600	303,400	822,900	319,200	2,570,700	299,900
Portugal	980,200	3,237,600	997,900	3,463,600	1,195,100	5,236,900
Russia	3,372,700	1,285,200	3,550,000	2,360,500	3,792,000	1,515,800
Spain	2,356,400	4,881,400	2,359,000	5,711,600	3,530,500	6,867,700
Sweden	9,132,100	1,620,600	9,584,200	1,487,500	11,154,400	1,265,900
Switzerland	1,995,900	2,493,300	3,190,200	3,999,500	2,624,800	6,298,600
Taiwan	1,016,700	1,972,800	1,091,900	2,041,900	1,457,700	1,010,000
UK	13,874,300	23,949,000	14,479,400	24,806,700	17,026,600	25,897,200
USA	12,840,400	14,708,000	13,502,900	18,299,700	19,540,200	18,031,400

COMMUNICATIONS

Roads

On 31 Dec. 1998 the length of the public roads (including roads in towns) was 12,689 km. Of these 8,213 km were main and secondary roads and 4,476 km were provincial roads. Total length of surfaced roads was 3,439 km. A ring road of 1,400 km runs just inland from much of the coast; about 80% of it is smooth-surfaced. Motor vehicles registered at the end of 1998 numbered 158,466, of which 141,916 were passenger cars and 16,550 trucks; there were also 1,379 motorcycles. There were 27 fatal road accidents in 1998 with 27 persons killed.

Rules of the Road

Driving in Iceland is on the right-hand side of the road. Most roads in Iceland, including parts of the national highways, are made up of loose gravel. Dipped headlights must be used by all vehicles at all times. The use of seat belts is obligatory in front and back seats. Driving under the influence of alcohol (more than 0·05% alcohol in the blood) is prohibited. The speed limit is 50 kph in built up areas, 80 kph elsewhere and 90 kph on asphalt roads. Mountain roads may be closed for large parts of the year due to unsuitable conditions; most open in June or July. The public roads administration (Tel: 564-1500) can advise on opening dates, but at some times it is only advisable to use 4WD vehicles. Petrol stations all accept credit cards and after closing times many, especially around Reykjavík, have automatic payment machines.

Rail
There is no railway system in Iceland.

Civil Aviation
There are a number of airports around Iceland and two in Reykjavík but all international arrivals will almost certainly be at Keflavík Airport (except from the Faroe Islands or Greenland). There is a 'Flybus' that picks up and drops off at all major hotels in the summer for each international flight. Icelandair is Iceland's national carrier and in 1998 it served 12 destinations in western Europe and 6 in north America as well as operating domestic services. In 1999 it carried 1·3m. passengers. In the summer, there are flights to New York JFK, London and Copenhagen at least once a day. Air Iceland is the main domestic airline and flies between many towns daily in summer. Services were also provided in 1998 by Atlantic Airways (Faroe Islands), Islandsflug, Greenlandair and SAS. Keflavík handled 1,226,395 passengers in 1998 (of which 366,824 transport travellers) and 27,534 tonnes of freight.

Icelandair
Laugavegur 7, Reykjavík
Tel: 505-0300 Fax: 505-0350

Flugfélag Islands (Air Iceland)
Tel: 570-3030 Fax: 570-3001 Web site: www.airiceland.is

Shipping
Total registered vessels, 955 (237,379 gross tonnage) on 31 Dec. 1998; of these, 799 were sea-going fishing vessels.

Telecommunications
At the end of 1998 the number of telephone subscribers was 162,000 (588 per 1,000 persons); mobile phone subscribers, 103,500. In 1995 there were 80,000 fax machines and 55,000 PCs (206 per 1,000 persons). There were 121,000 Internet users in Dec. 1998, or around 44% of the total population (the highest percentage of any country in the world).

In emergencies, dial 112. For operator services, dial 115 and for information, 114. The international code for telephoning or faxing Iceland is the code required to dial out of your own country followed by 354. All telephone numbers in Iceland have 7 digits. The prefix for a mobile telephone is 85. There are coin and card operated public telephones throughout the country; cards can be purchased for ISK500 at post offices and telephone kiosks. Fax services are also available at most post offices.

Postal Services
There are post offices in most towns and villages in Iceland. Opening times are usually 08.30-16.30, Monday-Friday. The main post office in Austurstræti, Reykjavík is also open on Saturday from June–Sept. 10.00-14.00. The cost of posting an airmail letter to European countries is ISK50 (up to 20g), ISK125 (100g) and outside Europe ISK75 (20g), ISK135 (50g).

At the end of 1998 the number of post offices was 87.

Internet Cafes

There is an internet cafe in Reykjavík at Nóatœn 17, open from 10.00 to 01.00 daily.

SOCIAL INSTITUTIONS

Justice

In 1992 jurisdiction in civil and criminal cases was transferred from the provincial magistrates to 8 new district courts, separating the judiciary from the prosecution. From the district courts there is an appeal to the Supreme Court in Reykjavík, which has 8 judges.

Religion

The national church, the Evangelical Lutheran, is endowed by the state. There is complete religious liberty. The affairs of the national church are under the superintendence of a bishop. At 1 Dec. 1998, 246,012 (89·4%) of the population were members of it (93·2% in 1980). 10,007 persons (3·0%) belonged to Lutheran free churches. 13,572 persons (4·9%) belonged to other religious organizations and 5,746 persons (2·1%) did not belong to any religious community.

Education

Primary education is compulsory and free from 6–15 years of age. Optional secondary education from 16 to 19 is also free. In 1998–99 there were about 42,400 pupils in primary schools, 20,400 in secondary schools (18,100 on day courses) and 8,800 tertiary-level students (8,158 on day courses). Some 16% of tertiary-level students study abroad.

There are 8 universities and specialized colleges at the tertiary level in Iceland. The largest is the University of Iceland in Reykjavík (founded 1911). There is also a university in Akureyri (founded 1987). Total enrolment of these 2 institutions was 6,100 students in 1997–98. In Reykjavík there are a teachers' university, a technical college, business colleges and an agricultural university.

In 1997 public sector spending on education was 5·4% of GNP. The adult literacy rate in 1997 was at least 99%.

Health

On 31 Dec. 1994 there were 57 hospitals with 3,924 beds, 797 doctors, 273 dentists, 1,952 nurses, and 176 pharmacists. In 1997 there were 3·6 doctors per 1,000 inhabitants. Iceland has one of the lowest alcohol consumption rates in Europe, at 4·8 litres of alcohol per adult a year, compared to a European Union average of 11·1 litres.

Welfare

The main body of social welfare legislation is consolidated in 6 acts:

(i) The social security legislation (a) health insurance, including sickness benefits; *(b)* social security pensions, mainly consisting of old age pension, disablement pension and widows' pension, and also children's pension; *(c)* employment injuries insurance.

(ii) The unemployment insurance legislation, where daily allowances are paid to those who have met certain conditions.

(iii) The subsistence legislation. This is controlled by municipal government, and social assistance is granted under special circumstances, when payments from other sources are not sufficient.

(iv) The tax legislation. Prior to 1988 children's support was included in the tax legislation, according to which a certain amount for each child in a family was subtracted from income taxes or paid out to the family. Since 1988 family allowances are paid directly to all children age 0–15 years. The amount is increased with the second child in the

family, and children under the age of 7 get additional benefits. Single parents receive additional allowances. The amounts are linked to income.

(v) The rehabilitation legislation.

(vi) Child and juvenile guidance.

Health insurance covers the entire population. Citizenship is not demanded and there is a 6 month waiting period. Most hospitals are both municipally and state run, a few solely state run and all offer free medical help. Medical treatment out of hospitals is partly paid by the patient; the same applies to medicines, except medicines of lifelong necessary use, which are paid in full by the health insurance. Dental care is partly paid by the state for children under 17 years old and also for old age and disabled pensioners. Sickness benefits are paid to those who lose income because of periodical illness. The daily amount is fixed and paid from the 11th day of illness.

The pension system is composed of the public social security system and some 90 private pension funds. The social security system pays basic old age and disablement pensions of a fixed amount regardless of past or present income, as well as supplementary pensions to individuals with low present income. The pensions are index-linked, i.e. are changed in line with changes in wage and salary rates in the labour market. The private pension funds pay pensions that depend on past payments of premiums that are a fixed proportion of earnings. The payment of pension fund premiums is compulsory for all wage and salary earners. The pensions paid by the funds differ considerably between the individual funds, but are generally index-linked. In the public social security system, entitlement to old age and disablement pensions at the full rates is subject to the condition that the beneficiary has been resident in Iceland for 40 years at the age period of 16–67. For shorter period of residence, the benefits are reduced proportionally.

Entitled to old age pension are all those who are 67 years old, and have been residents in Iceland for 3 years of the age period of 16–67. Entitled to disablement pension are those who have lost 75% of their working capacity and have been residents in Iceland for 3 years before application or have had full working capacity at the time when they became residents. Old age and disablement pension are of equally high amount; in the year 1999 the total sum was 198,645 kr. for an individual. Married pensioners are paid 90% of two individuals' pensions. In addition to the basic amount, supplementary allowances are paid according to social circumstances and income possibilities. Widows' pensions are the same amount as old age and disablement pension, provided the applicant is over 60 when she becomes widowed. Women in the age range 50–60 get a reduced pension. Women under 50 are not entitled to widows' pensions.

The employment injuries insurance covers medical care, daily allowances, disablement pension and survivors' pension and is applicable to practically all employees.

Social assistance is primarily municipal and granted in cases outside the social security legislation. Domestic assistance to old people and disabled is granted within this legislation, besides other services.

Child and juvenile guidance is performed by chosen committees according to special laws, such as home guidance and family assistance. In cases of parents' disablement the committees take over the guidance of the children involved.

CULTURE

Reykjavík is one of nine European Cities of Culture in the year 2000. The city's theme is 'Culture and Nature'. The other Cities of Culture are Avignon (France), Bergen (Norway), Bologna (Italy), Brussels (Belgium), Helsinki (Finland), Kraków (Poland), Prague (Czech Republic) and Santiago de Compostela (Spain). The title attracts large European Union grants.

Broadcasting

The state-owned public service, The Icelandic State Broadcasting Service, broadcasts 2 national and 3 regional radio programmes and 1 national TV channel. 20 privately owned radio stations and 9 private TV stations were in operation in 1998. At 31 Dec. 1998, 90,899 TV sets were licensed (89,990 colour by PAL and 1,909 black and white) and there were 101,775 radio licenses.

National Television Stations

RUV Ríkisútvarpid
Laugavegur 176, 150 Reykjavík
Tel 00 354 515 3900; fax 00 354 515 3008
Founded in 1930. The state broadcasting company. Broadcasts on 1 television channel 24 hours a day.

Íslenska Útvarpsfélagid (Icelandic Broadcasting Corporation)
Lynghals 5, 110 Reykjavík
Tel 00 354 515 6000; fax 00 354 515 6860
Private television company which broadcasts Channel 2 (subscription channel) and Vision TV (pay-TV). Also re-transmits satellite channels.

ICE TV
Kringlan 7, 108 Reykjavík
Tel 00 354 533 5600; fax 00 354 533 5699
Channel 3 is the latest private television station, having started broadcasting in 1995.

National Radio Stations

RUV

Efstaleiti 1, 150 Reykjavík

Tel 00 354 515 3000; fax 00 354 515 3010

State radio, broadcasting on 2 channels.

Bylgjan Radio

Lynghals 5, 110 Reykjavík

Tel 00 354 515 6000; fax 00 354 515 6860

Icelandic Broadcasting Corporation's national radio station.

Cinema

There were 25 cinemas with 45 screens in 1998 of which the capital had 7 cinemas and 26 screens. Total admissions numbered 1,510,388 in 1998, with the Reykjavík area accounting for 1,401,097.

Press

In 1998 there were 3 daily newspapers with a combined circulation of about 0·1m. There were 20 non-daily newspapers in 1998 (published 1–3 times per week) with a combined circulation of about 0·01m.

Book Publishers

Iceland publishes more books per person than any other country in the world. In 1998, 1,129 volumes of books and 457 volumes of booklets were published.

Bokautgafan Orn og Orlygur ehf

Founded 1966. Publishes biography, cookery, gardening, how-to, health and nutrition.

Dvergshoefda 27, IS-112 Reykjavík. Tel: 00 354 5671777. Fax: 00 354 5671240.

Fjolvi

Founded 1966. Publishes fiction, history and natural history.

Njoervasundi 15A, IS-104 Reykjavík. Tel: 00 354 5688433.

Fax: 00 354 5688142.

Heimskringla

Founded 1937. Publishes academic books.

Laugavegi 18, IS-101 Reykjavík. Tel: 00 354 5515199.

Fax: 00 354 5623523.

Hid Islenzka Bokmenntafelag

Founded 1816. Publishes literature, literary criticism, essays, art, language arts, linguistics, government, political science, history, natural history, psychology, psychiatry, social sciences and sociology. Sidumuli 21, IS-108 Reykjavík. Tel: 00 354 5889060.

Fax: 00 354 5889095.

Idunn

Founded 1945. Publishes fiction and general non-fiction; art, child care and development, health, history, nutrition, poetry and self-help. PO Box 294, IS-121 Reykjavík. Tel: 00 354 5528555.

Fax: 00 354 5528380.

Isafoldarprentsmidja hf

Founded 1877. Publishes fiction and education.

PO Box 455, IS-121 Reykjavík. Tel: 00 354 5517165.

Fax: 00 354 5517226.

Islendingasagnautgafan

Founded 1945. Publishes fiction and general non-fiction, poetry, self-help and Icelandic sagas in old Icelandic.

PO Box 488, IS-220 Hafnarfjörður. Tel: 00 354 8985868.

Mal og menning

Founded 1937. Publishes fiction and general non-fiction, education, literature, literary criticism, essays, poetry and travel.

Postholf 392, IS-121 Reykjavík. Tel: 00 354 515 2500. Fax: 00 354 5152505. Website: www.mm.is

Libraries

The National and University Library of Iceland is in Reykjavík and contains some 825,000 volumes. The 6 University libraries contain approximately 135,000 volumes, the 39 special libraries approximately 308,000 volumes and the 106 public libraries approximately 2,080,000 volumes.

Theatre and Opera

In 1997 there were 8 professional theatres operated on a yearly basis (of which 7 were in the capital region) and 18 professional theatre groups (all in the capital region). In the theatrical season 1997–98 there were 265,271 admissions to performances of the professional theatres, 79,899 admissions the the National Theatre and 81,072 admissions to the City Theatre and Idno Theatre. Total audience of the Icelandic Opera was 16,775.

There is one symphonic orchestra operated on a regular basis, the Icelandic Symphony Orchestra. In 1998 the orchestra performed 84 times within the country and abroad, with audiences totalling 61,000.

Museums and Galleries

In 1998 there were 99 museums, botanical gardens, aquariums and zoos in operation, with a total of about 1m. visitors. There were 27,257 visitors to the National Museum, 28,490 to the National Gallery and 70,000 to the Reykjavík Municipal Art Museum.

Tourism

There were 232,219 visitors in 1998, bringing revenue of 26,334m. kr. Overnight stays in hotels and guest houses in 1998 numbered 791,412.

Tourist Information Centre

Bankastræti 2, 101 Reykjavík

Tel: 562-3045 Fax: 562-3057

E-mail: tourinfo@mmedia.is

(USA) Iceland Tourist Board

655 Third Avenue, New York, NY 10017

Tel: 212 949-2333 Fax: 212 983-5260

(Germany) Isländisches Fremdenverkehrsamt

City Center, Carl-Ulrich-Strasse 11, 63263 Neu-Isenburg

Tel: (0)6102 254-484 Fax: (0)6102 254-570

Visas

Visas are not required to enter Iceland by citizens of EU countries, the USA, Canada, Australia or New Zealand for stays of up to three months. Citizens of other countries should contact their nearest Icelandic embassy or consulate for information on entry requirements.

Festivals

The Reykjavík Arts Festival, a biennial programme of international artists and performers, will be staging a special programme in May and June 2000 in conjunction with Reykjavík's status as one of the European Cities of Culture.

Public Holidays 2000

1 Jan.	New Year's Day.
20 April	Maundy Thursday.
21 April	Good Friday.
24 April	Easter Monday.
1 May	Labour Day.
1 June	Ascension Day.
12 June	Whit Monday.

17 June	National Day (proclamation of the Republic in 1944 and anniversary of birth of John Sigurdsson in 1811).
7 Aug.	Commerce Day
24 Dec.	Christmas Eve (half day).
25 Dec.	Christmas Day.
26 Dec.	Boxing Day.
31 Dec.	New Year's Eve (half day).

Business Etiquette

Icelanders are generally very well educated (the literacy rate is 100%) and most will speak at least one foreign language (probably English or Danish) to a reasonable level. Since few foreign companies can justify the costs of operating in Iceland, businessmen can usually expect to be warmly welcomed, especially if an effort is made to understand the local culture and learn a few words of Icelandic. Most companies will be family run organizations and may be very protective of their business interests. The Icelanders may seem very independent and reserved, but this should not be understood as disinterest or boredom. Do be punctual and use the 24 hour clock to avoid mistakes. The standard of living is good and high quality is expected, along with efficiency. Although Iceland is a former Danish colony, the two are vastly different and it is not advisable to treat the former as an extension of the latter, even in terms of your business operation. Be prepared to talk about and eat fish, but the subject of whaling is sensitive and may best be avoided.

DIPLOMATIC REPRESENTATIVES

Of Iceland in Great Britain (1 Eaton Terrace, London, SW1W 8EY)
Ambassador: Thorsteinn Pálsson.

Of Great Britain in Iceland (Laufásvegur 31, 101 Reykjavík)
Ambassador and Consul-General: James Ray McCulloch.
Of Iceland in the USA (1156 15th Street NW, Suite 1200, Washington,
D.C., 20005–1704)
Ambassador: Jón Baldvin Hannibalsson.
Of the USA in Iceland (Laufásvegur 21, 101 Reykjavík)
Ambassador: Barbara J. Griffiths.
Of Iceland to the United Nations
Ambassador: Thorsteinn Ingólfsson.
Of Iceland to the European Union
Ambassador: Gunnar Snorri Gunnarsson.

FURTHER READING

Statistics Iceland, *Landshagir* (Statistical Yearbook of Iceland). – *Hagtíðindi*
(Monthly Statistics)
Central Bank of Iceland. *Economic Statistics Quarterly. – The Economy of
Iceland.* May 1994
Hastrup, K., *A Place Apart: An anthropological study of the Icelandic world.*
Clarendon Press, Oxford, 1998
Lacy, T., *Ring of Seasons: Iceland – Its culture and history.* University of
Michigan Press, 1998
McBride F. R., *Iceland.* [Bibliography] 2nd ed. ABC-Clio, Oxford and Santa
Barbara (CA), 1996
National statistical office: Statistics Iceland, Skuggasund 3, IS-150 Reykjavík.
Website: http://www.statice.is/
National library: Landsbókasafn Islands. – Háskólabókasafn, Reykjavík,
Librarian: Einar Sigursson.

NORWAY

Kongeriket Norge
Kingdom of Norway

Capital: Oslo

Area: 323,758 sq. km

Population estimate, 2000: 4·46m.

Head of State: King Harald V

Head of Government: Jens Stoltenberg

TERRITORY AND POPULATION

Norway is bounded in the north by the Arctic Ocean, east by Russia, Finland and Sweden, south by the Skagerrak Straits and west by the North Sea. The total area of mainland Norway is 323,758 sq. km, including 17,506 sq. km of fresh water. Total coastline, including fjords, 21,340 km. There are more than 50,000 islands along the coastline. Exposed mountain (either bare rock or thin vegetation) makes up over 70% of the country. 25% of the land area is woodland and 4% tilled land.

Population (1990 census) was 4,247,546 (2,099,881 males; 2,147,655 females); population density per sq. km, 13·8. Estimated population in 1999, 4,445,000; population density, 15. With the exception of Iceland, Norway is the most sparsely peopled country in Europe.

The projected population for 2000 is 4·46m.

There are 19 counties (*fylke*). Land area, population and densities:

	Land area (sq. km)	Population (1990 census)	Population (1999 estimate)	Density per sq. km 1999
Oslo (City)	427	461,190	502,867	1,178
Akershus	4,587	417,653	460,564	100
Østfold	3,889	238,296	246,018	63
Hedmark	26,120	187,276	186,321	7
Oppland	23,827	182,578	182,239	8
Buskerud	13,856	225,172	235,018	17
Vestfold	2,140	198,399	210,707	98
Telemark	14,186	162,907	164,523	12
Aust-Agder	8,485	97,333	101,487	12
Vest-Agder	6,817	144,917	153,998	22
Rogaland	8,553	337,504	369,059	43
Hordaland	14,962	410,567	431,882	29
Sogn og Fjordane	17,864	106,659	107,648	6

Møre og Romsdal	14,596	238,409	242,538	17
Sør-Trøndelag	17,839	250,978	260,855	15
Nord-Trøndelag	20,777	127,157	126,797	6
Nordland	36,302	239,311	238,547	7
Troms	25,147	146,716	150,200	6
Finnmark	45,879	74,524	74,061	2
Mainland total	306,253 [1]	4,247,546	4,445,329	15

The Arctic territories of Svalbard and Jan Mayen have an area of 61,606 sq. km. Persons staying on Svalbard and Jan Mayen are registered as residents of their home Norwegian municipality.

[1]118,244 sq. miles.

In 1998, 74·4% of the population lived in urban areas. Population of the principal urban settlements on 1 Jan. 1998:

Oslo	750,404	Tønsberg	41,627	Moss	30,651
Bergen	200,243	Sarpsborg	39,885	Hamar	28,792
Trondheim	138,008	Sandnes	37,626	Arendal	25,502
Stavanger	108,802	Porsgrunn	36,319	Ålesund	24,635
Drammen	61,045	Haugesund	34,723	Larvik	21,748
Kristiansand	58,339	Sandefjord	34,514	Halden	20,909
Frederikstad	52,033	Bodø	33,972	Mo i Rana	19,703
Tromsø	47,936	Skien	30,825	Lillehammer	18,506

The official language is Norwegian, which has 2 versions: Bokmål (or Riksmål) and Nynorsk (or Landsmål).

The Sami, the indigenous people of the far north, number some 30,000 and form a distinct ethnic minority with their own culture and language.

Time Zone

Norway is 1 hour ahead of GMT.

POLITICAL AND SOCIAL CHRONOLOGY OF THE 20TH CENTURY

1905	Norway gains independence from Sweden
	Prince Carl of Denmark becomes King Haakon VII
1914	Norway declares its neutrality at the outbreak of war
1925	Kristiania is renamed Oslo
1933	Vidkun Quisling founds the National Unity Party
1935	The Labour Party is elected into office, a period in Government lasting, apart from the occupation period, until 1965
1939	Norway is again neutral at the start of World War II
1940	Germany invades and conquers Norway
	Norwegian soldiers sink the German cruiser 'Bluecher'
	Vidkun Quisling heads a pro-Nazi government
1944	Soviet Union attacks German forces from northern Norway
1945	German forces withdraw fully only at the end of the war
1949	Norway is a founding member of NATO
1969	Oil is discovered in the North Sea
1972	Norwegians vote not to join the EEC in a referendum
1986	Oil prices collapse
1994	Norway again rejects membership of the EU in a referendum

CULTURAL BRIEFING

Norway's status as a province of Denmark throughout its early modern history did little to encourage a Norwegian literary tradition. The reformation served merely to introduce Danish as the language of use in church texts and other works. Peter Dass, however, did manage to be patriotic about his home country and in 1772 Norske Selskab was founded in Copenhagen to further Norwegian culture. Things were made easier with the founding of a university in 1811 and the union with Sweden in 1814, but it was the 1840s that saw a cultural revolution, with Asbjørnsen and Moses' Norwegian folk tales and Ivar Aasen's progression to New Norwegian in the linguistic field. It was at this point too that PA Munch wrote his Norwegian history. There was more to come in the shape of Bjørnstjerne Bjørnson and Henrik Ibsen towards the close of the century, the former very much concerned with rural Norwegian life, the latter more with middle classes in the cities. A later romantic burst was evident at the turn of the century with writers like Knut Hamsum, but realism returned to the fore until the war. At this point there was much debate between conservative and radical writers on style and linguistic ideals, but in the inter-war period New Norwegian became more common. The occupation served as a source for much wartime and post war writing, but the folk story telling tradition was retained by Terje Stigen and Finn Carling, for example. Contemporary Norwegian literature, however, is just as progressive as in any other European country.

Architecture in Norway was encouraged when the country ceased to be a part of Denmark and Oslo grew in size and stature. Painting however, had to wait until the romantic period, when J. C. Dahl found this the perfect medium and style to portray the Norwegian landscape. Outdoor painting, a device borrowed from France, was important in allowing rugged landscape scenes, a national characteristic, to be pictured. Realism blossomed in the 1880s with artists like Erik Werenskiold, but it was the turn of the century pessimism of the sculptor Gustav Vigeland and the painter Edvard Munch that gave Norwegian art an international audience. Axel Revold and Per Krohg popularized fresco painting between the wars and there was also a renewed interest in expressionism due to influence from Germany.

Most of the music from Norway's early history has been lost or never written down, but folk music and dance retains a place in the nation's culture. L. M. Lindeman was instrumental in collating some of the traditional themes in the 1840s. Again, it was the separation from Denmark that saw a new wave of Norwegian music thrive and the golden age of Norway's musical scene was in the mid to late 19th century, pioneered especially be Johan Svendsson and Edvard Grieg. Romanticism and German influences were especially important, but in the 20th century there has been a harking back to folk influences under composers such as Harald Sæverud.

CULTURAL PROFILES

Henrik Ibsen

Henrik Ibsen is Norway's most important writer and dramatist and his plays have been performed the world over and translated into all major languages. He was born in 1828 to a merchant father, whose financial problems necessitated the end of Ibsen's schooling at the age of 15. He finally arrived in Oslo (then Christiania) to study at the university in 1850, but took instead to writing. Ibsen's early career earned him little fame as a dramatist but he aroused much controversy in political circles and after working in theatres in Bergen and Christiania he moved abroad in 1864. Two years later his poem *Brand* was critically acclaimed and the Norwegian government awarded him a grant. His most successful plays were written whilst living in Germany and Italy and *A Doll's House*, *Ghosts* and *Hedda Gabler* established his reputation as one of Europe's finest dramatists. Ibsen's plays are concerned largely with the family and family relationships and contain a series of strong female roles. In 1891 he returned to Norway, a year before *The Master Builder* was published. At the turn of the century Ibsen had a stroke and he died in 1906.

Edvard Munch

Edvard Munch was born in Christiania (now Oslo) in 1863 to a family plagued by illness and death. His mother died when he was only five and his older sister at the age of 15, both of tuberculosis, his younger sister was mentally ill and his brother Andreas, his only sibling to marry, died a few months after his wedding. Munch himself turned to art after studying at the technical college in Christiania and was initially influenced by French realism under the tutoring of Christian Krohg. In 1885 he travelled to Paris where he worked on his first piece that was to make a serious impact, *The Sick Child*, which marked a movement away from realism and was received badly. Munch returned to Paris in 1889 after receiving a state travel grant and became a pupil of Leon Bonnat. At this point the death of his father affected him greatly and the painting *Night* is an indication of the personal emotion that Munch is famous for expressing in his works. He exhibited in Kristiania (given by this time a new spelling but not yet a new name) in 1891 and then began to make preparatory sketches for *The Scream*, a painting that has been described as the first expressionist work. After an exhibition in Berlin in 1892 Munch moved there and showed a year later a series of paintings that were to become the first part of his *Frieze of Life*, subtitled *A Poem about Life, Love and Death*. He also befriended the Swedish writer August Strindberg and met up again with him when he returned to Paris in 1896. Munch exhibited the completed *Frieze of Life* in Berlin in 1902 and at this point struggled with alcoholism and a love affair that ended in a duel with a rival. After 1909 the artist lived in Norway and continued to paint landscapes and portraits, both in paints and other graphic mediums. However, he remains best known for his work at the end of the 19th century which so challenged the prevailing artistic tendencies and was of great influence to the Fauvists in France and Die Brücke group in Dresden, amongst others. Munch died in 1944, leaving his works to the city of Oslo.

Edvard Grieg

Grieg was born in Bergen on 15 June 1843 to a bourgeois family with a number of musical connections. His mother was a piano teacher, his grandparents had been involved in one of the world's oldest orchestras, Musikselskapet Harmonien in Bergen, and his uncle was Ole Bull, a famous violinist and founder of the first Norwegian Theatre. Grieg was not a successful pupil at school, and at the age of 15 Ole Bull persuaded Grieg's parents to send him to the music conservatory in Leipzig, founded in the year of Grieg's birth by Felix Mendelssohn. There he studied both classic and modern composers under many of the best teachers of the time and graduated in 1862. Unfortunately, he also caught a strain of tuberculosis in Leipzig and one lung collapsed, from which he never fully recovered. After his studies Grieg moved to Copenhagen in order that he might continue to learn abroad, yet remain in Scandinavia. There he met influential composers such as Niels Gade and notably Rikard Nordraak, who encouraged him to retain a Norwegian influence in his music. He also met his cousin and future wife, Nina Hagerup, in Copenhagen and it was there that his *Piano Concerto in A minor* was first performed in 1869, instantly confirming his status as an important composer. Grieg continued to travel widely with his wife, but bought in 1885 a house outside Bergen so that he could return to his native town regularly. The influence of Norway and the Norwegian environment cannot be underestimated in Grieg's music and he is perhaps most famous for his musical interpretation of *Peer Gynt*, one of a number of collabora-tions with Ibsen. Grieg toured continuously, seeking inspiration for his music to combine with summer experiences in Norway and meeting many of his contemporaries, including Brahms, Liszt and Tchaikovsky. At the beginning of a tour in 1907 he was waiting for a boat for England in Bergen when he collapsed of exhaustion and died in hospital.

CITY PROFILE

Oslo

Population 480,000

Oslo was officially founded around the year 1000 by King Harald, although there had been a settlement on the Oslo fjord since the 8th century. During the Viking era the town grew rapidly due to emerging trade and a ship building industry, but apart from archeological remains, little is known of the city before the Christian era. A plague in 1348 wiped out half of the population and the resulting decline in influence meant that Norway was absorbed into the Danish empire and Oslo became a provincial capital. The reformation of 1537 was violent and the remains of Catholic churches and monasteries can still be found in the city. The real growth of Oslo, however, took place after the entire city was destroyed by fire in 1624 and Christian IV decided to build a new town away from what is now called the old town. Akershus Fortress was the centre piece of the new city, which was constructed under new ideas of town planning and renamed Christiania. From then on Christiania grew in importance as the largest and most economically significant city in Norway, a trend not interrupted with the union with Sweden in 1814, but it was not until 1830 that Christiania overtook Bergen in population. Expansion continued until independence in 1905 and Kristiania (given a new spelling in the late 19th century) was declared the capital of Norway. In 1924 the city celebrated its 300th anniversary and it was decided that from the following year, the ancient name of Oslo would once again be adopted. Oslo is now the largest economic, industrial and cultural centre in Norway, the seat of the government and the home of the Norwegian royal family. The 1952 Olympic games were held there and the Nobel Peace Prize is presented in the city every year. In 2000 Oslo is celebrating its 1000 year anniversary with festivities the whole year round.

Landmarks

Akershus Fortress

Akershus Fortress and castle were built by Håkon V at the end of the 13th century and have withstood a number of attacks. Akershus castle was redecorated by Christian IV in the 1600s, but there is still a decidedly medieval feel to the buildings. The fortress is also the site of Norway's Resistance museum, poignant especially as the Nazis used Akershus as a prison and a number of resistance fighters were killed there. Admission to the fortress itself is free, although there is a charge for the castle and chapel, where Norway's post-independence Kings are buried.

Vigeland Park

Vigeland Park, or Frognerparken, is a large park east of the city centre that also serves as a huge sculpture garden, filled with almost 200 works by Norway's finest sculptor, Gustav Vigeland. All of the pieces are life size humans, and the artist portrays young and old in every possible emotional and physical state. The statues line the central alleyway in the park and at one end a circular series of steps leads up to a mass of contorted bodies which is supposed to be the largest granite sculpture in the world. There is also a Vigeland museum at Nobels gate 32, closed on Mondays.

Museums and Galleries

A museum dedicated to the life and works of Edvard Munch contains the drawings, paintings and writings that were left to the city of Oslo on the artist's death.

Munch Museum
Tøyengata 53, 0608 Oslo
Tel: 22-67-37-74. Fax: 22-67-33-41

The National gallery has a large collection of Norwegian and European art, including Munch's famous 'The Scream' and works by

many other prominent artists. Admission is free and the museum is
open daily except Tuesdays.
Nasjonalgalleriet (National Gallery)
Universitetsgata 13, 0164 Oslo
Tel: 22-20-04-04. Fax: 22-36-11-32
Web: www.nasjonalgalleriet.no

There is a museum of contemporary Scandinavian art, closed on
Mondays, for which admission is also free. The collection contains
post war work from all aspects of the visual arts.
The National Museum of Contemporary Art
Bankplassen 4, 0034 Oslo
Tel: 22-33-58-20. Fax: 22-33-57-90
Web: www.mfs.no

Opera House
Den Norske Opera
Storgaten 23, PO Box 8800 Younstorvet, 0028 Oslo
Tel: 23-31-50-00. Fax: 23-31-50-30
Web: www.norskopera.no E-mail: informasjon@norskopera.no

Theatre
Nationaltheatret
Stortingsgata 15, 0161 Oslo
Tel: 22-41-27-10. Fax: 22-00-16-90
Web: www.nationaltheatret.no E-mail: salg@nationaltheatret.no

Hotels
Continental Hotel, Stortingsgate 24–26, 0161 Oslo
Tel: 22-82-40-00

Grand Hotel, Karl Johans Gate 31, 0159 Oslo
Tel: 22-42-93-90

Radisson SAS Scandinavia Hotel Oslo, Holbergs Gate 30, 0166 Oslo
Tel: 22-11-30-00

SOCIAL STATISTICS

Statistics for calendar years:

	Marriages	Divorces	Births	Still-born	Outside marriage[1]	Deaths
1994	20,605	10,934	60,092	276	27,581	44,071
1995	21,677	10,360	60,292	236	28,680	45,190
1996	23,172	9,982	60,927	276	29,435	43,860
1997	23,815	9,961	59,801	230	29,133	44,595
1998	. . .	. . .	58,352	247	28,573	44,112

[1]Excluding still-born.

Rates per 1,000 population, 1998, birth, 13·2; death, 10·0; marriage, 5·4 (1997); divorce, 2·3 (1997). Population growth rate, 1998, was 0·63%. Over 1990–95 the suicide rate per 100,000 population was 15·5 (men, 23·3; women, 8).

Expectation of life at birth, 1998, was 75·54 years for males and 81·28 years for females. Infant mortality, 1998, 4·0 per 1,000 live births; fertility rate, 1·81 births per woman. 49% of births are to unmarried mothers.

At 1 Jan. 1998 the immigrant population totalled 244,705, including 20,924 from Pakistan, 19,546 from Sweden, 18,388 from Denmark and 14,595 from Vietnam. In 1998 Norway received 8,374 asylum applications (2,271 in 1997), equivalent to 1·9 per 1,000 inhabitants. Most were from Croatia (2,415), Yugoslavia (1,623) and Iraq (1,296).

Central Bureau of Statistics

PO Box 8131 Dep., 0033 Oslo.
Web site: www.ssb.no

CLIMATE

There is considerable variation in the climate because of the extent of latitude, the topography and the varying effectiveness of prevailing westerly winds and the Gulf Stream. Winters along the whole west coast are exceptionally mild but precipitation is considerable. Oslo, Jan. 24·3°F (−4·3°C), July 61·5°F (16·4°C). Annual rainfall 30·0" (763 mm). Bergen, Jan. 34·7°F (1·5°C), July 58·1°F (14·5°C). Annual rainfall 88·6" (2,250 mm). Trondheim, Jan. 26°F (−3·5°C), July 57°F (14°C). Annual rainfall 32·1" (870 mm). Bergen has one of the highest rainfall figures of any European city. The sun never fully sets in the northern area of the country in the summer and even in the south, the sun rises at around 3 a.m. and sets at around 11 p.m.

CONSTITUTION AND GOVERNMENT

Norway is a constitutional and hereditary monarchy.

The reigning King is **Harald V**, born 21 Feb. 1937, married on 29 Aug. 1968 to Sonja Haraldsen. He succeeded on the death of his father, King Olav V, on 21 Jan. 1991. *Offspring:* Princess Märtha Louise, born 22 Sept. 1971; Crown Prince Haakon Magnus, born 20 July 1973. The king receives a tax-free annual allowance of 19·8m. kroner from the civil list. Women have been eligible to succeed to the throne since 1990. There is no coronation ceremony. The royal succession is in direct male line in the order of primogeniture. In default of male heirs the King may propose a successor to the Storting, but this assembly has the right to nominate another, if it does not agree with the proposal.

The Constitution, voted by a constituent assembly on 17 May 1814 and modified at various times, vests the legislative power of the realm in the *Storting* (Parliament). The royal veto may be exercised;

but if the same Bill passes two Stortings formed by separate and subsequent elections it becomes the law of the land without the assent of the sovereign. The King has the command of the land, sea and air forces, and makes all appointments.

The 165-member Storting is directly elected by proportional representation. The country is divided into 19 districts, each electing from 4 to 15 representatives.

The Storting, when assembled, divides itself by election into the *Lagting* and the *Odelsting*. The former is composed of one-fourth of the members of the Storting, and the other of the remaining three-fourths. Each Ting (the Storting, the Odelsting and the Lagting) nominates its own president. Most questions are decided by the Storting, but questions relating to legislation must be considered and decided by the Odelsting and the Lagting separately. Only when the Odelsting and the Lagting disagree, the Bill has to be considered by the Storting in plenary sitting, and a new law can then only be decided by a majority of two-thirds of the voters. The same majority is required for alterations of the Constitution, which can only be decided by the Storting in plenary sitting. The Storting elects 5 delegates, whose duty it is to revise the public accounts. The Lagting and the ordinary members of the Supreme Court of Justice (the *Høyesterett*) form a High Court of the Realm (the *Riksrett*) for the trial of ministers, members of the *Høyesterett* and members of the Storting. The impeachment before the *Riksrett* can only be decided by the Odelsting.

The executive is represented by the King, who exercises his authority through the Cabinet. Cabinet ministers are entitled to be present in the Storting and to take part in the discussions, but without a vote.

National Anthem
'Ja, vi elsker dette landet' ('Yes, we love this land'); words by B. Bjørnson, tune by R. Nordraak.

RECENT ELECTIONS

At the elections for the Storting held on 16 Sept. 1997 the following parties were elected: Labour Party, 65 seats (with 35·0% of the vote); Christian Democratic Party, 25 (15·3%); Progress Party 25 (13·7%); Conservative Party, 23 (14·3%); Centre Party, 11 (7·9%); Socialist Left Party, 9 (6·0%); Liberal Party, 6 (4·5%); Coastal Party, 1 (0·4%).

During the election campaign, Prime Minister Thorbjørn Jagland announced his decision to resign if the Labour Party failed to attract at least 36·9% of the vote, the same share that the party received in 1993. He resigned on 14 Oct. 1997 and on 17 Oct. Kjell Magne Bondevik formed a coalition government of the 3 centrist parties (Christian Democratic, Centre and Liberal) with a combined 26·1% of the vote.

CURRENT ADMINISTRATION

In March 2000 the minority Coalition government comprised:

Prime Minister: Jens Stoltenberg.

Deputy Prime Minister, Minister of Local Government: Odd Roger Enoksen.

Minister of Cultural Affairs: Aaslaug Marie Haga. *Children and Family Affairs:* Valgerd Svarstad Haugland. *Industry and Trade:* Lars Sponheim. *Foreign Affairs:* Knut Vollebæk. *Fisheries:* Lars Peder Brekk. *Finance:* Gudmund Restad. *Labour and Government Administration:* Laila Daavoy. *Agriculture:* Kåre Gjønnes. *Justice and Police:* Odd Einer Dørum. *National Defence:* Eldbjørg Løwer. *Transport and Communication:* Dag Jostein Fjaervoll. *Education, Research and Church Affairs:* Jon Lilletun. *Social Affairs:* Magnhild Meltveit Kleppa. *Health:* Dagfinn Høybråten.

Oil and Energy: Marit Arnstad. *Environment:* Guro Fjellanger.
International Development Aid and Human Rights: Hilde Frafjord
Johnson.

LOCAL GOVERNMENT

There are 18 counties and the urban district of Oslo, in each of which
the central government is represented by a county governor. The
counties are divided into 435 municipalities, each of which usually
corresponds in size to a parish. The municipalities are administered
by municipal councils, whose membership may vary between 25 and
85 directly-elected councillors. Elections were held in Sept. 1995;
turn-out was 62·8%. The Labour Party gained 30·5% of all votes cast;
the Conservative Party, 20·2%; the Centre Party, 11·6%; the Progress
Party, 10·5%.

DEFENCE

Conscription is for 12 months, with 4 to 5 refresher training periods.
In 1998 defence spending totalled US$3,133m. (US$711 per capita),
representing 2·2% of GDP. Expenditure per capita was the highest of
any European country in 1998.

Army

There are a Northern and a Southern command, and within these the
Army is organized in 4 district commands, 1 divisional headquarters
and 14 territorial commands.

Strength (1999) 15,200 (including 10,000 conscripts). The fast
mobilization reserve numbers 184,000.

Navy

The Royal Norwegian Navy has 3 components: the Navy, Coast Guard and Coastal Artillery. Main Naval combatants include 12 coastal submarines (including 6 new German-built Ula class), and 4 frigates.

The personnel of the navy totalled 8,200 in 1999, of whom 3,300 were conscripts. 1,000 served in Coastal Artillery and 700 in the Coast Guard. The main naval base is at Bergen (Håkonsvern), with subsidiary bases at Horten, Ramsund and Tromsø.

The naval elements of the Home Guard on mobilization can muster some 5,000 personnel.

Air Force

The Royal Norwegian Air Force comprises the Air Force and the Anti-air Artillery.

Total strength (1999) is about 6,700 personnel, including 3,200 conscripts. There were 79 combat aircraft in operation including F-5A/Bs and F-16A/Bs.

Home Guard

The Home Guard is organized in small units equipped and trained for special tasks. Service after basic training is 1 week a year. The Home Guard consists of the Land Home Guard (strength, 1999, 77,000), Sea Home Guard and Anti-Air Home Guard organized in 18 districts. *See also under* NAVY, *above.*

INTERNATIONAL RELATIONS

Norway is a member of the UN, NATO, EFTA, OECD, Council of Europe, OSCE, CERN, Council of Baltic Sea States, Nordic Council,

Inter-American Development Bank, Asian Development Bank, IOM and the Antarctic Treaty, and an Associate Member of the WEU. Norway has acceded to the Schengen Accord abolishing border controls between Norway and Austria, Belgium, Denmark, Finland, France, Germany, Greece, Iceland, Italy, Luxembourg, Netherlands, Portugal, Spain and Sweden.

In a referendum on 27–28 Nov. 1994, 52·2% of votes cast were against joining the EU. The electorate was 3,266,182; turn-out was 88·88%.

ECONOMY

Norway's economy was transformed in the 1960s with the discovery of North Sea Oil. Norway is now the second largest exporter of oil in the world behind Saudi Arabia. In 1986, at the time of the crash in oil prices, the oil industry accounted for 35% of state revenue and after this severe economic lesson, the Norwegian economy of the 1990s has not been so dependent on oil. Service industries now make up 30% of GDP and the fishing industry continues to be important. Paper and wood products, chemicals and metals are the other main products as well as the manufacturing industries, although machinery and other manufactured goods make up over half of all exports. Norway has the fourth largest merchant fleet in the world. The economy is generally in very good shape; Norway has no foreign debt and although two referenda have rejected EU membership against the advice of economists and politicians, membership of the EEA means that Europe is still the most important trading market for Norway. Unemployment is relatively low (3·2% in 1998), as is inflation (2·3% in 1998) and Norway can afford to spend more per capita on international aid than virtually any other country.

Agriculture accounted for 2% of GDP in 1997, industry 30% and services 68%.

According to the anti-corruption organization *Transparency International*, Norway ranked equal 9th in the world in a survey of the countries with the least corruption in business and government. It received 8·9 out of 10 in the annual index published in 1999.

Real GDP growth was estimated at 2·2% in 1998 (3·4% in 1997), with a forecast for 1999 of growth of 2·3%.

Budget

Central government current revenue and expenditure (in 1m. kroner) for years ending 31 Dec.:

	1995	1996	1997[1]	1998[1]
Revenue	381,585	423,896	466,950	462,493
Expenditure	349,065	363,949	375,637	399,329

[1]Provisional

The 1999 budget, presented in Oct. 1998, projected the central government surplus to rebound by 23·5bn. kroner to over 52bn. kroner – almost 50% of the increase is due to a narrowing of the non-oil budget deficit. As in 1998 the entire budget surplus will be allocated to the government Petroleum Fund.

Currency

The unit of currency is the *Norwegian krone* (NOK) of 100 *øre*. After Oct. 1990 the krone was fixed to the ecu in the EMS of the EU in the narrow band of 2·25%, but it was freed in Dec. 1992. Annualized inflation was 1·3% in 1996, 2·6% in 1997 and 2·1% in 1998, but was forecast to rise to 3·5% in 1999. In Feb. 1998 foreign exchange reserves were US$22,884m. and gold reserves were 1·18m. troy oz. In Jan. 1998 total money supply was 421bn. kroner.

Banking and Finance

Norges Bank is the central bank and bank of issue. Supreme authority is vested in the Executive Board consisting of 7 members appointed by the King and the Supervisory Council consisting of 15 members elected by the Storting. The *Governor* is Svein Gjedrem. Total assets and liabilities at 31 Dec. 1997 were 318,728m. kroner.

There are 3 major commercial banks: Den Norske Bank, Christiana and Fokus. Total assets and liabilities of the 21 commercial banks at 31 Dec. 1997 were 621,019m. kroner.

The number of savings banks at 31 Dec. 1997 was 133; total assets and liabilities were 361,698m. kroner.

Banks

Norges Bank

The Central Bank of Norway was founded in 1816. The bank issues bank notes and advises on monetary, credit and foreign exchange policy. Based in Oslo with 12 regional branches. The present Central Bank Governor is Svein Gjedrem.

Head office: Bankplassen 2, PO Box 1179 Sentrum, 0107 Oslo.
Tel: 22-31-60-00. Fax: 22-41-31-05.
Web site: www.norges-bank.no

Den Norske Bank (DnB)

Norway's largest financial services group is 52% owned by the government. DnB has nearly one million retail customers and its share of the corporate market is estimated at around a quarter. A subsidiary, DnB Markets, is Norway's largest investment firm, handling currency exchange, insurance and asset management.
E-Mail: central.bank@norges-bank.co Web site: www.dnb.no

Stock Exchange

The Oslo Stock Exchange is the only one in Norway and opened in 1819. It is a self-owned and self-financed institution, with the Stock

Exchange Council being appointed by the Ministry of Finance. 232 companies were listed on 1 Aug. 1998 and 32 stockbroking firms and banks were members, nine of these being foreign owned. Decentralized trading was introduced in Sept. 1998, opening up the market to foreign participants.

Oslo Stock Exchange (Oslo Børs)

Tollbugaten 2, PO Box 460 Sentrum, 0105 Oslo.

Tel: 22-34-17-00. Fax: 22-41-65-90.

E-mail: info@ose.no Web site: www.ose.no

Chambers of commerce

USA

880 Third Avenue, New York, NY 10022

Tel: 212 421-1655. Fax: 212 838-0374

Web: www.norway.org/nacc E-mail: nacc@ntcny.org

Trade Associations

The Norwegian Trade Council provides a service to Norwegian companies operating abroad, helping to solve potential problems, improve competitiveness and advise on local markets and strategies. They can also provide information for foreign companies wishing to do business in Norway.

Norwegian Trade Council (NTC)

(Norges Eksportråd) Drammensvein 40, 0243 Oslo.

Tel: 22-92-63-00. Fax: 22-92-64-00.

Web site: www.nortrade.com E-mail: oslo@ntc.no

UK

Charles House, 5 Lower Regent St., London SW1Y 4LR

Tel: (0)20 7389-8800. Fax: (0)20 7973-0189

Web: www.norway.org.uk E-mail: london@ntc.no

USA

880 Third Avenue, New York, NY 10022

Tel: 212 421-9210. Fax: 212 838-0374

Web: www.ntcusa.org

Invest in Norway assists foreign firms wanting to set up in Norway or to collaborate with Norwegian firms.

Invest in Norway

Akersgata 13, PO Box 448 Sentrum, 0104 Oslo

Tel: 22-00-25-00. Fax: 22-42-47-27

Web: www.norwayinvest.com

Weights and Measures

The metric system is obligatory.

ENERGY AND NATURAL RESOURCES

Electricity

Norway is a large producer of hydro-electric energy. The potential total hydro-electric power was estimated at 179,647m. kWh in 1998. Installed electrical capacity in 1994 was 26·43m. kW, more than 95% of it hydro-electric. Production, 1998 estimate, was 116,987m. kWh (of which 116,259m. kWh was hydro-electric). Consumption per capita in 1996, at 23,830 kWh, was the highest in the world.

Oil and Gas

There are enormous oil reserves in the Norwegian continental shelf. In 1966 the first exploration well was drilled. Production of crude oil, 1998, 150,006,000 tonnes. Norway is the world's second biggest oil exporter after Saudi Arabia, producing around 3·5m. bbls. a day in

1996. It had proven reserves of 11·2bn. bbls. in Sept. 1997. In March 1998 Norway announced that it would reduce its output for the year by 100,000 bbls. per day as part of a plan to cut global crude production.

Output of natural gas, 1998, 48,146m. cu. metres.

Minerals

Production, 1996 (in tonnes): iron ore, 1,554,599; ferrotitanium ore, 758,711; copper concentrates, 31,736; lead ore (1995), 3,721; zinc ore, 8,619.

Agriculture

Norway is barren and mountainous. The arable area is in strips in valleys and around fiords and lakes.

In 1998 the agricultural area[1] was 1,046,300 ha, of which 632,900 ha were meadow and pasture, 167,100 ha were sown to barley, 92,500 ha to oats, 69,000 ha to wheat and 16,300 ha to potatoes. Production (in 1,000 tonnes) in 1997: barley, 663; oats, 360; wheat, 256; potatoes, 471; hay, 2,633; vegetables, 134; meat, 258.

Livestock, 1998[1], 1,036,400 cattle (347,700 milch cows), 941,500 sheep, 54,500 goats, 1,385,200 pigs, 3,205,900 hens, 104,000 silver and platinum fox, 528,000 blue fox, 388,000 mink, 191,600 reindeer.

[1]Holdings with at least 50 ha agricultural area in use.

Forestry

In 1995 the total area under forests was 8·07m. ha, or 26·3% of the total land area (7·94m. ha and 25·9% in 1990). Productive forest area, 1997, approximately 67,375 sq. km. About 80% of the productive forest area consists of conifers and 20% of broadleaves. In 1997, 8·56m. cu. metres of roundwood were cut: 37m. cu. metres were special and saw timber and 36m. cu. metres pulpwood.

Fisheries

The total number of fishermen in 1998 was 21,123, of whom 6,153 had another chief occupation. In 1998 the number of registered fishing vessels (all with motor) was 13,252, and of these 4,788 were open boats.

The catch in 1998 totalled 2,844,438 tonnes (provisional), almost entirely from sea fishing. The catch of herring totalled 830,950 tonnes and cod 320,314 tonnes. 9,067 seals were caught in 1998 (including 27 harp seal and 19 hodded seal for research purposes). Commercial whaling was prohibited in 1988, but recommenced in 1993: 624 whales were caught in 1998.

Environment

In 1998 there were 18 national parks (total area, 1,386,840 ha), 1,319 nature reserves (243,019 ha), 86 landscape protected areas (506,303 ha) and 76 other areas with protected flora and fauna (11,052 ha).

INDUSTRY

Industry is chiefly based on raw materials. Paper and paper products, industrial chemicals and basic metals are important export manufactures. In the following table figures are given for industrial establishments in 1996. The values are given in 1m. kroner.

Industries	Establish-ments	Number of Employees	Gross value of produc-tion	Value added
Coal and peat	8	292	125	9
Metal ores	7	1,011	901	269
Other mining and quarrying	346	3,015	4,138	1,598

Food products	1,729	52,450	96,608	23,680
Beverages and tobacco	54	6,204	14,154	10,242
Textiles	315	5,079	3,867	1,481
Clothing, etc.	160	2,407	1,526	542
Leather and leather products	43	730	479	161
Wood and wood products	987	14,491	14,678	3,895
Pulp, paper and paper products	108	10,553	19,375	5,884
Printing and publishing	1,870	36,406	28,982	12,208
Basic chemicals	65	8,245	19,814	6,282
Other chemical products	112	5,620	110,313	4,079
Coal and refined petroleum products	8	1,206	18,845	1,627
Rubber and plastic products	356	6,605	7,052	2,472
Other non-metallic mineral products	600	9,437	12,497	4,176
Basic metals	121	15,140	35,546	8,376
Metal products, except machinery/ equipment	1,178	17,791	14,698	6,209
Machinery and equipment	1,164	22,867	26,236	8,418
Office machinery and computers	25	746	1,129	402
Electrical machinery and apparatus	316	9,587	11,264	3,806
Radio, television, communication equipment	75	4,471	6,411	2,165
Medical, precision and optical instruments	333	5,397	6,720	2,178
Oil platforms	91	17,413	19,731	6,515
Motor vehicles and trailers	97	4,832	4,888	1,565
Other transport equipment	524	17,582	19,753	5,741
Other manufacturing industries	742	12,892	10,547	3,704
Total (all industries)	11,380	286,265	396,122	117,441

Norway's top exporting companies.

Company	Head Office	Value of exports in 1998 (1,000Nkr)	Exports as %age of total turnover
Den Norske Stats Oljeskap AS	Stavanger	92,666	86·9
Norsk Hydro ASA	Oslo	88,940	91·3
Kværner ASA	Lysaker	68,132	81·9
Asea Brown Boveri AS	Billingstad	20,751	71·6
Aker RGI ASA	Oslo	19,167	55·1
Orkla ASA	Oslo	16,745	54·3
Norske Skogindustrier AS	Lysaker	12,097	81·1
Hydro Aluminium ASA	Oslo	12,087	80·1
Dyno ASA	Oslo	10,681	90·0
Elkem ASA	Oslo	9,100	91·4

Labour

Norway has a tradition of centralized wage bargaining. Since the early 1960s the contract period has been for 2 years with intermediate bargaining after 12 months, to take into consideration such changes as the rate of inflation.

The labour force (i.e. employed persons plus non-employed persons seeking work aged 16–74) averaged 2,317,000 in 1998 (1,071,000 females). The total number of employed persons in 1998 averaged 2,242,000 (1,036,000 females), of whom 2,056,000 were salaried employees and wage earners, 172,000 self-employed and 14,000 family workers.

Distribution of employed persons by occupation in 1995 showed 560,000 in technical, physical science, humanistic and artistic work; 146,000 administrative executive work; 197,000 clerical; 222,000 sales; 105,000 agriculture, forestry, fishing etc.; 8,000 mining and quarrying; 131,000 transport and communication;

385,000 manufacturing; 285,000 service; and 39,000 military and occupation not specified.

There were 75,000 registered unemployed in 1998, giving an unemployment rate of 3·2%.

There were 36 work stoppages in 1997: 286,407 working days were lost.

Trade Unions

There were 1,479,634 union members at the end of 1998.

Norwegian Confederation of Trade Unions
Landesorganisasjonen i Norge (LO)

Founded in 1899, LO is Norway's largest and most influential workers' organization with more than 800,000 members of national unions which are affiliated to LO. Women represent 45% of the membership.

Youngs gate 11, 0181 Oslo.

Tel: 23-06-10-50. Fax: 23-06-17-43.

Web site: www.lo.no

Employers Associations

Confederation of Norwegian Business and Industry
Næringslivets Hovedorganisasjon (NHO)

The main organization for employers in the manufacturing industries, services and crafts with a membership of over 13,800 companies.

PO Box 5250, Majorstua, 0303 Oslo.

Tel: 22-96-50-00. Fax: 22-69-55-93.

Web site: www.nho.no

Sector federations belonging to NHO:

Federation of Norwegian Engineering Industries (THO)

PO Box 7072, Majorstua, 0306 Oslo.

Tel: 22-59-66-00. Fax: 22-59-66-69.

Federation of Process Industries (PIL)
PO Box 2724, St. Hanshaugen, 0131 Oslo.
Tel: 22-96-10-00. Fax: 22-96-10-99.

National Federation of Fish and Aquaculture Industries (FHL)
PO Box 5471, Majorstua, 0305 Oslo.
Tel: 22-96-50-18. Fax: 22-60-15-42.

INTERNATIONAL TRADE

Imports and Exports

Total imports and exports in calendar years (in 1m. kroner):

	1994	1995	1996	1997	1998
Imports	192,963	208,626	229,720	252,232	282,638
Exports	244,475	265,883	320,128	342,421	304,653

Major import suppliers in 1998 (value in 1m. kroner): Sweden, 41,677·0; Germany, 38,074·5; UK, 27,918·4; USA, 22,670·1; Denmark, 18,802·9; Netherlands, 12,751·2; Japan, 12,630·5; Italy, 11,660·1; France, 11,068·1; Finland, 9,535·4. Imports from economic areas: EU, 191,443·2; Nordic countries, 70,851·4; EFTA, 4,550·1.

Major export markets in 1998 (value in 1m. kroner): UK, 51,567·2; Germany, 37,597·5; Netherlands, 29,403·5; Sweden, 29,790·5; France, 25,691·9; USA, 18,539·7; Denmark, 17,252·0; Canada, 10,570·1; Belgium, 9,624·6; Finland, 8,205·9; Italy, 7,644·0. Exports to economic areas: EU, 234,273·0; Nordic countries, 57,264·0; EFTA, 3,140·6.

Principal imports in 1998 (in 1m. kroner): motor vehicles, 25,881·7; other transport equipment, 24,309·1; general industrial machinery and equipment, 16,661·6; electrical machinery, 14,698·8; passenger cars including station wagons, 13,989·6; office machines and computers, 13,588·1; specialized machinery for particular industries, 12,346·9; ships over 100 tonnes, 12,093·8; iron and steel, 12,012·7; manufactures of metals, 11,554·9; clothing and accessories, 10,775·5; telecommunications and sound apparatus and equipment, 10,024·6; metalliferous ores and metal scrap, 9,511·1. Principal exports in 1998 (in 1m. kroner): petroleum, petroleum products and related materials, 101,628·8 (including crude petroleum, 91,083·2); natural and manufactured gas, 29,718·9 (including natural gas, 27,220·2); fish, crustaceans and molluscs, and preparations thereof, 26,478·1; non-ferrous metals, 24,730·4 (including aluminium, 17,350·3); transport equipment excluding road vehicles, 11,850·7; paper, paperboard and products, 9,907·9; iron and steel, 9,782·0.

COMMUNICATIONS

Roads
In 1998 the length of public roads (including roads in towns) totalled 91,254 km. In 1996 there were 67,500 km of paved roads. Total road length in 1998 included: motorways, 109 km; national roads, 26,611 km; provincial roads, 27,108 km; local roads, 37,022 km. Number of registered motor vehicles, 1998, included: 1,786,404 passenger cars (including station wagons and ambulances), 224,084 tractors and special purpose vehicles, 208,955 vans, 113,868 mopeds, 107,221 combined vehicles, 74,653 goods vehicles (including lorries), 70,479 motorcycles and 36,218 buses. In 1998 there were 8,864 road accidents with 315 fatalities.

Rules of the road
Driving in Norway is on the right-hand side of the road. The wearing of seatbelts is compulsory in the front seats and, if fitted, in the back.

Dipped headlights must be used by all vehicles at all times. Helmets must be worn by motorcycle and moped drivers. A warning triangle should be carried by all motorists. Although not compulsory, studded or chained snow tyres are recommended for winter driving off main routes. Unless otherwise indicated, speed limits are 90 kph on motorways, 80 kph on other roads and 50 kph in built-up areas, although in residential areas the limit may be 30 kph. Ramps and speed control humps are not always signposted. There are toll charges on some roads and highways and entrance charges for a number of cities and towns. Driving under the influence of alcohol (more than 0·05% alcohol in the bloodstream) is severely prohibited. A green card is not necessary in Norway. Only a small number of petrol stations will accept credit cards. Vegmeldingssentralen (Tel: 22-65-40-40) can give information on the state of roads. In case of breakdown, Norges Automobilförbund (NAF) (Tel: 22-34-14-00) can help.

Rail

The length of state railways in 1997 was 4,021 km (2,456 km electrified). Operating receipts of the state railways in 1998 were 3,958m. kroner; operating expenses, 4,180m. kroner. The state railways carried 7,458,000 tonnes of freight and 46,972,000 passengers in 1998. As recently as 1995, 20,909 tonnes of freight had been carried in the year.

There are direct trains from Norway to Sweden (Stockholm, Gothenburg and Helsingborg are the main lines) and to Denmark via Helsingborg. There are also links to Sweden in the north but timetables may be subject to seasonal variations.

Norwegian State Railways (NSB)
Prinsensgate 7–9, 0048 Oslo. Tel: 81-50-08-88
Web site: www.nsb.no

There is a metro (98 km) and tram/light rail line (54 km) in Oslo.

Civil Aviation

The main international airports are at Oslo (Fornebu), Bergen (Flesland) and Stavanger (Sola). Kristiansand and Trondheim also have a few international flights.

Established in 1946 as a consortium of Norway, Denmark and Sweden's national airlines, Scandinavian Airlines System (SAS) is the biggest airline in Scandinavia and the fourth largest in Europe. SAS flies around 21m. passengers a year and has an annual turnover of around NOK 39bn. SAS collaborates with Lufthansa and United Airlines amongst others in an integrated network called Star Alliance. Denmark and Norway each hold two-sevenths and Sweden three-sevenths of the capital of SAS, but they have joint responsibility towards third parties. 23,744,601 passengers, 87,489 tonnes of freight and 50,154 tonnes of mail were carried on all domestic and international flights in 1996. Braathens is the Norwegian national airline and the largest wholly Norwegian owned carrier. The airline serves 16 Norwegian airports and 7 in Sweden as well as 10 direct flights to other countries, and has a link up to another 400 destinations due to their participation in the KLM/Northwest alliance. It carried 5,162,200 passengers in 1996.

In 1998 services were also provided by Aeroflot, Air Canada, Air France, Air Lithuania, Air Malta, Air Stord, Air Team, Aviosarda, British Airways, British Midland, Coast Air, Continental Airlines, Czech Airlines, Delta Air Lines, Finnair, Golden Air Flyg, Hemus Air, Iberia, Icelandair, Interimpex-Avioimpex, KLM, KLM UK, LOT, Lufthansa, Maersk Air, Muk Air, Ryanair, SABENA, Skyways, Swissair, TAP, Teddy Air, Thai Airways International, Tyrolean Airways, United Airlines and Wideroe's Flyveselskap. In 1996 Oslo (Fornebu) handled 10,845,000 passengers (6,514,000 on domestic flights) and 50,600 tonnes of freight. Bergen was the second busiest in 1996 for passenger traffic, with 3,064,000 (2,573,000 on domestic flights), and Stavanger second busiest for freight, with 7,100 tonnes.

SAS

Snaröyveien 57, 0080 Oslo.

Tel: 64-81-60-50. Fax: 64-81-15-35

Web: www.scandinavian.net

Braathens ASA

Oksenøyvein 3, PO Box 55, 1330 Fornebu

Tel: 67-59-70-00. Fax: 67-59-70-10

Web: www.braathens.no

Oslo International Airport Gardermoen

Oslo's new airport was opened in Oct. 1998 and is situated 45 km northeast of the city. The Airport Express Train takes 19 minutes from Oslo Central Station with trains leaving every 15 minutes. Buses or Flytaxis are also available from Oslo city centre.

Shipping

The Norwegian International Ship Register was set up in 1987. At 31 Dec. 1998, 713 ships were registered (494 Norwegian) totalling 19,547,000 GRT. 171 tankers accounted for 8,716,000 GRT. There were also 969 ships totalling 2,799,000 GRT on the Norwegian Ordinary Register. These figures do not include fishing boats, tugs, salvage vessels, icebreakers and similar special types of vessels. Norway's merchant fleet represents 4·3% of total world tonnage.

In 1997, 45,199,000 passengers were carried by coastwise shipping on long distance, local and ferry services.

The warm Gulf Stream ensures ice-free harbours throughout the year.

Telecommunications

Number of telephone connections on 31 Dec. 1998 was 2,935,053. By the end of 1998 there were 2·1m. mobile phone subscribers (48% of the total population). In 1997 there were 1,589,000 PCs (361 for every 1,000 persons) and 220,000 fax machines. There were around 601,000 Internet users in Jan. 1998.

Emergency numbers are as follows; Fire – 110, Police – 112, Ambulance – 113. International access code for Norway is 47. For directory enquiries dial 180 for numbers in Norway, Sweden and Denmark and 181 for all other countries. To make an international call, dial 00 first. Payphones accept either coins (minimum charge 2 Nkr), phone cards (available from post offices and kiosks) or credit cards.

There are no area codes in Norway and telephone numbers have 8 digits which must all be dialled.

Postal Services

There were 1,587 post offices in 1997. In 1995 a total of 2,176m. items of mail were processed, or 499 per person. Postal System Post offices can be found everywhere in Norway and poste restante can be received at any of them. A postcard or letter weighing less than 20g costs 4·50 Nkr to Nordic countries, 5·50N kr to other European countries or 6 Nkr to send elsewhere. Faxes can be sent from most post offices.

Main post office

Oslo Sentrum Postkontor, Dronningens gate 15, 0101 Oslo.

SOCIAL INSTITUTIONS

Justice

The judicature is common to civil and criminal cases; the same professional judges preside over both. These judges are state officials. The participation of lay judges and jurors, both summoned for the individual case, varies according to the kind of court and kind of case.

The 96 city or district courts of first instance are in criminal cases composed of one professional judge and 2 lay judges, chosen by ballot from a panel elected by the local authority. In civil cases 2 lay judges may participate. These courts are competent in all cases except criminal cases where the maximum penalty exceeds 6 years imprisonment.

In every community there is a Conciliation Board composed of 3 lay persons elected by the district council. A civil lawsuit usually begins with mediation by the Board which can pronounce judgement in certain cases.

The 5 high courts, or courts of second instance, are composed of 3 professional judges. Additionally, in civil cases 2 or 4 lay judges may be summoned. In serious criminal cases, which are brought before high courts in the first instance, a jury of 10 lay persons is summoned to determine whether the defendant is guilty according to the charge. In less serious criminal cases the court is composed of 2 professional and 3 lay judges. In civil cases, the court of second instance is an ordinary court of appeal. In criminal cases in which the lower court does not have judicial authority, it is itself the court of first instance. In other criminal cases it is an appeal court as far as the appeal is based on an attack against the lower court's assessment of the facts when determining the guilt of the defendant. An appeal based on any other alleged mistakes is brought directly before the Supreme Court.

The Supreme Court *(Høyesterett)* is the court of last resort. There are 18 Supreme Court judges. Each individual case is heard by 5 judges. Some major cases are determined in plenary session. The Supreme Court may in general examine every aspect of the case and the handling of it by the lower courts. However, in criminal cases the Court may not overrule the lower court's assessment of the facts as far as the guilt of the defendant is concerned.

The Court of Impeachment *(Riksretten)* is composed of 5 judges of the Supreme Court and 10 members of Parliament.

All serious offences are prosecuted by the State. The Public Prosecution Authority consists of the Attorney General, 18 district attorneys and legally qualified officers of the ordinary police force. Counsel for the defence is in general provided for by the State.

Religion

There is freedom of religion, the Church of Norway (Evangelical Lutheran), however, being the national church, endowed by the State. Its clergy are nominated by the King. Ecclesiastically Norway is divided into 11 bishoprics, 96 archdeaconries and 626 clerical districts. There were 251,009 members of registered and unregistered religious communities outside the Evangelical Lutheran Church, subsidized by central government and local authorities in 1997. At 1 Jan. 1997 there were 59 Muslim congregations with 46,500 members. The Roman Catholics are under a Bishop at Oslo, a Vicar Apostolic at Trondheim and a Vicar Apostolic at Tromsø.

Education

Free compulsory schooling in primary and lower secondary schools was extended to 10 years from 9, and the starting age lowered to 6 from 7, in July 1997. All young people between the ages of 16 and 19 have the statutory right to 3 years of upper secondary education. In 1997 there were 6,260 kindergartens (children up to 6 years old) with 184,514 children and 51,793 staff. In 1997–98 there were 3,273 primary and lower secondary schools with 558,247 pupils and 43,568 teachers; 707 upper secondary schools with 201,925 pupils and 21,134 teachers; and 71 colleges, with 97,257 students and 5,264 teachers.

There are 4 universities: Bergen, founded 1946; Oslo, 1811; Tromsø, 1968; and the Norwegian University of Science and Technology, 1996 (formerly the University of Trondheim and the Norwegian Institute of Technology); and 10 specialized institutions of equivalent status. In 1997–98 these had 83,484 students and 6,485 academic staff. The University of Tromsø is responsible for Sami language and studies.

In 1996 total expenditure on education came to 7·5% of GNP. The adult literacy rate in 1997 was at least 99%.

Health

The health care system, which is predominantly publicly financed (mainly by a national insurance tax), is run on both county and municipal levels. Persons who fall ill are guaranteed medical treatment, and health services are distributed according to need. In 1996 there were 15,368 doctors (equivalent to 1 for every 284 persons), 5,222 dentists and 65,232 nurses. In 1994 provision of hospital beds was 51 per 10,000 population.

In 1997, 34·0% of men and 32·7% of women smoked. The rate among women is one of the highest in the world.

Hospitals and health care

Chemists are called Apotek and there is usually one in each area open for emergencies at night and on weekends. Prescriptions written abroad cannot be processed by law.

Welfare

In 1997 there were 628,247 old age pensioners who received a total of 53,333·2m. kroner, 246,541 disability pensioners who received 25,182·8m. kroner, 29,956 widows and widowers who received 1,806·6m. kroner and 44,986 single parents who received 2,5065·0m. kroner. In 1997, 921,230 children received family allowances. Maternity leave is for 1 year on 80% of previous salary; unused portions may pass to a husband. In 1997 sickness benefits totalling 27,310·0m. kroner were paid: 14,787·9m. kroner in sickness allowances and 12,522·1m. kroner in medical benefits. Expenditure

on benefits at childbirth and adoption totalled 6,614·9m. kroner to
95,294 cases in 1997.

CULTURE

Bergen is one of 9 European Cities of Culture in the year 2000. Its
theme will be 'Art, Work and Leisure', part of which will coincide with
the Bergen International Festival held in May 2000. The other Cities
of Culture are Avignon (France), Bologna (Italy), Brussels (Belgium),
Helsinki (Finland), Kraków (Poland), Prague (Czech Republic),
Reykjavík (Iceland) and Santiago de Compostela (Spain). The title
attracts large European Union grants.

Broadcasting

The Norwegian Broadcasting Corporation (Norsk Rikskringkastning)
is a non-commercial enterprise operated by an independent state
organization and broadcasts 1 programme (P1) on long, medium,
and short-waves and on FM and 1 programme (P2) on FM. Local
programmes are also broadcast. It broadcasts 1 TV programme from
2,259 transmitters. Colour programmes are broadcast by PAL
system. Number of television licences, 1997, 1,678,140. In 1996
there were 4m. radio receivers. NRK no longer has the state
monopoly that prevailed until relatively late. There are now
commercial terrestrial and satellite TV channels and many local FM
radio stations as well as a nationwide commercial radio station.
Radio Norway can be received in Oslo on 93MHZ FM, elsewhere on
shortwave.

Television Stations

NRK (Norsk Rikskringkasting)
Bjørnstjerne Bjørnsons Plass 1, N-0340 Oslo

Tel 00 47 23 04 7000

Website: www.nrk.no

Commenced broadcasting in 1960, The Norwegian Broadcasting Corporation broadcasts on 2 channels – NRK1 and NRK2.

TV2

Postboks 2, N-5002 Bergen

Tel 00 47 55 90 8070; fax 00 47 55 90 8090

Commercial public service television, founded in 1992.

TV Norge

Sagveien 17, N-0459 Oslo 4

Tel 00 47 22 38 7800; fax 00 47 22 35 1000

Satellite-to-cable television.

Radio Stations (National)

NRK (Norsk Rikskringkasting)

Bjørnstjerne Bjørnsons Plass 1, N-0340 Oslo

Tel 00 47 23 04 7000

Website: www.nrk.no

Founded 1933; broadcasts nationally on 5 channels with 17 regional stations and NRK Sámi Radio which broadcasts in the Sámi language.

Cinema

There were 396 cinemas in 1997, with a seating capacity of 90,105. Attendances totalled 10·95m.

Press

There were 63 daily newspapers with a combined average net circulation of 2·22m. in 1998, and 92 weeklies and semi-weeklies with 753,000. Norway has the highest circulation rate of daily newspapers in Europe, at 596 per 1,000 inhabitants in 1995. In 1994 a survey discovered that 85% of Norwegians read a newspaper each day and spent an average of 45 minutes a day doing so.

Norway's five largest national newspapers with place of publication and circulation (average for 1996):

Verdens Gang	Oslo	356,861
Aftenposten	Oslo	283,915
Dagbladet	Oslo	205,740
Bergens Tidende	Bergen	95,400
Adresseavisen	Trondheim	91,912

Book Publishers

H. Aschehoug & Co (W. Nygaard) A/S

Founded 1872. Publishes fiction and general non-fiction, sociology, general and social science.

Postboks 363, 0102 Sentrum, Oslo. Tel: 00 47 22 400400.

Fax: 00 47 22 206395

J. W. Cappelens Forlag A/S

Founded 1829. Publishes fiction, general non-fiction and religion.

Postboks 350, 0101 Sentrum, Oslo. Tel: 00 47 22 365000.

Fax: 00 47 22 365040.

N. W. Damm og Søn A/S

Founded 1845. Publishes fiction and general non-fiction.

Postboks 1755, Vika, 0122 Oslo. Tel: 00 47 22 471100.

Fax: 00 47 22 360874.

Ex Libris Forlag A/S

Founded 1982. Publishes cookery, health, nutrition, humour, human relations, publishing and book trade reference.

Postboks 2130, Grünerløkka, 0505 Oslo. Tel: 00 47 22 384450.

Fax: 00 47 22 385160.

Gyldendal Norsk Forlag A/S

Founded 1925. Publishes fiction, science fiction, fantasy, art, dance, biography, government, political science, history, how-to, music, social sciences, sociology, poetry, philosophy, psychology, psychiatry and religion.

Postboks 6860, 0130 St Olaf, Oslo. Tel: 00 47 22 034100.
Fax: 00 47 22 034105.

Hjemmets Bokforlag AS

Founded 1969. Publishes fiction and general non-fiction.
Postboks 1755, Vika, N–0055 Oslo. Tel: 00 47 22 471000.
Fax: 00 47 22 471098.

NKS-Forlaget

Founded 1971. Publishes accountancy, child care and development, English as a second language, health, nutrition, mathematics, natural history, sociology, general and social sciences.

Postboks 5853, 0308 Oslo. Tel: 00 47 22 596000.
Fax: 00 47 22 596300. Website: www.nks.no

Tiden Norsk Forlag

Founded 1933. Publishes fiction, general non-fiction, essays, literature, literary criticism, science fiction, fantasy and management.

PO Box 8813, Youngstorget, 0028 Oslo. Tel: 00 47 22 007100.
Fax: 00 47 22 426458.

Libraries

In 1997 there were 1,108 public libraries, 3,521 school libraries, and 394 special and research libraries (9 national).

Theatre and Opera

There were 6,703 theatre and opera performances attended by 1,290,621 people at 20 theatres in 1997. Den Nationale Scene was the first national theatre founded in Norway and remains an important stage for productions of Norwegian and foreign drama.

Den Nationale Scene
Engen 1, Postboks 78 Sentrum, 5803 Bergen
Tel: 55-54-97-00. Fax: 55-54-97-30
Web: www.den-nationale-scene.no
E-mail: dns@den-nationale-scene.no

Museums and Galleries
There were 539 museums in 1997 (37 art, 451 social history, 15 natural history and 36 mixed social and natural history), with 9,109,609 visitors.

Tourism
In 1997 there were 2,702,000 foreign tourists. In 1996 there were 1,186 hotels and 744 camping sites. Receipts from foreign tourism totalled US$2·5bn.

Norwegian Tourist Board
Norway: PO Box 2893 Solli, Drammensvein 40, 0230 Oslo.
Tel: 22-92-52-00. Fax: 22-56-05-05.
E-mail: norway@nortra.no Web site: www.tourist.no

UK: 5th Floor, Charles House, 5 Lower Regent Street, London SW1Y 4LR.
Tel: (0)20 7839 6255. Fax: (0)20 7839 6014.

USA: 655 Third Avenue, Suite 1810, New York, NY 10017.
Tel: 212 885 9700. Fax: 212 885 9710.

France: 28 rue Bayard, 75008 Paris.
Tel: 1 53-23-00-50. Fax: 1 53-23-00-59.

Germany/Austria/Switzerland: PO Box 760820, 22058 Hamburg.
Tel: (0)40 2271-0810. Fax: (0)40 4022-1588.

Holland/Belgium/Luxembourg: PO Box 75120, 1070 AC Amsterdam.

Visas

Visas are not required by citizens of EU countries, the USA, Canada, Australia or New Zealand for stays of less than 3 months. Residents of other countries should contact the Norwegian Embassy in their own country for details of entry requirements.

Festivals

The National Theatre's next biennial International Ibsen Festival will be held in Skien in the summer of 2001.

Public Holidays in 2000

1 Jan.	New Year's Day
16 April	Palm Sunday
20 April	Maundy Thursday
21 April	Good Friday
23 April	Easter Sunday
24 April	Easter Monday
1 May	May Day
17 May	Constitution Day
1 June	Ascension Day
11 June	Whitsun
12 June	Whitmonday
25 Dec.	Christmas Day
26 Dec.	Boxing Day

Business Etiquette

Norway is a conservative country. There is little in the way of conversational banter. Norwegians prefer to be direct, and believe it is better to be straightforward. Beware of comparing Norway to Sweden and do not give the impression that you consider the two countries to be one homogenous area. Whaling is a sensitive subject and best avoided. Businesses are generally small and staff will have more say than in companies outside Scandinavia. Dress is likely to be more informal than in other countries but it will be expected that foreigners will dress formally if this is their custom. It is important to shake hands on meeting and parting with business colleagues. The use of technology is widespread and this will be expected of business partners. Payments will normally be made promptly and the same will be expected or interest will usually be charged. Do be punctual and use the 24 hour clock to avoid mistakes. Business and social relationships will almost certainly be kept separate, but if invited into a home be punctual and take a small gift for the hostess. If going to a restaurant it should be noted that the mark-up on wine can be anything from 200% to 400%. Many Norwegians will only indulge in wine or the popular aquavit at home.

DIPLOMATIC REPRESENTATIVES

Of Norway in Great Britain (25 Belgrave Sq., London, SW1X 8QD)
   Ambassador: Tarald Brautaset.
Of Great Britain in Norway (Thomas Heftyesgate 8, 0244 Oslo, 2)
   Ambassador: R. Dales, CMG.
Of Norway in the USA (2720 34th St., NW, Washington, D.C., 20008)
   Ambassador: Tom Eric Vraalsen, GCVO.
Of the USA in Norway (Drammensvein 18, 0244 Oslo, 2)
   Ambassador: David B. Hermelin.
Of Norway to the United Nations
   Ambassador: Ole Peter Kolby.
Of Norway to the European Union
   Ambassador: Einar Bull.

FURTHER READING

Central Bureau of Statistics. *Statistisk Årbok; Statistical Yearbook of Norway .– Economic survey* (annual, from 1935; with English summary from 1952, now published in *Økonomiske Analyser*, annual). *– Historisk Statistikk; Historical Statistics. – Statistisk Månedshefte* (with English index)

Norges Statskalender. From 1816; annual from 1877

Arntzen, J. G. and Knudsen, B. B., *Political Life and Institutions in Norway.* Oslo, 1981

Derry, T. K., *A History of Modern Norway,* 1814–1972. OUP, 1973. *– A History of Scandinavia.* London, 1979

Petersson, O., *The Government and Politics of the Nordic Countries.* Stockholm, 1994

Sather, L. B., *Norway.* [Bibliography] ABC-Clio, Oxford and Santa Barbara (CA), 1986

Selbyg, A., *Norway Today: An Introduction to Modern Norwegian Society.* Oslo, 1986

National library: The National Library of Norway, Drammensvein 42b, 0255 Oslo.

National statistical office: Statistics Norway, PB 8131 Dep., N-0033 Oslo.

Website: http://www.ssb.no/

SWEDEN

Konungariket Sverige
(Kingdom of Sweden)

Capital: **Stockholm**

Area: **449,964 sq. km**

Population estimate, 2000: **8·9m.**

Head of State: **King Carl XVI Gustaf**

Head of Government: **Göran Persson**

TERRITORY AND POPULATION

Sweden is bounded in the west and northwest by Norway, east by Finland and the Gulf of Bothnia, southeast by the Baltic Sea and southwest by the Kattegat. The area is 449,964 sq. km. At the 1990 census the population was 8,587,353. Estimate, Dec. 1998, 8,854,322; density 20 per sq. km. In 1997, 83·2% of the population lived in urban areas.

The UN gives a projected population for 2000 of 8·9m.

Area, population and population density of the counties (*län*):

	Land area (in sq. km)	Population (1990 census)	Population 31 Dec 1998	Density per sq. km 31 Dec. 1998
Stockholm	6,490	1,640,389	1,783,440	275
Uppsala	6,989	268,503	291,413	42
Södermanland	6,062	255,546	256,269	42
Östergötland	10,562	402,849	412,411	39
Jönköping	9,944	308,294	328,059	33
Kronoberg	8,458	177,880	178,078	21
Kalmar	11,171	241,149	238,104	21
Gotland	3,140	57,132	57,643	18
Blekinge	2,941	150,615	151,414	51
Skåne	11,027	1,068,587	1,120,426	102
Halland	5,454	254,568	272,539	50
Västra Götalands	23,942	1,458,166	1,486,918	62
Värmland	17,586	283,148	278,313	16
Örebro	8,517	272,474	274,584	32
Västmanland	6,302	258,544	257,661	41
Kopparberg	28,193	288,919	282,898	10
Gävleborg	18,192	289,346	282,226	16
Västernorrland	21,678	261,099	251,884	12
Jämtland	49,443	135,724	131,766	3
Västerbotten	55,401	251,846	257,803	5
Norrbotten	98,911	263,546	260,473	3

There are some 17,000 Sami (Lapps).
On 31 Dec. 1998 aliens in Sweden numbered 410,621. Of these, 116,543 were from Nordic countries; 142,797 from the rest of Europe; 24,441 from Africa; 12,666 from North America; 17,936 from South America; 92,238 from Asian countries; 1,975 from the former USSR; 1,928 from Oceania; and 97 country unknown.

Immigration: 1997, 44,818; 1998, 49,391. Emigration: 1997, 38,543; 1998, 38,518.

Population of the 50 largest communities, 31 Dec. 1998:

Stockholm	736,113	Huddinge	81,339	Sollentuna	57,067
Göteborg	459,593	Karlstad	79,664	Örnsköldsvik	56,658
Malmö	254,904	Södertälje	75,836	Solna	55,806
Uppsala	187,302	Kristianstad	73,854	Mölndal	55,224
Linköping	131,948	Växjö	73,698	Falun	54,576
Västerås	124,780	Skellefteå	73,499	Trollhättan	52,795
Örebro	122,641	Nacka	73,029	Varberg	52,392
Norrköping	122,415	Luleå	71,360	Norrtälje	51,552
Helsingborg	116,337	Botkyrka	70,949	Skövde	49,437
Jönköping	115,987	Haninge	67,764	Hässleholm	49,046
Umeå	103,517	Kungsbacka	63,142	Nyköping	49,000
Lund	97,975	Karlskrona	60,429	Uddevalla	48,969
Borås	96,106	Täby	60,274	Borlänge	47,838
Sundsvall	93,923	Järfälla	59,839	Motala	42,444
Gävle	90,105	Kalmar	58,808	Piteå	40,458
Eskilstuna	88,027	Östersund	58,673	Lindingö	40,373
Halmstad	84,538	Gotland	57,643		

A fixed link with Denmark will be opened in July 2000 when the Öresund motorway and railway bridge between Malmö and Copenhagen is completed.

The official language is Swedish.

Time Zone

Sweden is 1 hour ahead of GMT.

POLITICAL AND SOCIAL CHRONOLOGY OF THE 20TH CENTURY

1905   Norway granted independence

1907   Gustav V becomes king

1909   Universal suffrage for males introduced

1914   Sweden declares its neutrality at start of First World War

1917   Social democrats first elected to parliament

1920   Sweden joins League of Nations

1921   Women given the vote

1939   Sweden declares its neutrality at start of Second World War

1946   Sweden joins UN

Tage Erlander elected Prime Minister and holds post until 1969

1950   Gustav VI Adolf becomes king

1971   Second parliamentary chamber abolished

1973   Carl XVI Gustaf becomes king

1974   New constitution adopted

1980   Order of succession to the throne altered to disregard gender

1982   Olof Palme elected prime minister

1986   Palme assassinated

1995   Sweden joins EU after a referendum

CULTURAL BRIEFING

Swedish cultural history starts with bronze-age rock carvings which date from between 1500 and 500 BC. Almost nothing is known about this period other than what the carvings themselves can tell us, namely that a culture involving fertility rites and sun worship existed. The first works of art about which we have more information are Viking runestones, which told stories in pictures and words of journeys and individuals' lives. It was during the middle ages that the visual arts became important in Sweden, for with the conversion to Christendom came the need to build and decorate churches. Swedish art was from this period heavily influenced by continental styles and the nobility generally decorated their homes with traditional Swedish tapestries and craft work or with the work of foreign artists. It was not until the 1700s that Swedish artists received any encouragement, and even then it was generally in the form of education abroad. The Rococo artist Carl Gustaf Pilo, for instance, spent 30 years in Copenhagen as a court painter, but there were also portrait artists schooled at the 'Kongliga Ritarakademien' (founded 1735) who stayed at home. The 1800s saw the fashion for landscape painting reach Sweden and a romantic theme began to develop under influence from Germany. It was in the late nineteenth century that a real explosion took place in Swedish art, and artists such as Carl Larsson, the impressionist Anders Zorn and Per Hasselberg, schooled in France, began to rebel against the traditionalist approach at home under the encouragement of Ernst Josephson. Trends continued to filter through from Paris in the twentieth century; fauvism was popular with artists like Isaac Grünewald and Nils Dardel, whilst others flirted with cubism and later surrealism. Pop art and experimental art changed the post war scene considerably, and although there may not be many world renowned Swedish artists of this period there is considerable interest at home and the art world is still generously subsidized.

Swedish film is best known abroad through the work of Ingmar Bergman, but the industry stretches back to the beginning of the century, when Victor Sjöstrom and Mauritz Stiller first instilled the nation with an interest in the big screen. Their move to Hollywood in the 1920s caused something of a crisis and it was not until the Second World War that the industry was revived. In the 1940s approximately 40 feature films were made each year, the most important by Alf Sjöberg. It was Bergman, however, that brought an international audience to the industry, whilst the 1960s saw a critical response in the films of Bo Widerberg and Vilgot Sjöman. Politicization of films in the late '60s by directors such as Jan Troell was perhaps inevitable, but after this point the Swedish film industry fell into decline under competition from abroad.

Viking sagas and inscriptions on runestones are the earliest known works of 'literature' that Sweden can lay claim to, and during the early Christian era there was little writing that was not in Latin. The reformation brought new possibilities and the Swedish lyrical tradition began to appear in written form. The mystic Emmanuel Swedenborg was perhaps the earliest writer known outside his own country, but in the 1700s Gustav III especially encouraged poets and writers and in the next century a romantic age, influenced by German writers, took hold. Poets and lyricists remained the most important writers until Johan Ludvig Runeberg introduced some realism into Swedish writing in the middle of the century. It was Strindberg who revolutionized the Swedish literary world, and thereafter writers such as Victoria Benedictsson could raise issues such as the position of women. Towards the end of the century Selma Lagerlöf achieved international fame with her novels and children's books. In the twentieth century Vilhelm Moberg achieved fame with proletarian novels, but whist the Swedish folk tradition has been retained by poets, literary trends set abroad have largely been adopted in Sweden.

Swedish folk music remains important today and many songs have been passed down for generations. Sweden lacks a composer of international stature, but since the renaissance has encouraged concerts and recitals of works by foreign and native composers. Johan Helmich Roman was important in the 1700s in organizing truly public concerts in Stockholm and Uppsala was also active in attracting musicians to perform. Franz Berwald was the first Swedish composer of note and the 1800s saw many Swedes compose operas and romantic pieces, but Swedish music is probably best represented by the folk songs of Sven-Bertil and Evert Taube or by the modern pop industry that started with Abba and remains disproportionately large today with respect to the size and population of the country.

CULTURAL PROFILES

Ingmar Bergman

Bergman was born the son of a Lutheran pastor in Uppsala, Sweden, on 14 July 1918. His childhood, and in particular his strict religious upbringing, was to have a major influence in the development of the themes and ideas of his filmmaking life.

It was at Stockholm University (where he studied art, history and literature) that he became involved with the theatre. He went on to get a job as a director at Hälsingborg municipal theatre where he met Anders Dymling, the head of the 'Svensk Filmindustri'. Dymling commisioned Bergman to write his first screenplay ('Hets') in 1944. As a result of the enormous success of this film he got the chance to write and direct a film of his own, 'Kris' ('Crisis'), in 1945. Bergman's early films were largely autobiographical; concerned with young people in a changing society, love and military service. With 'Kvinnors vänton' ('Waiting Women') and 'Sommaren med Monika' ('Summer with Monika') in 1952 his mature work began, focusing on his new preoccupations of marriage: its pressures and effects.

Bergman achieved widespread international success with 1955's 'Sommernattens leende' ('Smiles of a Summer Night'). This was the beginning of his most famous period of work, including 'The Seventh Seal' (1956), a symbolic morality play set in the middle ages, and 'Wild Strawberries' (1957), a meditation on old age. Universally recognized as classics, Bergman was one of the first filmmakers to write and direct a series of films which developed the same central ideas, perceptions and preoccupations.

Bergman continued to make films until 1992 when he announced his retirement from international filmmaking with his final screenplay, 'The Best Intentions'. His later work includes: the trilogy 'Såsom i en spegel' ('Through a Glass Darkly'), 'Nattsvardsgästerna' ('Winter Light') and 'Tystnaden' ('The Silence'), dealing with sanity and madness; the bleak island dramas of 'Persona', 'Vartimmen' ('Hour of the Wolf'), 'Skammen' ('Shame') and 'En Passion' ('The Passion'); and the intimate family portraits of 'Viskingar och rop' ('Cries and Whispers'), 'Scener ur ett aktenskap' ('Scenes from a Marriage') and 'Herbstsonate' ('Autumn Sonata').

Bergman's work is the cinematic embodiment of the internalized emotional life of the Swedish character and the harsh Scandinavian landscape which helped form it. His work is perhaps most remembered for its visual representation of evil which was greatly influenced by the religious imagery of the rural Swedish churches he knew as a child.

Carl Larsson

Carl Larsson, born in 1853, was a painter who was influenced in Paris by the Barbizon school and his idyllic outdoor scenes are universally known in Sweden. However, he achieved fame not merely as a painter, but as an advocate of a simple, elegant way of life and as a critic of the contemporary world and its bourgeois taste for ostentatious design. Born to a poor family in Stockholm, Larsson found work as a newspaper illustrator before travelling to Paris and on to Grez-sur-Loing in 1882, where he was the central figure in a Scandinavian artists colony that included his wife to be, Karin Bergöö. It was at this time that he ceased to paint in oils and took to light and airy impressionistic water-colours, of which his wife was often the subject. In 1885 the couple returned to Sweden and Larsson taught painting in Gothenburg, at which point art nouveau became a major influence. *Ett Hem* (A Home), Larsson's first book, was published in 1889, and two years later he and his wife moved to the village of Sundborn in the cultural heart of Sweden, Dalarna, where the couple furnished their house with a contrast of traditional artisan and avant garde furniture and decorations. Karin was responsible for much of the interior design, making wallpaper, textiles and rugs and painting the furniture in simple, bright colours. The house, Lilla Hytnäs, was sparsely furnished in comparison to the prevalent style of the times and was simple, yet attractive and functional. It became the background for many of Larsson's paintings and further books, notably *Spardarfvet* (1906) and *Ät Solsidan* (1910) which sold hundreds of thousands of copies in Sweden and abroad, establishing the Larssons' reputations as initiators of 'The Swedish Style', a movement that was to have an impact on interior design the world over throughout the twentieth century. Larsson's water-colours are now almost seen as Swedish national emblems and Lilla Hytnäs is a museum. He died in 1919, 9 years before his wife.

August Strindberg

Strindberg was born in Stockholm in 1849 to a middle class family, a fact he was later to play down. Although he portrayed his childhood as proletarian and unhappy, this was probably not the case and he was able to study at Uppsala University before returning to Stockholm to work in the Royal Library. His earliest literary attempts were largely unsuccessful plays and novels and his first work of significance, the play *Master Olof* (1876), was rejected by theatres until after his reputation had been made. He married the aristocratic actress Siri von Essen in 1877, the first of three unhappy marriages, and in 1879 finally achieved success with his satirical novel *Röda Rummet* (The Red Room). Hailed as the first modern Swedish novel, The Red Room introduced realism to Swedish literature and owed much to Dickens. He continued to write critiques of contemporary society, largely in prose form, and in 1883 moved with his family to France and then Switzerland and wrote the first part of his autobiography in 1886. Strindberg was deeply unhappy and mentally unstable, but continued to write humorous novels such as *Hemsöborna* (1887), before returning to Sweden in 1889. In 1892 he met Edvard Munch in Berlin, with whom he had much in common, especially concerning their psychological insecurity and attitudes to women. The following year he was married again, this relationship lasting only 12 months. He moved to Paris in 1894 and became interested in the occult and alchemy, but was soon to enter a prolific period in which he wrote novels and plays, such as *Inferno*, which were concerned with his own difficulties as well as issues like religion and guilt. In the early twentieth century he also turned to historical dramas and became an advocate of expressionist theatre, founding Intima Teatern in Stockholm with August Falck in 1907. Strindberg wrote a number of other autobiographical works and during his career even turned to painting as a form of expression. He died in 1912, having that year been awarded a state grant to free him of his life long debt.

MAJOR CITIES

The international code for telephoning or faxing Sweden is the code required to dial out of your own country followed by 46.

Stockholm

Population 1·5m. (Greater Stockholm)

There have been settlements in the Stockholm area since the 9th century which survived by way of trade during Viking times, not only with the rest of Scandinavia but also Russia and Europe and trade routes that stretched into Asia. The city is built upon numerous islands around the archipelago that separates Lake Mälaren from the Baltic Sea. The first mention of the city in writing dates back to 1252, and the rapid expansion of Stockholm was due largely to the German hanseatic trade on the Baltic. German influence was great for the next few hundred years, but it was in 1523 when Gustav Vasa was crowned king that the city became Sweden's capital and royal seat. Gustav Vasa also constructed city defences and his immediate successors constructed a royal castle and a number of the city's oldest surviving churches. It was not until 1634 that Stockholm actually became administratively independent, having previously governed by the county of Uppsala. This coincided with the city's rapid expansion, from only 9,000 in 1630 to 43,000 less than half a century later and the construction of new parts of the city that now make up the centre. In 1697 the Royal Castle was burned to the ground and replaced by the structure that still stands today. Gustav III encouraged the cultural growth of the city and the Opera House, theatres and concert halls were built as the city continued to grow in size and importance. The loss of Finland to Russia in 1809 removed Stockholm from its central position in the realm, however, and its importance as a trading centre was thus reduced. The abolition of the guilds in 1846 helped remove the stranglehold on industry, though, and the industrial revolution saw Stockholm once again rise in importance. In 1900 there were over 300,000 inhabitants in the city. In 1912 the Olympic Games were held in Stockholm and the 20th century has seen the city become ever more cosmopolitan. It remains the financial heart of Sweden and the seat of the

Government and the Royal Family, but immigration has given Stockholm a more international feel (15% of greater Stockholm's inhabitants are immigrants). The Nobel Institute is based in the city and the Nobel Prizes (apart from the Peace Prize) are presented in Stockholm every year. Stockholm was the European city of Culture in 1998. There are a total of 10 Royal Castles in the Stockholm area, including the largest Royal Palace still used by a monarch.

Public Transport
Storstockholms Lokaltrafik runs public transport in the city and the surrounding area. The tunnelbana (T) or metro is the most efficient way of getting around and there is a collection of modern art in the blue line stations. T-Centralen is the hub of the network and is connected to the Central Station. Tickets for public transport are valid for 1 hour after validation and the number of coupons used for each journey is one more than the zones travelled through. SL Tourist Cards and the Stockholm Card give unlimited use of public transport and entry to some attractions and museums. Buses in the centre converge on Sergels Torg and there are accurate timetables at each bus stop.
Storstockholms Lokaltrafik's information office is located in T-Centralen (Tel: (0)8 686-1197)
    Taxis are generally expensive but can be hailed anywhere or picked up at taxi ranks throughout the city.

Landmarks
Gamla Stan
Gamla Stan, on the island at the geographical centre of the city, is Stockholm's historic centre (rather than the modern financial and commercial centre on Norrmalm), and the winding narrow streets appear to have changed little since medieval times. Most of Stockholm's oldest buildings and churches are in Gamla Stan and the Royal Palace is on the north side of the island.

Royal Palace

The Royal Palace has 608 rooms, a large number of which can be viewed by the public in the summer. The Palace is home to the Royal Apartments, the Royal Armoury and the Royal Treasury, where the crown jewels are kept. The Palace was originally decorated in Baroque and Rococo styles and has been added to and altered ever since. The exterior, designed by Tessin, is not particularly impressive, but there is a fine Rococo chapel.

Skansen

In the Djurgården, Skansen was the world's first ever open-air museum and is in fact the site of a collection of small museums and attractions founded in 1891 by Artur Hazelius. In the summer there are Swedish folk dancing displays and there are historical buildings from all parts of Sweden.

Hotels

The Grand Hotel is Stockholm's most luxurious and central hotel. Grand Hotel, Södra Blasieholmshamnen 8, Box 16424, 10327 Stockholm. Tel: (0)8 679-3550 Fax: (0)8 611-8686

Museums and Art Galleries

Nationalmuseum

The Nationalmuseum holds come 12,500 paintings and sculptures by European and Swedish artists. The collection includes paintings by Rembrandt and Watteau and a number of French impressionists as well as a large collection of Russian icons. Swedish artists from the 16th to 19th centuries are well represented.

Södra Blasieholmen, 10324 Stockholm

Tel: (0)8 5195-4300 Fax: (0)8 5195-4450

Web: www.nationalmuseum.se

Moderna Museet

Moderna Museet was reopened in 1998 in a new building designed by Rafael Moneo on the island of Skeppsholmen in central

Stockholm. The collection includes a wide variety of 20th century art, sculpture, photography and film including paintings by Picasso and Matisse and a good representation of modern Swedish artists.

Box 16382, 10327 Stockholm

Tel: (0)8 5195-5200

Web: www.modernamuseet.se

Opera House

Kungliga Operan

The Royal Opera House was founded in 1773 and is the home of Sweden's national operatic and ballet companies.

Jacobs Torg 4, Stockholm

Tel: (0)8 791-4300

Web: www.kungligaoperan.se

Theatres

Riksteatern is the National Theatre company and has toured Sweden with a variety of performances for over 60 years. The oldest theatre in Sweden, Södra Teatern in Stockholm is one of many stages that Riksteatern perform on and is a part of the National Theatre Company.

Riksteatern, 14583 Norsborg

Tel: (0)8 5319-9100 Fax: (0)8 5318-3102

Web: www.riksteatern.se

Södra Teatern, Mosebacke Torg 1–3, Stockholm

Tel: (0)8 644-9900

Gothenburg (Göteborg)

Population 500,000

Gothenburg is Sweden's second largest city and after greater Stockholm, Gothenburg and the surrounding area is the most densely populated part of Sweden. The area has been populated since c.1000 and during the middle ages there was a healthy trade centre in the area, but present day Gothenburg was founded by Gustav II Adolf in 1619. The town quickly became important in trade with the Netherlands, England, Scotland and Germany as well as the rest of Scandinavia and quickly grew in importance, becoming a bishops' seat in 1665. The royal residence followed in 1700 and in the following century Gothenburg became an administrative centre for the whole of western Sweden and an important port for the export of Swedish iron and timber. In 1731 the Ostindiska (East-Indian) company was founded, boosting trade, and the fishing industry also became Sweden's largest. The 1800s saw ever closer ties with England and with the industrial revolution further expansion. By the 20th century, Gothenburg was the most important city for Swedish export and its position as an industrial heartland was secured when the city became the centre for Sweden's engineering businesses. www.gothenburg.se

Gothenburg Tourist Office

Kungsportsplatsen 2

Tel: (0)31 100740)

Web: www.gbg-co.se

Landmarks

Liseberg

Liseberg is Sweden's largest amusement park and is dominated by Spaceport Liseberg, a ride that takes you 80 metres above the ground with a stunning view of the city. There are also gardens and other attractions. Liseberg is open in the summer only.

Konstmuseet

The Konstmuseet collection (on Götaplatsen) is impressive, with works by major European artists such as Picasso, Van Gogh and Rembrandt.

SOCIAL STATISTICS

Statistics for calendar years:

	Total living births	To mothers single, divorced or widowed	Stillborn	Marriages	Divorces	Deaths exclusive of still-born
1996	95,297	51,348	330	33,484	21,612	94,133
1997	90,502	48,945	314	32,313	21,470	93,326
1998	89,028	48,658	306	31,598	21,187	93,271

Rates, 1998, per 1,000 population: births, 10·1; deaths, 10·5; marriages, 3·6. Sweden has the highest rate of births outside marriage in Europe, at nearly 55% in 1998. In 1998 the most popular age range for marrying was 25–29 for women and 30–34 for men. Expectation of life in 1997: males, 76·3 years; females, 80·8. Infant mortality, 1998, 3·5 per 1,000 live births (the lowest rate of any country). Fertility rate, 1998, 1·5 births per woman. In 1998 Sweden received 13,000 asylum applications, equivalent to 1·48 per 1,000 inhabitants.

Statistiska centralbyrån

PO Box 24300, 10451 Stockholm.
Tel: (0)8 783-4000
Web site: www.scb.se

CLIMATE

The north has severe winters, with snow lying for 4–7 months. Summers are fine but cool, with long daylight hours. Further south, winters are less cold, summers are warm and rainfall well distributed

throughout the year, although slightly higher in the summer.
Stockholm, Jan. 0·4°C, July 17·2°C. Annual rainfall 385 mm.

CONSTITUTION AND GOVERNMENT

The reigning King is **Carl XVI Gustaf**, b. 30 April 1946, succeeded
on the death of his grandfather Gustaf VI Adolf, 15 Sept. 1973,
married 19 June 1976 to Silvia Renate Sommerlath, b. 23 Dec. 1943
(Queen of Sweden). *Daughter* and *Heir Apparent:* Crown Princess
Victoria Ingrid Alice Désirée, Duchess of Västergötland, b. 14 July
1977; *son:* Prince Carl Philip Edmund Bertil, Duke of Värmland,
b. 13 May 1979; *daughter:* Princess Madeleine Thérèse Amelie
Josephine, Duchess of Hälsingland and Gästrikland, b. 10 June
1982. *Sisters of the King.* Princess Margaretha, b. 31 Oct. 1934,
married 30 June 1964 to John Ambler; Princess Birgitta (Princess of
Sweden), b. 19 Jan. 1937, married 25 May 1961 (civil marriage) and
30 May 1961 (religious ceremony) to Johann Georg, Prince of
Hohenzollern; Princess Désirée, b. 2 June 1938, married 5 June
1964 to Baron Niclas Silfverschiöld; Princess Christina, b. 3 Aug.
1943, married 15 June 1974 to Tord Magnuson. *Uncles of the King.*
Count Sigvard Bernadotte of Wisborg, b. on 7 June 1907; Count Carl
Johan, Bernadotte of Wisborg, b. on 31 Oct. 1916. *Aunt of the King.*
Queen Ingrid (Princess of Sweden, Dowager Queen of Denmark),
b. 28 March 1910, married 24 May 1935 to Frederik, Crown Prince of
Denmark (King Frederik IX), died 14 Jan. 1972.

Under the 1975 Constitution Sweden is a representative and
parliamentary democracy. The King is Head of State, but does not
participate in government. Parliament is the single-chamber *Riksdag*
of 349 members elected for a period of 4 years in direct, general
elections.

The manner of election to the *Riksdag* is proportional. The country is divided into 29 constituencies. In these constituencies 310 members are elected. The remaining 39 seats constitute a nationwide pool intended to give absolute proportionality to parties that receive at least 4% of the votes. A party receiving less than 4% of the votes in the country is, however, entitled to participate in the distribution of seats in a constituency, if it has obtained at least 12% of the votes cast there.

A parliament, the *Sameting*, was instituted for the Sami (Lapps) in 1993.

National Anthem

'Du gamla, du fria' ('Thou ancient, thou free'); words by R. Dybeck; folk-tune.

RECENT ELECTIONS

At the elections of 20 Sept. 1998 turn-out was 81·4%. A total of 5,374,588 votes were cast of which 5,261,122 were valid votes. The Social Democratic Party (SDP) won 131 seats with 36·4% of votes cast (162 with 45·3% in 1994), the Moderate Party 82 with 22·9% (80 with 22·4%), the Left Party (ex-Communists) 43 with 12·0% (22 with 6·2%), the Christian Democratic Party 42 with 11·8% (14 with 4·1%), the Centre Party 18 with 5·1% (27 with 7·7%), the Liberal Party 17 with 4·7% (26 with 7·2%) and the Green Party 16 with 4·5% (18 with 5%). Of the 349 Members of Parliament there are 200 men (57·3%) and 149 women (42·7%), the highest percentage of women for any parliament in the world.

European Parliament. Sweden has 22 representatives. At the June 1999 elections turn-out was 38·3%. The Social Democratic Party won

6 seats with 26·1% of votes cast (group in European Parliament: Party of European Socialists); the Moderate Party, 5 with 20·6% (European People's Party); V (Far Left), 3 with 15·8% (Confederal Group of the European United Left/Nordic Green Left); the Liberal Party, 3 with 13·8% (Liberal, Democrat and Reform Party); MP, 2 with 9·4% (Greens); the Christian Democratic Party, 2 with 7·7% (European People's Party); the Centre Party, 1 with 6·0% (Liberal, Democrat and Reform Party).

CURRENT ADMINISTRATION

A minority Social Democratic government was formed in Oct. 1998, which comprised in March 2000:

Prime Minister: Göran Persson (b. 1949; sworn in 21 March 1996).

Deputy Prime Minister: Lena Hjelm-Wallén.

Minister of Justice: Laila Freivalds. *Foreign Affairs:* Anna Lindh. *Agriculture and Lapp Affairs:* Margareta Winberg. *Culture:* Marita Ulvskog. *Defence:* Björn von Sydow. *Education:* Thomas Östros. *Environment:* Kjell Larsson. *Finance:* Bosse Ringholm. *Social Affairs:* Lars Engqvist. *Trade and Industry:* Björn Rosengren.

The *Speaker* is Birgitta Dahl.

LOCAL GOVERNMENT

The country is divided into 21 counties *(län)* subdivided into 288 municipalities, each with an elected council. The government appoints a Governor to each county who is chair of a 14-member board, elected from the county by the county council for a 4-year period.

Gotland consists of only one municipality. The parishes, 2,528 in 1997, are the local units of the Swedish Lutheran Church and have the same status as municipalities. The publicly elected parochial church council is the supreme decision-making body in larger parishes. Small parishes have the parish meeting, a form of direct democracy.

Regional and local elections took place simultaneously with the parliamentary elections on 20 Sept. 1998.

DEFENCE

The Supreme Commander is, under the government, in command of the 3 services. He is assisted by the Swedish Armed Forces HQ.

There is conscription of 7–15 months for males. Females have the possibility to serve on a voluntary basis.

In 1998 military expenditure totalled US$5,536m. (US$623 per capita, the highest in non-NATO Europe), representing 2·5% of GDP. Sweden's national security policy is currently undergoing a shift in emphasis. Beginning with the decommissioning of obselete units and structures, the main thrust of policy is the creation of contingency forces adaptable to a variety of situations.

The government stressed that Sweden's membership of the EU (in 1995) did not imply any change in Sweden's traditional policy of non-participation in military alliances, 'with the aim of making it possible to be neutral in the event of war in Sweden's vicinity'.

Sweden is equipped with modern air raid shelters with capacity for some 7m. people. Since this is short of the full population evacuation and relocation operations would be necessary in the event of war.

Preparations for 'psychological defence' in wartime have also been made. It is headed by the National Board of Psychological Defence whose main task is to safeguard the free, undisrupted transmission of news 'regarded in Sweden as the best possible antidote to the enemy propaganda, disinformation and rumour-mongering that can be expected in war'.

Army

The peacetime Army consists for training purposes of 38 mechanized, cavalry, infantry, artillery and other units. Army strength, 1999, 19,300 (11,800 conscripts). The Army can mobilize a reserve of 350,000.

Navy

Naval forces are divided between 2 branches: the Fleet and Coastal Artillery. There are 4 Naval Command Areas, covering the coast area surrounding Sweden. The fleet includes 9 diesel submarines.

The personnel of the Navy in 1999 totalled 16,800 including a coastal defence force, a Naval Air Wing and 3,700 conscripts. The Navy can mobilize about 45,000 reserves.

Air Force

Combat aircraft include JAS 39 Gripens, JA 37 Viggens and AJS 37 Viggens.

Strength (1999) 6,000 (2,500 conscripts), with approximately 253 combat aircraft. The Air Force can mobilize about 70,000.

During peacetime all the helicopters of the Army, Navy and Air Force are organized into a joint Helicopter Wing with a staff and 4 helicopter battalions.

INTERNATIONAL RELATIONS

Sweden is a member of the UN, NATO Partnership for Peace, BIS, OECD, EU, Council of Europe, OSCE, CERN, Nordic Council, Council of Baltic Sea States, Inter-American Development Bank, Asian Development Bank, IOM and the Antarctic Treaty. Sweden is a signatory to the Schengen Accord, which abolishes border controls between Austria, Belgium, Denmark, Finland, France, Germany, Greece, Iceland, Italy, Luxembourg, the Netherlands, Norway, Portugal, Spain and Sweden.

ECONOMY

After suffering heavily in the late 1980s and early 1990s, the Swedish economy is now once again relatively healthy. Sweden was long famed for high taxes, high standards of living, low unemployment and an unrivalled social welfare system, but this is no longer quite the case. Taxes have come down, standards of living are still relatively good and the Swedes are unwilling to let their social welfare net be reduced further, but unemployment was for a number of years extremely high before falling to the level of around 6·5% today. The future looks reasonably bright, with the Krona now stable after losing much of its value in the early 1990s and economic controls seem to have been proved successful. Adult education schemes have done much to re-educate those made redundant and the economy is growing at a steady rate. Youth unemployment does, however, remain a problem at over 11%. This figure should fall a little in the coming years, as it is predicted to do for all age groups, and the economy is set to continue its growth. State controls are not what they once were, and deregulation of many public utilities has been introduced, very successfully, for example, in the telecoms industry. Although Sweden is not one of the Euro zone countries, it may well join soon and the economic conditions that this would place on the currency should not be a problem. Inflation is low, cutbacks in benefits have boosted the economy significantly and although the bill for the welfare system does still make up a high proportion of government spending, this now looks sustainable. Exports are important for the Swedish economy and although the crises in Asia and Russia had an effect, this was largely offset at the time by increased demand at home. The major industries are engineering, which accounts for almost half of the entire industrial output, two thirds of which is exported, the automobile industry, which makes up 13% of Swedish exports, and modern technologies such as telecommunications and information technology. Sweden is also one of only a few smaller nations to have its own established aviation industry.

Whatever happens elsewhere in Scandinavia, an economic boom can be confidently predicted for the Öresund region. In July 2000 a new link will open between Copenhagen and Malmö. For the first time, it will be possible to cross the stretch of water between Denmark and Sweden in a matter of ten minutes. The achievement outranks the Channel tunnel as a feat of engineering. The 16-kilometre route consists of a tunnel, an artificial island four kilometres long and a bridge incorporating one high bridge and two lower approach bridges. The acceleration in communication will be all the more impressive for offering road and rail services. Infrastructure improvements on both sides of the water include new motorways and huge building projects. Malmö will have a city tunnel and Copenhagen a state-of-the-art light railway. Leading companies are expected to choose the region for their northern European headquarters.

Services accounted for 67% of GDP in 1997, industry 31% and agriculture 2%.

According to the anti-corruption organization *Transparency International*, Sweden ranked equal 3rd in the world in a survey of the countries with the least corruption in business and government. It received 9·4 out of 10 in the annual index published in 1999.

Performance

Real GDP growth was 1·3% in 1996, 1·8% in 1997 and 2·6% in 1998, with a forecast of growth of 3·6% in 1999 and 3·0% in 2000.

The OECD reported in 1999 that 'Overall, the improvement in economic performance . . . has continued and the short-term outlook is favourable. Firm control of inflation has established the credibility of monetary policy, which, in turn, has effectively anchored inflation expectations. Underlying these favourable trends is the successful completion of the fiscal consolidation process, which has brought public finances back into surplus. Product-market competition, though incomplete, has been significantly extended. The longer-run supply potential of the economy has been enhanced. But restoring the position of Sweden in terms of GDP per capita requires further substantial action, to complete regulatory reform, modify transfers and reduce labour and capital taxes, subject to the overriding requirement of a sustained structural budget surplus. Such action is needed to improve incentives to work, seek education and invest. The long-term pay-off to employment creation and capital formation would be substantial. The benign climate now emerging may be politically less favourable to reforms than the situation of macroeconomic imbalance that characterized the mid-1990s insofar as there is less urgency. But the return to macroeconomic balance should actually be seen as providing the opportunity for implementing further structural reforms at a relatively low short-term cost, while serving to realise the country's full economic potential in the longer term.'

In 1998 the state debt amounted to 1,448,861m. kr.

Budget

Revenue and expenditure of the total budget (Current and Capital) for financial years ending 30 June (in 1m. kr.):

	1996–97	1997–98	1998–99
Revenue	648,928	706,314	715,217
Expenditure	655,156	696,652	649,312

Revenue and expenditure for 1999 (1,000 kr.):

Revenue	
Taxes on income	39,943
Tax on income–legal entities	72,868
Other revenue	5,246
Social security fees	227,183
Estate tax	27,840
Other taxes on property	11,611
VAT	162,625
Excise duties	79,498
Compensation for municipalities and county councils	20,525
Income from government activities	32,131
Income from sale of assets	15,001
Loans repaid	3,135
Computed revenue	5,300
Contributions, etc., from the EU	10,241
Total revenue	696,368

Expenditure	
The Swedish political system	4,180
Economy and fiscal administration	1,705
Tax administration and collection	5,811
Justice	21,919
Foreign policy administration andinternational co-operation	2,871
Total defence	44,108
International development assistance	11,900

Immigrants and refugees	4,324
Health care, medical care, social services	24,012
Financial security in the event of illness and disability	80,503
Financial security in old age	34,315
Financial security for families and children	39,896
Financial security in the event of unemployment	33,789
The labour market and working life	48,274
Study support	22,447
Education and university research	29,031
Culture, the media, religious organizations and leisure	7,452
Planning, housing supply and construction	20,463
Regional balance and development	2,743
General environment and conservation	1,549
Energy	1,681
Communications	25,501
Agriculture and forestry, fisheries, etc.	11,974
Business sector	2,898
General grants to municipalities	103,565
Interest on Central Government Debt, etc.	84,560
Contribution to the European Community	21,908
Total Expenditure	680,368

VAT is 25% (reduced rate, 12%). In 1998 tax revenues were 53·0% of GDP.

Currency

The unit of currency is the *krona* (SEK), of 100 *öre*. Inflation was –0·6% in Dec. 1998, and by Dec. 1999 stood at 1·2%. Foreign exchange reserves were US$18,001m. and gold reserves 5·96m. troy oz in Jan. 2000.

Banking and Finance

The central bank and bank of issue is the *Sveriges Riksbank*. The bank has 11 trustees, elected by parliament, and is managed by a directorate, including the governor, appointed by the trustees. The *governor* is Urban Bäckström, appointed for 6 years. On 31 Dec. 1998 there were 41 commercial banks. Their total deposits amounted to 946,884m. kr.; advances to the public amounted to 902,689m. kr. On 31 Dec. 1997 there were 85 savings banks. The largest banks are Svenska Handelsbanken, MeritaNordbanken (formed in 1997 when Nordbanken of Sweden merged with Merita of Finland), Förenings-Sparbanken and Skandinavska Enskilda Banken.

Banks

Riksbanken (Central Bank of Sweden)

The main issuing bank in Sweden is an independent institution. Its position with regard to the government was confirmed with a new act of parliament that came into force on 1 Jan. 1999, bringing Sweden into line with the conditions stipulated in the Maastricht treaty. The Central Bank sets interest rates and makes decisions with regard to monetary policy.

Brunkebergstorg 11, 10337 Stockholm

Tel: (0)8 787-0000

Web: www.riksbank.se

Svenska Bankföreningen

(Swedish Bankers' Association)

Regeringsgatan 38, PO Box 7603, 10394 Stockholm

Tel: (0)8 453-4400 Fax: (0)8 796-9395

Nordbanken

Nordbanken is a part of the Merita Nordbanken group, which has more than 6·5m private customers and 400,000 commercial

customers and is the largest banking group in the Nordic area.
Merita Nordbanken has over 1m. Internet Banking users and the
largest telephone banking service in Sweden.
Drottninggatan 4, Box 16081
10322 Stockholm
Web: www.nb.se, www.meritanordbanken.com

ForeningsSparbanken (Swedbank)
Foreningsbanken and Sparbanken Sverige merged in 1997 following
their individual foundations, both in 1992, out of many of Sweden's
local and savings banks.
Brunkebergstorg 8, 10534 Stockholm
Tel: (0)8 585-9000
Web: www.foreningssparbanken.se

Skandinaviska Enskilda Banken
Sergels Torg 2, 10640 Stockholm
Tel: (0)8 763-5000 Fax: 205408
Web: www.seb.se

Stock Exchange
Stockholm's Fondbörs
is Sweden's only stock exchange and was founded in 1863. It was
made a company in 1993 and merged with the Swedish derivatives
exchange in 1998. The Stockholm Exchange and the Copenhagen
Stock Exchange have signed the NOREX agreement to create a
common Nordic securities market and the SAX2000 trading system
has in 1999 enabled trading of Danish shares on the Swedish
exchange and vice versa.
Börshuset, Källargränd 2, Box 1256, 11182 Stockholm
Tel: (0)8 613-8800
Web: www.xsse.se

Business Centres

Kommerskollegium

(Board of Commerce), Drottninggatan 89, 11386 Stockholm

Tel: (0)8 690-4800

Chambers of Commerce

Sweden

Federation of Swedish Chambers of Commerce, PO Box 16050,
10322 Stockholm.

Tel: (0)8 555-10000

Web: www.ci.se

British-Swedish Chamber of Commerce

Jakobs Torg 3, PO Box 16050, 10321 Stockholm

UK

Swedish Chamber of Commerce for the UK, 73 Welbeck Street,
London W1M 7HA.

Tel: (0)20 7486 4545 Fax: (0)20 7935 5487

E-mail: link@swedish-chamber.org.uk

Web site: www.swednet.org.uk

USA

The Swedish-American Chamber of Commerce of the US
(Nationwide Secretariat), 599 Lexington Avenue, Suite 1204,
New York, NY 10022

Tel: 212 838-5530 Fax: 212 755-7953

E-mail: business.services@saccny.org

Germany

Schwedische Handelskammer in der BRD, Berliner Allee 32, 40212
Düsseldorf

Tel: (0)211 320-014 Fax: (0)211 324-488

France

Chambre de Commerce Suédoise en France, 67 Boulevard Hausmann, 75081 Paris

Tel: (0)1 42-66-05-85 Fax: (0)1 42-66-63-04

Trade Associations

Exportrådet

(The Swedish Trade Council) is mostly involved in aiding Swedish companies and exporters abroad.

Sweden

Storgatan 19, Box 5513, 11485 Stockholm

Tel: (0)8 783-8500

Web site: www.swedishtrade.se

England

73 Welbeck Street, London W1M 8AN

Tel: (0)20 7935 9601 Fax: (0)20 7935 4130

E-mail: swed-info@swedishtrade.org.uk

USA

150 N. Michigan Avenue, Suite 1200

Chicago, IL 60601

Tel: (312) 781-6222 Fax: (312) 346-0683

Website: www.swedentrade.com

Invest in Sweden Agency (ISA)

is a government supported agency aiming to attract businesses to and investment in Sweden.

Tel: (0) 402-7800 Fax: (0)8 402-7878

E-mail: isa@isa.se Web site: www.isa.se

Weights and Measures

The metric system is obligatory.

ENERGY AND NATURAL RESOURCES

Environmental Policies

A new Environmental Code (Miljöbalken) came into effect on 1 Jan. 1999, which places strict environmental controls on businesses and individuals. A guiding principle is that environmental damage must be paid for by the organization responsible for causing it. Furthermore, there are five Environmental Courts with jurisdiction to fine organizations for negligence or breach of laws and to grant permits to operate in environmentally protected areas. The environmental impact of any large-scale project must be taken into account at the earliest stages of planning. Detailed goals and strategies are now being drawn up by environmental agencies and local authorities with respect to the new code and will be published early in the new millennium. Recycling is constantly being encouraged and it is now an obligation to recycle materials as far as possible. A returnable deposit must legally be paid on all bottles to stimulate recycling programmes and the recycling of packing materials is the responsibility of the manufacturer. In 1999 government spending on environmental incentives and improvements was expected to total 8bn. kr. Around 15% of Sweden's energy supply comes from Hydro-electricity and 15 nuclear reactors provide the same amount. A long-standing commitment to phase out nuclear power by 2010 has been postponed.

Electricity

Sweden is rich in hydro-power resources. Installed capacity was 34,536 MW in 1997, of which 16,462 MW was in hydro-electric plants, 10,083 MW in nuclear plants and 7,869 MW in thermal plants. Electricity production in 1996 was 135,192m. kWh; consumption per capita was 16,423 kWh. A referendum of 1980 called for the phasing out of nuclear power by 2010. In Feb. 1997 the government began denuclearization by designating one of the 10 reactors for decommissioning. The state corporation Vattenfall was given the responsibility of financing and overseeing the transition to the use of non-fossil fuel alternatives.

Minerals

Sweden is a leading producer of iron ore. There are also deposits of copper, lead, zinc and alum shale containing oil and uranium. Iron ore produced, 1996, 20·3m. tonnes; copper ore, 1994, 297,999 tonnes.

Agriculture

In 1998 the total area of land given over to farms of 2 ha or more was 7,916,607 ha; of this 2,783,755 was arable land; 448,855 natural pasture; 3,928,340 forest; and 755,657 other. Of the land used for arable farming, 2–5 ha holdings covered a total area of 51,681 ha; 5·1–10 ha holdings covered 124,320 ha; 10·1–20 ha, 256,710; 20·1–30 ha, 243,919; 30·1–50 ha, 464,441; 50·1–100 ha, 775,465 and holdings larger than 100 ha covered 867,220 ha. There were 90,488 agricultural enterprises in 1996 compared to 150,014 in 1971 and 282,187 in 1951. Around 40% of the enterprises were between 5 and 20 ha.

Agriculture accounts for 5·8% of exports and 7·9% of imports. The agricultural sector employs 3% of the workforce.

Chief crops	Area (1,000 ha)			Production (1,000 tonnes)		
	1996	1997	1998	1996	1997	1998
Wheat	334·6	344·2	398·0	2,029·9	2,056·2	2,248·7
Rye	33·6	29·4	34·6	165·7	138·7	160·5
Barley	468·6	482·9	445·0	2,113·4	2,086·3	1,686·9
Oats	283·6	315·5	311·5	1,199·8	1,274·3	1,136·2
Potatoes	36·6	35·8	33·7	853·2	874·3	792·5
Sugarbeet	59·2	60·5	58·7	2,430·0	2,639·1	2,570·8
Ley	772·4	746·8	742·1	3,365·2	3,202·8	. . .
Oil linseed	72·8	. . .	. . .	9·9	12·2	6·4

Milk production (in 1,000 tonnes) 1998 (1997): 3,331 (3,334); butter production: 53 (59); cheese: 125 (118).

Livestock 1998: cattle, 1,738,500; sheep and lambs, 421,200; pigs, 2,286,050; poultry, 7,516,450. There were 238,567 reindeer in Sami villages in 1997. Harvest of moose during open season 1998: 101,930.

Forestry

Forests form one of the country's greatest natural assets. The growing stock includes 46% Norway spruce, 36% Scots pine, 12% birch and 6% other. In the period 1993–97 forests covered 22,621,000 ha (55% of the land area). Public ownership accounts for 9·4% of the forests, limited companies own 39·8% and the remaining 50·7% is in private hands. Of the 60·6m. cu. metres of wood felled in 1998, 31·5m. cu. metres were sawlogs, 22·2m. cu. metres pulpwood, 5·9m. cu. metres fuelwood and 0·9 cu. metres other.

Fisheries

In 1998 the total catch was 402,841 tonnes, worth 1,048m. kr.

INDUSTRY

Manufacturing is mainly based on metals and forest resources. Chemicals (especially petro-chemicals), building materials and decorative glass and china are also important.

Industry groups	No. of establishments 1996	Average no. of wage-earners 1996	Sales value of production (gross) in 1m. kr. 1996
Mines and quarries	149	5,328	9,780
Manufacturing industry	8,707	405,790	931,782
Food products, beverages and tobacco	842	41,518	102,694

Textiles and textile products, leather and leather products	270	8,450	9,765
Wood and wood products	714	23,747	41,015
Pulp, paper and paper products, publishers and printers	1,197	54,253	132,481
Coke, refined petroleum products and nuclear fuel	16	1,228	26,373
Chemicals, chemical products and man-made fibres	317	14,339	65,778
Rubber and plastic products	407	15,656	23,115
Other non-metallic mineral products	357	11,543	16,234
Basic metals	159	23,913	67,848
Fabricated metal products, machinery and equipment	4,018	196,655	427,358
Other manufacturing industries	410	14,488	19,116

Ten largest engineering companies, 1997

Name	Sales (bn. kr.)	Foreign sales (%)
Volvo	183·6	89
Ericsson	167·7	94
Svedala Industri	135·9	92
Electrolux	113·0	95
SKF	36·9	94
ABB Sverige	34·5	54
Sandvik	34·1	93
Scania	33·7	95
Atlas Copco	30·0	96
Saab Automobile	22·3	81

Labour

In 1998 there were 3,979,000 persons in the labour force, employed as follows: 770,000 in health and social work; 803,000 in manufacturing, mining, quarrying, electricity and water services; 774,000 in trade and communication; 466,000 in financial services and business activities; 323,000 in education, research and development; 310,000 in personal services and cultural activities, and sanitation; 208,000 in public administration; 102,000 in agriculture, forestry and fishing. The unemployment rate in 1998 was 6·5%. In 1998, 73·5% of men and 69·4% of women between the ages of 15 and 64 were in employment. No other major industrialized nation has such a small gap between the employment rates of the sexes.

Trade Unions

At 31 Dec. 1998 the Swedish Trade Union Confederation (LO) had 19 member unions with a total membership of 2,093,726; the Central Government Organization of Salaried Employees (TCO) had 20, with 1,233,448; the Swedish Confederation of Professional Associations (SACO) had 26, with 461,958; the Central Organization of Swedish Workers had 8,446 members.

In March 1997 employers' organizations and trade unions signed an agreement on the conduct of wage negotiations in 1998. The agreement involved 0·8m. workers, and provided for the establishment of an Industrial Committee to promote the development of industry.

Landsorganisationen (LO)

This is the umbrella organization for 19 affiliated Swedish trades unions and has some 2·1m. members, of whom nearly 1m. are women and 1·17m. work in the private sector.
Barnhusgatan 18, 10553 Stockholm
Tel: (0)8 796-2500

Centralorganisationen (SACO/SR)
The Swedish Confederation of Professional Associations has over 460,000 members and is politically independent.
Lilla Nygatan 14, Box 2206, 10315 Stockholm

Tjänstemännens Centralorganisation (TCO)
Central Organization of Salaried Employees has 20 affiliates with more than 1·2m. members
Linnégatan 14, 11494 Stockholm
Tel: (0)8 782-9100

Employers' Associations
Svenska Arbetsgivareföreningen (SAF)
The Swedish Employers' Confederation is made up of 39 employers' associations which have a total of 43,000 companies as members.
S. Blasieholmshamnen 4A, 10330 Stockholm
Tel: (0)8 762-6000

INTERNATIONAL TRADE

Imports and Exports
Imports and exports (in 1m. kr.):

	1994	1995	1996	1997	1998
Imports	399,152	460,578	448,739	501,098	542,160
Exports	471,602	567,836	569,167	632,709	673,091

Breakdown by Standard International Trade Classification (SITC, revision 3) categories (value in 1m. kr.; 1998 figures are estimates):

| | Imports | | Exports | |
	1997	1998	1997	1998
0. Food and live animals	29,127	30,602	14,524	14,177
1. Beverages and tobacco	3,932	4,520	2,081	2,305
2. Raw materials	15,573	16,313	41,322	38,091
3. Fuels and lubricants	38,608	28,217	16,281	12,313
4. Animal and vegetable oils	1,466	1,460	1,016	1,032
5. Chemicals	50,251	53,951	55,643	60,534
6. Manufactured materials	72,817	76,873	136,289	139,754
7. Machinery and transport equipment	207,138	229,073	300,990	331,768
8. Manufactured items	62,721	68,801	52,433	54,566
9. Other	83	62	941	832

Principal exports in 1998 (in tonnes): paper and board, 4,988,771; lumber, sawn and planed, 10,985,000 sq. metres; power-generating non-electrical machinery, 16,805; chemical wood pulp, 2,542,010; newsprint, 2,269,787; mechanical handling equipment, 156,931; flat-rolled products of iron, 1,304,128; pumps and centrifuges, 60,011.

Imports and exports by countries (in 1m. kr.):

| | Imports from | | Exports to | |
	1997	1998	1997	1998
Belgium	18,625	20,420	25,502	30,333
Denmark	36,181	33,226	38,859	39,322
Finland	26,308	26,770	33,791	34,942
France	28,709	31,939	29,060	33,344
Germany	92,507	96,661	70,042	73,617
Italy	15,212	17,198	20,050	24,122
Netherlands	38,208	41,431	35,186	38,546
Norway	38,453	38,810	52,906	57,556
Switzerland	8,240	8,669	10,288	11,559
UK	49,199	52,087	57,975	59,914
USA	29,863	31,723	52,395	57,740

Business Fairs

A full list of business and trade fairs, which change regularly, can be found on the Industrilitteratur website.
www.industrilitteratur.se

COMMUNICATIONS

Roads

In 1997 there were 210,760 km of roads comprising: main roads, 14,615 km; secondary roads, 83,447 km; other roads, 112,698 km. A total of 77·2% were surfaced. There were also 1,428 km of motorway. Motor vehicles in 1998 included 3,792,000 passenger cars, 338,000 lorries, 15,000 buses and 285,000 motorcycles and mopeds.

Sweden, along with the United Kingdom, has the lowest death rates in road accidents of any industrialized country, at less than 6 deaths per 100,000 people.

Rules of the Road

Driving in Sweden is on the right-hand side of the road. The wearing of seatbelts is compulsory in the front seats and, if fitted, in the back. Dipped headlights must be used by all vehicles at all times. Helmets must be worn by motorcycle and moped drivers. Strict drink-drive laws are enforced with fines or imprisonment for those over the limit of 0·02% alcohol in the bloodstream. Service stations are often open 24 hours and mostly accept credit cards. Petrol on sale is generally unleaded. Studded or snow tyres may be needed in winter although they are not compulsory. Maximum speeds, unless otherwise indicated, are 110 kph on motorways, 90 kph on other roads and 50 kph in built up areas.

Rail

Total length of railways at 31 Dec. 1998 was 10,998 km (7,614 km electrified). The state railway operator SJ carried 111m. passengers and 29m. tonnes of freight in 1998. Some lines are run under contract by private operators. There is a metro in Stockholm (108 km), and tram/light rail networks in Stockholm, Göteborg (81 km) and Norrköping.

Direct trains from Sweden can be caught to Norway, the main routes being to Oslo and Trondheim (via Storlien) or in the north to either Norway or Finland, although some northern routes may not run all year round. There are also rail links to Denmark and Germany (Copenhagen and Berlin, via Helsingborg-Helsingør and Trelleborg-Sassnitz respectively) when trains run directly onto ferries. The Öresund rail and road bridge between Denmark and Sweden, to open early in the millennium, will create a new route to Denmark.

Swedish Railways (Statens Järnvägen)
10550 Stockholm
Tel: (0)8 696-7540
Web site: www.sj.se

Civil Aviation

Sweden's busiest airport is Arlanda, north of Stockholm and also close to Uppsala. Both buses and trains (including a new high speed rail link) run from the airport to Stockholm city centre (Central Station). There is also an airport at Nyköping, south of Stockholm, where some flights from England may arrive, and a more central airport at Bromma which is used mainly for domestic and Scandinavian destinations. Gothenburg's Landvetter airport has some European flights and other main cities and towns also have their own airports, but for most international flights, travellers will have to change at Arlanda or Copenhagen.

Scandinavian Airlines System (SAS) was established in 1946 as a consortium of Norway, Denmark and Sweden's national airlines, SAS is the biggest airline in Scandinavia and the fourth largest in Europe. SAS flies around 21m. passengers a year and collaborates with Lufthansa and United Airlines amongst others in an integrated network called Star Alliance. SAS has a joint paid-up capital of 14,241m. Sw. kr. Capitalization of SAS Sverige AB, 5,560m. Sw. kr., of which 50% is owned by the government and 50% by private enterprises.

In 1997, the total distance flown was 109·0m. km; passenger-km, 8,893·7m.; goods, 294·7m. tonne-km. These figures represent the Swedish share of the SAS traffic (Swedish domestic and three-sevenths of international traffic). Malmö Aviation and Skyways AB, both Sweden-based carriers, operate some international as well as domestic flights. In 1998 services were also provided by Aer Lingus, Aeroflot, Air Baltic, Air Canada, Air China, Air Express, Air France, Air Lithuania, Air Malta, Air Ukraine, Airborne of Sweden, Alitalia, American Airlines, Austrian Airlines, Balkan, Belavia, Braathens, British Airways, Continental Airlines, Croatia Airlines, Czech Airlines, Delta Air Lines, Deutsche BA, Egyptair, El Al, Estonia Air, Falcon Air, Finnair, Flying Enterprise, Guard Air, Iberia, Icelandair, Interimpex-Avioimpex, Iran Air, JAT, Kenya Airways, KLM, KLM UK, Lithuanian Airlines, LOT, Lufthansa, Maersk Air, Malév, Minskavia, Muk Air, Royal Air Maroc, Ryanair, SABENA, Skargardsflyg, Swedeways Air Lines, Swissair, Syrian Arab Airlines, TAP, Thai Airways International, Trans Travel Airlines, Turkish Airlines, Tyrolean Airways, United Airlines, West Air Sweden and Wideroe's Flyveselskap.

In 1998 Stockholm (Arlanda) handled 16,147,971 passengers (10,035,978 on international flights) and in 1996 it handled 112,497· tonnes of freight. Göteborg (Landvetter) was the second busiest airport in 1998, handling 3,678,776 passengers (2,490,629 on international flights) and (in 1996) 32,044 tonnes of freight.

SAS

Frösundsaviksallé 1, 16187 Solna, Sweden

Tel: (0)8 797-0000

Web site: www.scandinavian.net

Shipping

The mercantile marine consisted on 31 Dec. 1998 of 412 vessels of 2·71m. GRT. Cargo vessels entering Swedish ports in 1998 numbered 23,250 (134·35m. GRT) while passenger ferries numbered 96,819 (831·76m. GRT). The number of cargo vessels leaving Swedish ports in 1998 totalled 23,293 (133.35 GRT) and the number of passenger ferries leaving was 96,780 (831·21m. GRT).

The busiest port is Göteborg. In 1997 a total of 31·29m. tonnes of goods were loaded and unloaded there (27·03m. tonnes unloaded from and loaded to foreign ports). Other major ports are Brofjorden, Helsingborg, Trelleborg and Luleå.

Telecommunications

There were 6,010,000 main telephone lines in 1997, or 678 per 1,000 population. In 1995 there were 6,830 telephone exchanges. 3·8m. mobile phones were in use in 1998. More than 47% of Swedes are mobile phone subscribers – one of the highest penetration rates in the world. There were 3,100,000 PCs in 1997 (350 per 1,000 population) and 450,000 fax machines in 1996. In Nov. 1998 there were 2·9m. Internet users, or nearly a third of the total population.

For emergencies in Sweden, dial 112. The country code for Sweden is 46. To make an international call, dial 009 first. Directory enquiries is charged for; dial 07975, or 07977 for international numbers. Public phones can be found everywhere, but most take cards only, which cost 35, 60 or 100 kr. – the more expensive the card, the more economical it is. Phone boxes may also accept credit cards. Faxes can be sent and received at post offices, although this service is generally expensive.

Postal Services

Post offices are usually open from 08.30 to 18.00 on weekdays and until the early afternoon on Saturdays, but stamps can also be bought at kiosks. Poste restante can be received at main post offices in major cities only. Postcards and letters weighing less than 20g cost 5 kr. to Sweden, 6 kr. to Scandinavian and Baltic countries, 7 kr. to other European countries and 8 kr. elsewhere.

There were 1,800 post offices at the end of 1998. A total of 5,377m. pieces of mail were processed in 1997, equivalent to 608 per person.

Internet Cafes

There is an internet cafe called Cafe Access (Tel: (0)8 5083-1488) in the Kulturhuset, an arts complex on Sergels Torg, the main city square in Stockholm, but note that the entire Kulturhuset is closed on Mondays.

SOCIAL INSTITUTIONS

Justice

The administration of justice is independent. The Attorney-General (appointed by the government) and 4 Parliamentary Commissioners for the Judiciary and Civil Administration (appointed by the Parliament), or Ombudsmen, exercise a check on judicial affairs administration. In 1998–99 the Ombudsmen received altogether 4,791 cases, of which 147 were instituted on their own initiative.

Sweden has no constitutional court. However, in each particular case the courts do have a certain right to ascertain whether a statute meets the standards set out by superordinate provisions.

The courts can be divided into general or ordinary courts and special courts. There are 2 general court organizations: the courts of general jurisdiction and the general administrative courts. These organizations are, in all essentials, parallel and are structured as a triple instance system. The general courts handle criminal cases and civil disputes between individuals. The general administrative courts primarily deal with cases which relate to matters between the community at large and a private individual. A number of courts of special jurisdiction exist beside the courts, such as the labour court.

There is a 3-tier hierarchy of courts: the Supreme Court; 6 intermediate courts of appeal; and 95 district courts. Of the district courts 24 also serve as real estate courts, 7 as maritime courts and 5 as environmental courts. When a permanent judge is appointed by the government, he cannot, in principle, be dismissed.

District courts are courts of first instance and deal with both civil and criminal cases. Petty cases are tried by 1 judge. Civil and criminal cases are tried as a rule by 3 to 4 judges or in minor cases by 1 judge. Disputes of greater consequence relating to the Marriage Code or the Code relating to Parenthood and Guardianship are tried by a judge and a jury of 3–4 lay assessors. More serious criminal cases are tried by a judge and a jury of 5 members (lay assessors) in felony cases, and of 3 members in misdemeanour cases. The cases in courts of appeal are generally tried by 4 or 5 judges.

Those with low incomes can receive free legal aid out of public funds. In criminal cases a suspected person has the right to a public defence, paid mainly out of public funds.

The Attorney-General and the Ombudsmen supervise the application in the public sector of acts of Parliament and regulations.

In Nov. 1999 there were some 60 penal institutions with a population of 9,500 inmates (including persons detained in custody).

Religion

The national church is the Swedish Lutheran Church, due to be disestablished in 2000. It is headed by Archbishop Karl Gustaf Hammar (b. 1943) and has its metropolitan see at Uppsala. In 1996 there were 13 bishoprics and 2,544 parishes. The clergy are chiefly supported from the parishes and the proceeds of the church lands. Other denominations, in 1996: Pentecostal Movement, 91,939 members; The Mission Covenant Church of Sweden, 70,072; Salvation Army, 26,089; Orebo Missionary Society, 22,801; Swedish Evangelical Mission, 26,089; The Baptist Union of Sweden, 18,548; Swedish Alliance Missionary Society, 12, 846; Holiness Mission, 6,393. There were also 164,015 Roman Catholics (under a Bishop resident at Stockholm).

Education

In 1998–99 there were 706,913 pupils in primary education (grades 1–6 in compulsory comprehensive schools); secondary education at the lower stage (grades 7–9 in compulsory comprehensive schools) comprised 303,314 pupils. In secondary education at the higher stage (the integrated upper secondary school), there were 309,143 pupils in Oct. 1998 (excluding pupils in the fourth year of the technical course regarded as third-level education). The folk high schools, 'people's colleges', had 29,341 pupils on courses of more than 15 weeks in 1998.

In municipal adult education there were 237,510 students in 1998.

There are also special schools for pupils with visual and hearing handicaps (809 pupils in 1998) and for those who are mentally retarded (16,095 pupils).

In 1997–98 there were in integrated institutions for higher education 305,581 students enrolled for undergraduate studies. The number of students enrolled for postgraduate studies in 1998 was 18,230.

In 1997 total expenditure on education came to 7·65% of GDP. The adult literacy rate is at least 99%.

Health

In 1998 there were 23,600 doctors, 4,200 dentists, 75,800 nurses and midwives and in 1997 there were 34,885 hospital beds. In 1994 the total cost of healthcare was 112,983m. kr., representing 7% of GDP.

Welfare

Social insurance benefits are granted mainly according to uniform statutory principles. All persons resident in Sweden are covered, regardless of citizenship. All schemes are compulsory, except for unemployment insurance. Benefits are usually income-related. Most social security schemes are at present undergoing extensive discussion and changes. Recent proposals include the introduction of a new pension scheme.

Type of scheme	Beneficiaries	Expenditure 1998 (in 1m. kr.)
Sickness and parental insurance	All residents	36,770
Work injury insurance	All gainfully occupied persons	6,010
Unemployment insurance	Members of unemployment insurance societies	32,663
Basic and supplementary pensions (old-age, disability, survivors)	All resident or gainfully occupied persons (2,134,425)	181,772
Partial pensions	All gainfully occupied persons between 61 and 64 (5,680)	585
Child allowance	All children below 16 (1,770,000)	16,830

In 1996, 34·8% of GNP was spent on social security – the highest
percentage of any EU-member country.

CULTURE

Broadcasting

3,350,000 combined radio and TV reception fees were paid in 1998.
There were an estimated 8m. radio receivers in 1997 and 4·7m.
television sets in 1997. There were 1·93m. cable TV subscribers in
1997. *Sveriges Radio AB* is a non-commercial semi-governmental
corporation, transmitting 3 national programmes and regional
programmes. It also broadcasts 2 TV programmes (colour by PAL).
There are 3 commercial satellite channels (TV3, TV4 and Nordic),
and a land-based commercial channel.

Television stations

Sveriges Television

Oxenstiernsgatan 26-34, S-10 510 Stockholm

Tel 00 46 8 784 0000; fax 00 46 8 784 1500; Website: www.svt.se

Founded in 1956 and funded entirely by licence fees. Public
service broadcasting on 2 channels: STV1 and STV2. Digital broadcasting since April 1999 offers 6 new channels. SVT Europe
broadcasts to Swedish-speaking viewers abroad via satellite.

TV4

Storangskroken 10, S-11 579 Stockholm

Tel 00 46 8 459 4000; fax 00 46 8 459 4444

Website: www.tv4.se

The commercial terrestrial television broadcaster.

Radio stations (National)

Sveriges Radio (SR)

S-10 510 Stockholm

Tel 00 46 8 784 5000; fax 00 46 8 784 1500

Website: www.sr.se

Public service radio, broadcast on 6 national channels – P1, P2, P3, P4, P6 and P7 – and 26 local.

Cinema

In 1998 there were 1,167 cinemas. Total attendances in 1998 were 15·8m.

Press

In 1998 there were 171 daily newspapers with an average weekday net circulation of 4,173,000.

Ten largest daily newspapers with circulation figures

	Monday–Saturday	Sunday
Expressen	418,300	519,800
Dagens Nyheter	381,800	434,700
Aftonbladet	353,000	470,400
Göteborgs-Posten	273,600	306,700
Svenska Dagbladet	200,300	214,500
Idag	136,900	200,300
Sydsvenska Dagbladet	126,300	146,200
Arbetet	97,100	90,600
Dagens Industri	95,200	
Nerikes Allehanda	70,600	

Business Magazines/Newspapers

Affärsvärlden

Klara Södra Kyrkogata 1, 10612 Stockholm

Tel: (0)8 796-6500 Fax: (0)8 202157

Web: www.afv.se

Dagens Industri
Torsgatan 21, 11390 Stockholm
Web: www.di.se

Dagens Nyheter
Gjörwellsgatan 30, 10515 Stockholm
Tel: (0)8 738-1000 Fax: (0)8 738-2190
Web: www.dn.se

Finanstidningen
Kungsgatan 18, Box 70347, 10723 Stockholm
Tel: (0)8 5062-4500 Fax: (0)8 149-930
Web: www.fti.se

Privata Affärer
10544 Stockholm
Tel: (0)8 736-5300
Web: www.privataaffarer.se

Svenska Dagbladet
Gjörwellsgatan 28, 10517 Stockholm
Tel: (0)8 135-000
Web: www.svd.se

Veckans Affärer
11390 Stockholm
Tel: (0)8 736-5200 Fax: (0)8 736-5022
Web: www.va.se

Book Publishers

Albert Bonniers Förlag AB
Founded 1837. Publishes fiction and general non-fiction.
Box 3159, S–103 63 Stockholm.
Tel: 00 46 8 6968620. Fax: 00 46 8 6968359.

Bokförlaget Bra Böcker AB
Founded 1965. Publishes fiction, geography, geology and history.
Södra Vägen, S–26380 Höganäs. Tel: 00 46 42 339000.
Fax: 00 46 42 330504.

Brombergs Bokförlag AB
Founded 1973. Publishes fiction, general non-fiction, government,
political science and general science.
Box 12886, S–112 98 Stockholm.
Tel: 00 46 8 6503390. Fax: 00 46 8 56262085.

Bokförlaget Forum AB
Founded 1944. Publishes fiction and general non-fiction.
PO Box 70321, S–107 23 Stockholm.
Tel: 00 46 8 6968440. Fax: 00 46 8 6968368.

Bokförlaget Natur och Kultur
Founded 1922. Publishes fiction and general non-fiction, biography,
history, psychology, psychiatry and general science.
Box 27323, S–102 54 Stockholm.
Tel: 00 46 8 4538600. Fax: 00 46 8 7893038.

Norstedts Förlag AB
Founded 1823. Publishes fiction and general non-fiction.
Box 2052, S–103 12 Stockholm.
Tel: 00 46 8 7893000. Fax: 00 46 8 7893038.

AB Rabén och Sjögren Bokförlag
Founded 1942. Publishes general non-fiction.
PO Box 42052, S–103 12 Stockholm.
Tel: 00 46 8 7893000. Fax: 00 46 8 7893052.

Richters Förlag AB
Founded 1942. Fiction publishers.
Ostra Förstadsgatan 46, 205 75 Malmö. Tel: 00 46 40 380600.
Fax: 00 46 40 933708.

B Wählströms Bokförlag AB
Founded 1911. Publishes fiction and general non-fiction.
Box 30022, S–104 25 Stockholm. Tel: 00 46 8 6198600.
Fax: 00 46 8 6189761.

Libraries

In 1998 there were 1 national library, 326 public libraries, 33
university libraries and 33 special libraries.

Theatre and Opera

State-subsidised theatres gave 14,450 performances for audiences
totalling 2,731,351 during 1998.

Museums and Galleries

Sweden had 240 public museums and art galleries in 1998 with a
combined total of 17,882,602 visits.

Tourism

There were 2,386,000 foreign tourists in 1997, bringing revenue of
US$3·78bn. In 1998 foreign visitors stayed 4,408,654 nights in hotels
and 864,649 in holiday villages and youth hostels. In 1998 there were
2,522 accommodation establishments with 251,368 beds.

Tourist Organizations

Sweden
Svenska Turistföreningen, Box 25, 10120 Stockholm
Tel: (0)8 463-2100; Web site: www.stfturist.se

UK
Swedish Travel and Tourism Council, 11 Montagu Place, London
W1H 2AL
Tel: (0)20 7724-5868
E-mail: sttc-info@swedish-tourism.org.uk

USA
Swedish Travel and Tourism Council, Grand Central Station,
New York, NY 10017-5617
Tel: 212 885-0700
E-mail: info@gosweden.org

Germany
Schweden-Werbung für Reisen und Touristik, Lilienstrasse 19, 20095
Hamburg
Tel: (0)40 3255-2355
E-mail: info@swetourism.de

France
Office Suédois du Tourism et des Voyages, 18 Boulevard
Malesherbes, 75008 Paris
Tel: (0)1 53-43-26-27

Visas
Visas are not required for stays of longer than three months for
citizens of EU countries, the USA, Canada, Australia or New Zealand.
Citizens of other countries should check with their local Swedish
embassy or consulate before travelling.

Festivals
The Stockholm Water Festival is the biggest event in Stockholm's
calendar, lasting for 10 days at the beginning of Aug. each year.
There are concerts, special events, exhibitions, fireworks and
sporting events throughout the festival that attracts thousands of
visitors and spreads all over the city. The festival is a celebration of
Stockholm's position on the water and although a pass is needed to
see many of the concerts and events, the venue for the festival is the
city itself, so much is free.

Public Holidays 2000

New Year's Day	1 Jan.
Twelfth Night	6 Jan.
Good Friday	21 April
Easter Monday	24 April
Labour Day	1 May
Ascension Day	1 June
Whit Monday	12 June
Midsummer's Day	24 June
All Saints' Day	4 Nov.
Christmas Day	25 Dec.
Boxing Day	26 Dec.

Business Etiquette

Sweden considers itself the leading economy in the region. Companies in Sweden are more hierarchical than in other Nordic countries but staff will have more say than in companies outside Scandinavia. Dress is likely to be more informal than in other countries but it will be expected that foreigners will dress formally if this is their custom. It is important to shake hands on meeting and parting with business colleagues. The use of technology is widespread (there are more mobile phones per capita than any other country apart from Finland and internet use is extremely common) and this will be expected of business partners. Payments will normally be made promptly and the same will be expected or interest will usually be charged. Do be punctual and use the 24 hour clock to avoid mistakes. Business and social relationships will almost certainly be kept separate, but if invited into a home be punctual and take a small gift for the hostess.

DIPLOMATIC REPRESENTATIVES

Of Sweden in Great Britain (11 Montagu Pl., London, W1H 2AL)
Ambassador: Mats Bergquist, CMG.
Of Great Britain in Sweden (Skarpögatan 6–8, S-115 93 Stockholm)
Ambassador: J. D. K. Grant.
Of Sweden in the USA (1501 M Street, NW, Suite 900, Washington,
D.C., 20005-1702)
Ambassador: Rolf Ekéus.
Of the USA in Sweden (Strandvägen 101, S-115 89 Stockholm)
Ambassador: Lyndon L. Olson, Jr.
Of Sweden to the United Nations
Ambassador: Hans Dahlgren.

FURTHER READING

Statistics Sweden. *Statistik Årsbok/Statistical Yearbook of Sweden. – Historisk statistik för Sverige* (Historical Statistics of Sweden). 1955 ff. *– Allmän månadsstatistik* (Monthly Digest of Swedish Statistics). *– Statistiska meddelanden* (Statistical Reports). From 1963
Andersson, L., *A History of Sweden.* Stockholm, 1962
Grosskopf, G., *The Swedish Tax System.* Stockholm, 1986
Gustafsson, A., *Local Government in Sweden.* Stockholm, 1988
Hadenius, S., *Swedish Politics during the Twentieth Century.* Stockholm, 1988
Heelo, H. and Madsen, H., *Policy and Politics in Sweden: Principled Pragmatism.* Philadelphia, 1987
Henrekson, M., *An Economic Analysis of Swedish Government Expenditure.* Aldershot, 1992
Lindström, E., *The Swedish Parliamentary System.* Stockholm, 1983
Olsson, S. E., *Social Policy and Welfare State in Sweden.* Lund, 1990

Peterson, C.-G., *Local Self-Government and Democracy in Transition.* Stockholm, 1989

Petersson, O., *Swedish Government and Politics.* Stockholm, 1994

Sather, L. B. and Swanson, A., *Sweden.* [Bibliography] ABC-Clio, Oxford and Santa Barbara (CA), 1987

Scott, F. D., *Sweden: the Nation's History.* Univ. of Minnesota Press, 1983

Sveriges statskalender. Published by Vetenskapsakademien. Annual, from 1813

National library: Kungliga Biblioteket, Stockholm.

National statistical office: Statistics Sweden, S-11581 Stockholm.

Website: http://www.scb.se/

Swedish Institute Website: http://www.si.se